D0897605

Gateway to Equality

GATEWAY TO
EQUALITY

Black Women and the Struggle for Economic Justice in St. Louis

KEONA K. ERVIN

UNIVERSITY PRESS OF KENTUCKY

Copyright © 2017 by The University Press of Kentucky

Scholarly publisher for the Commonwealth,
serving Bellarmine University, Berea College, Centre College of Kentucky, Eastern
Kentucky University, The Filson Historical Society, Georgetown College, Kentucky
Historical Society, Kentucky State University, Morehead State University, Murray
State University, Northern Kentucky University, Transylvania University,
University of Kentucky, University of Louisville, and Western Kentucky University.
All rights reserved.

Editorial and Sales Offices: The University Press of Kentucky
663 South Limestone Street, Lexington, Kentucky 40508-4008
www.kentuckypress.com

Library of Congress Cataloging-in-Publication Data

Names: Ervin, Keona K., author.
Title: Gateway to equality : Black women and the struggle for economic
    justice in St. Louis / Keona K. Ervin.
Description: Lexington, Kentucky : University Press of Kentucky, 2017. |
    Series: Civil rights and the struggle for Black equality in the twentieth
    century | Includes bibliographical references and index.
Identifiers: LCCN 2017019635| ISBN 9780813168838 (hardcover : acid-free
    paper) | ISBN 9780813169873 (PDF) | ISBN 9780813169866 (ePub)
Subjects: LCSH: African American women—Missouri—Saint Louis—Social
    conditions—20th century. | African American women—Missouri—Saint
    Louis—Economic conditions—20th century. | Working class
    women—Missouri—Saint Louis—History—20th century. |
    Equality—Missouri—Saint Louis—History—20th century. | Social
    justice—Missouri—Saint Louis—History—20th century. | Saint Louis
    (Mo.)—Social conditions—20th century. | Saint Louis (Mo.)—Race
    relations—20th century. | Saint Louis (Mo.)—Economic conditions—20th
    century.
Classification: LCC F474.S29 N4334 2017 | DDC 305.48/896073077866—dc23
LC record available at https://lccn.loc.gov/2017019635

A portion of this work was originally published in slightly different form in
International Labor and Working-Class History, Journal of Civil and Human Rights,
and *Souls: A Critical Journal of Black Politics, Culture and Society.*

This book is printed on acid-free paper meeting the requirements of the American
National Standard for Permanence in Paper for Printed Library Materials.

Manufactured in the United States of America.

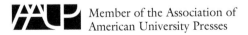 Member of the Association of
American University Presses

For my parents

Contents

Photographs follow page 120

Abbreviations

ACTION	Action Committee to Improve Opportunities for Negroes
AFL	American Federation of Labor
CCC	Colored Clerks' Circle
CCRC	Citizens Civil Rights Committee
CIO	Congress of Industrial Organizations
CORE	Committee (Congress) of Racial Equality
CPUSA	Communist Party USA
FEPC	Fair Employment Practices Committee
HDC	Human Development Corporation
HL	St. Louis Housewives' League
ILGWU	International Ladies' Garment Workers Union
MOWM	March on Washington Movement
NAACP	National Association for the Advancement of Colored People
NIRA	National Industrial Recovery Act
SLHA	St. Louis Housing Authority
TUUL	Trade Union Unity League
UC	Unemployed Council
UCAPAWA	United Cannery, Agricultural, Packing and Allied Workers of America Union
UL	Urban League

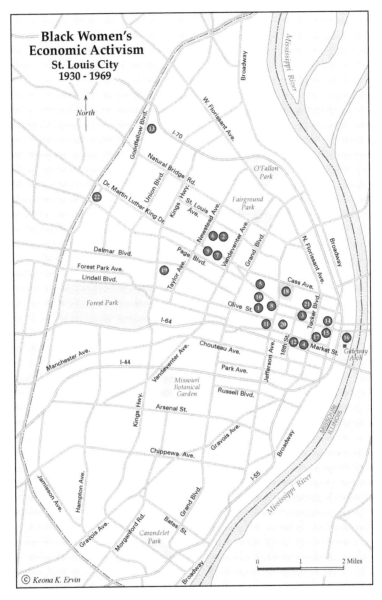

Black Women's Economic Activism
St. Louis City
1930 - 1969

North

Goodfellow Blvd.

I-70

W. Florissant Ave.

Broadway

Mississippi River

Natural Bridge Rd.

O'Fallon Park

Union Blvd.

Dr. Martin Luther King Dr.

Kings Hwy.

St. Louis Ave.

Newstead Ave.

Fairground Park

Vandeventer Ave.

Grand Blvd.

N. Florissant Ave.

Broadway

Delmar Blvd.

Page Blvd.

Taylor Ave.

Forest Park Ave.

Lindell Blvd.

Cass Ave.

Tucker Blvd.

Forest Park

Olive St.

I-64

Manchester Ave.

I-44

Vandeventer Ave.

Chouteau Ave.

Park Ave.

Jefferson Ave.

18th St.

Market St.

Gateway Arch

Missouri Botanical Garden

Russell Blvd.

Kings Hwy.

Arsenal St.

Gravois Ave.

MISSOURI
ILLINOIS

Chippewa Ave.

Grand Blvd.

I-55

Mississippi River

Jamieson Ave.

Hampton Ave.

Gravois Ave.

Morganford Rd.

Bates St.

Carondelet Park

Broadway

0   1   2 Miles

© Keona K. Ervin

(1) Phillis Wheatley YWCA, (2) Poro Building, (3) Funsten Nut Company, (4) City Hall, (5) Labor Lyceum, (6) Colored Clerks' Circle Headquarters, (7) Woolworth Store, (8) Woolworth Store, (9) Gerken's Hat Shop, (10) St. Louis Urban League Headquarters, (11) March on Washington Movement Headquarters, (12) Municipal Auditorium, (13) U.S. Cartridge Small Arms Plant, (14) Stix, Baer and Fuller, (15) Famous-Barr Company, (16) "Mississippi Revels" Revue, (17) ILGWU Labor Stage, (18) Pruitt-Igoe Housing Project, (19) St. Louis City Welfare Office, (20) St. Louis Housing Authority, (21) Plymouth House, (22) California Manufacturing Company.

Introduction

The Labor of Dignity

Black Working-Class Women's Organizing in the Gateway City

Not long after St. Louisans entered into the new year of 1969, the final year of a decade of significant social upheaval at the local and national level, thousands of public-housing tenants struck against the St. Louis Housing Authority (SLHA). Together, the black working-class women whose lives were at the center of the debate over the future of the city staged one of the largest and earliest demonstrations of its kind. National news outlets provided coverage, politicians at the local, state, and national level weighed in and amended or adopted policies as a result, and several strike leaders emerged as national figures. While they issued numerous demands to city officials, above all, dissidents called for dignity and control. Drawing upon support from key leaders, public sympathy, and the sustainable political communities that they had built over time, strikers demanded the redistribution of power and a greater allocation of resources to manage their own affairs and become key brokers in decision-making processes. Their hard-hitting politics and critical views about municipal authority and governance were deeply rooted in their insistence on making black working-class women's survival a matter of public concern.[1]

Winning their demands after months of mobilization, the strikers put St. Louis on the proverbial map as a site of transformative black working-class struggle, and they also made it possible for the St. Louis public-housing system to emerge as a national exemplar of the tenant management model. Most importantly, however, by engaging in collective action that exposed the connections between housing, employment, and working-class residency in a declining, deindustrializing American city, the tenants

1

who refused to pay rent cemented black women's status as influential members of the city's working class. Women selected the strike method as their political weapon of choice, they established close ties with unions to advance their cause, and they articulated their battle over housing as a problem of a lack of access to jobs and economic dignity. These elements not only reflected their political sophistication; they also pointed to black working-class women's political legacies in the Gateway City. While contemporaries tended to hold the view that the rent strike was at best a spontaneous and disorganized eruption of working-class disaffection with those in power, an accurate examination reveals that what transpired did not emerge in a vacuum. Instead, the strike was the culmination of three decades of black working-class women's economic activism and labor organizing. The organizing tradition that black working-class women in St. Louis inspired and led set the stage for and accentuated the conceptualization of the rent strike as a struggle waged by black working-class women for economic dignity.

Beginning in the early 1930s, black working-class women played an integral role in formulating and shaping at the local level the basic premise of what George Lipsitz calls the "Age of the CIO," a "social warrant" that "took the form of a socially agreed upon understanding certifying that working people deserved respect, dignity, and self-determination." Used here less as a marker of the work of a particular labor organization, in this case the Congress of Industrial Organizations, than as a means to name a larger guiding ethos, this "warrant" that imbued working people's living concerns with political and social importance serves as a useful construction for framing an era of significant political work developed by black working-class women in St. Louis. It points out how and why class mattered to black working women and it opens doors for articulating the ways in which black women challenged conceptions of the working class and worker justice.[2]

Although the "Age of the CIO" dawned unevenly and asynchronously in cities and towns across the United States, in St. Louis the era began in the spring of 1933, two years before labor organizers founded the CIO. In that year, comrades Carrie Smith and Cora Lewis, two black working-class radical women, led a strike of two thousand predominantly black female industrial workers. They staged one of the most important episodes of labor militancy and economic justice struggle in St. Louis since the 1877 General Strike, when thousands of mostly white and male railroad workers shut down the city. Two generations later, Smith, Lewis, and their coconspirators, all nut shellers in St. Louis and East St. Louis, battled the R. E. Funsten Nut Company after managers implemented severe wage cuts. "We think we are entitled to a wage that will provide us with ample food and clothing," Smith told gatherers at a hearing. Smith, who was in her early forties, had been working for Funsten for eighteen years. Overwork and financial insecurity had taken their toll; so too, had the unrelenting demands of political leadership. The day before the hearing, which included company representatives, she addressed demonstrators at the conclusion of a march through downtown. The first to speak, she bore witness to black working-class women's economic suffering, summoning the broader public sphere to embrace concern and responsibility for black women's survival. Lewis, also in her early forties, spoke at the hearing too, and shared that her three-dollar average weekly wage kept her household, comprising her mother and her four children, mired in poverty. A shop committee chair, Lewis told St. Louis mayor Bernard F. Dickmann that working women's *low wages*, not paid labor itself, made mothering difficult. The strike leaders had joined forces with the Communist Party, espousing the need for workers to engage in militant action to fight the ravages of industrial capitalism; some participants opposed industrial capitalism itself. They fiercely resisted red-baiting, persuasively criticized liberal reformism, creatively bridged local struggles for economic justice and black freedom, and broke new ground for working-class women's leadership.[3]

It was indeed no small feat that strikers won all of their demands, but their victory echoed deeper. Smith and Lewis's political project set the stage for a wave of struggle over the following two decades that prioritized economic dignity and firmly established black women's role in the local working-class struggle. *Gateway to Equality* explains how the roots of the rent strike ran much deeper than the decade in which it occurred. It turns the lens to focus on the forms of labor for economic dignity that black women workers performed and inspired during the thirties, forties, and fifties to show how black laboring women had effectively grounded working-class struggle in the framework of black women's changing economic experiences before the rise of antipoverty activism of the 1960s. Examining this prehistory sheds light on an era of significant worker self-organization in the city's history.

Across the era of American racial and economic liberalism, from the 1930s to the 1960s, many black working-class women forged a most expansive social justice struggle for economic dignity or the right to jobs, a living wage, welfare, decent working conditions, affordable housing, state-based economic projections, and unfettered access to public accommodations and the consumer marketplace. Women merged feminist, labor, black freedom, and antipoverty agendas to construct broad visions of community empowerment and democratically controlled urban landscapes. Women's economic activism questioned the role of the state, the terms of who and what concerns composed urban politics, the limits and possibilities of American citizenship and democracy, and the reach of economic power. Through their expansive, intersectional, and community-based working-class politics, black working-class women disrupted prevailing conceptualizations of "worker," "the working class," "labor organizing," and "the labor movement." The definitional parameters of such historically contingent constructions depended upon the legibility or illegibility of black women workers' political subjectivity. Through various acts of resistance and collective struggle, black working-class women made themselves visible by drawing attention to their roles as economic actors and activists and inserting their laboring bodies into political discourse and practice through testimony, quotidian resistance, and mass protest. Their struggle to counter misapprehensions about the existence and meaning of their political work, to challenge political cultures that rendered their politics unintelligible, was deeply connected to their quest for freedom from economic misery.[4]

I argue throughout this book that black working-class women's socioeconomic status and economic experiences were central to the formation of progressive black urban political agendas and the means by which black middle-class reformers established power and prestige in their communities. Using black working-class women's narratives, I illuminate some of the mechanisms of intraracial class politics, revealing the gendered aspects of black economic self-determination. The chapters that follow examine how black working-class women's paid and unpaid labors shaped the black freedom and economic justice struggle in St. Louis. The book's conceptual and methodological framework aligns with historical studies in black women's activism that tend to feature the politics of low-income and radical black women, illustrating black women's central role in community organizing, civic engagement, and civil rights and Black Power politics and the means by which black women engendered urban politics, social movement agendas, and urban policy. The scholarship positions black working-class women as key contributors to black women's activism, situating their politics as a critical form of unpaid labor. These writings also select as their core theme black women's economic and political marginalization in the labor market and within the political cultures of progressive movements.[5]

There are multiple ways to tell the story of black women's activism, but this book centers labor in its telling. It identifies black working-class women's unpaid labor in terms of its political, reform-based, and community-based dimensions and reveals the deep connections between that labor and the labors that women performed in the workplace. While many books on black women's activism center around the postwar period, covering in particular the 1950s through the 1970s, this book argues for the importance of the earlier decades, bridging Great Depression–era resistance, 1940s wartime activism, and postwar organizing with actions that occurred during the War on Poverty, creating a new periodization for economic justice work among black women. Revealing the gendered aspects of racial economies and black economic self-determination, *Gateway to Equality* highlights the extent to which economic issues, in their multiple forms, were central to black working-class women's struggle for dignity.

The following examination of black working-class women's economic politics reveals how people along the margins of society, those with little access to power, used the few resources they had to improve the conditions of their lives. It analyzes the political work of those deemed least likely to organize or those regarded as inauthentic political subjects. It centers the voices of black working-class women by relating the story of a local social justice movement through their lives, perspectives, and contributions and examines connections between struggles for black freedom and economic justice.

Defining Black Women's Labors

Examining black working-class women's economic activism reimagines historical narratives of labor and working-class history. David Roediger identifies the tendency to define "'American labor' as white and male" and asks, "What if labor weren't white and male?" One possible answer comes in the form of an invitation to make more visible the economic experiences of those groups left out of narratives driven by the activities of historically conservative unions and labor associations. In 1930s St. Louis approximately 92 percent of employed black women in the city's aboveground economy were manual laborers in domestic and personal service or industrial workers in marginal factories. Two decades later, the figure stood at approximately 49 percent. Over the time span covered by this study, the number of black women workers in domestic service decreased as more African American women entered clerical and professional occupations and public sector employment, but black women continued throughout the twentieth century to be a disproportionate share of the working classes. Such figures and developments explode myths about labor's composition. In addition to more adequately picturing the twentieth-century US working class, they urge a closer examination of black women as workers. From the 1930s to the 1960s, the majority of employed black women in St. Louis's aboveground economy worked for a wage; they were workers without access to the means of production or to professional jobs in fields such as medicine, law, and social work, which required postsecondary education or training and afforded employees a degree of mobility, flexibility, and autonomy. Trapped in low-wage positions, most black women workers were designated by the capitalist class as "unskilled," interchangeable, and disposable. Black women workers in industrial, domestic, and retail work, and the many without access to steady employment are the focus of this book. For them, working-class status profoundly shaped the conditions under which they constructed their lives.[6]

Laboring for dignity anchored and connected multiple meanings and uses of black working-class women's paid and unpaid labor in St. Louis. Marginal workers in the paid labor force, black working-class women toiled in homes, factories, and shops, earning wages that, while meager, sustained families and communities and kept households intact. Through cleaning, cooking, sorting, selling, weighing, sewing, and riveting, for example, these workers made major contributions to the local and national economies, their relatively high rates of labor-force participation indicating not only need but also impact. While paid labor constituted an important arena of struggle, black working-class women navigated poverty and racism not only in the context of their employment but also in the context of their lives on a day-to-day basis. *Gateway to Equality* attempts to define and more fully capture black working-class women's economic experiences, including their daily struggles to survive.

This book seeks a broader definition of laboring for dignity, which necessitates situating black working-class women's labor and economic experiences in the context of family, neighborhood, and community. It also requires connecting black working-class women's employment and unionism to the factors that propelled them into the work of job seeking: poor housing, food scarcity, discrimination, mass unemployment, and neighborhood and environmental racism. From this more comprehensive standpoint, we can connect traditional understandings of labor history, which primarily emphasize workplace issues, with an inclusive examination of workers' lives, including their living concerns and the multiple points at which they engaged in political struggle to improve their existence. In St. Louis, black working-class women's struggles for employment, a living wage, a union, and decent working conditions were intimately bound up with public-housing battles and welfare-rights activism, for example, or the push to challenge negative images of black low-income women and the effort to make unions more hospitable to those who disrupted dominant notions about the look of labor. Finally, laboring for dignity also encompassed the work that black working-class women's bodies, images, and narratives performed in the service of defining racial and economic inequality and the scope and trajectory of black freedom and economic justice struggles.[7]

The scholarship in women's history and black feminist theory that highlights the multidimensionality of women's labor, the ways different forms overlap and reinforce each other, and how black women's labor, in particular, shaped the development of race- and gender-based systems of economic exploitation and black middle-class reform informs this study.

Recent, groundbreaking works on the history of the carceral state, for example, show how such regimes extracted and exploited the labor of black women to drive profit-making enterprises of "Jim Crow modernity" and postbellum industrial development in the New South. Recent studies of domestic-worker organizing move black working-class women out of the shadows as subjugated, apolitical subjects and into the center of movements for social justice, revising US labor and working-class history. Finally, studies of the history of underground economies invite us to rethink the parameters of black women's working lives. They show us how black women in the sex industry and black female numbers runners used economic illegality as a means to struggle against poverty and carve out a space for themselves in racial politics. Connecting recent examinations and earlier works of black feminist intellectual production are the bedrock historical designation of black women's labor as exploited labor and the necessity of examining how race and gender shaped black women's economic experiences and activism. *Gateway to Equality* takes its cue from such works by making black women's labor a category of analysis to examine the social, political, and economic landscape of twentieth-century St. Louis.[8]

This book focuses on one crucial dimension of black working-class women's unpaid labor—economic justice struggle, which took on multiple forms. Black working-class women vigorously sought access to expanded work opportunities and fair employment; they were the political architects, organizers, participants, and emblems of some of the most important battles for social justice; they were engaged in organizational leadership; and even within the crucible of progressive social movements, they labored in the struggle to assert their own political subjectivities. In striving for dignity through paid and unpaid forms of labor, black working-class women fashioned what Xiomara Santamarina calls "African American working womanhood." They did so as they struck against companies, made creative use of community institutions to build a collective relationship with their employers, challenged workplace hierarchies through quotidian resistance, testified at public hearings, resisted union and factory discipline, and formed associations to challenge employer power, all while navigating competing conceptions of their roles as breadwinners, wage earners, wives, and mothers. Black working-class women's work to establish economic dignity in tangible form also proved generative for black middle-class women's reform efforts. This study shows that ideas about and responses to black women's paid labor and unpaid labor activism were not only central to black freedom and economic justice struggle; they were also especially important to the political development of St. Louis's black female professional class. Black women in social work, law, education, and civil rights used platforms created by black working-class women to make their mark on the local movement for civil rights and racial reform.[9]

Gendering Black Economic Self-Determination

Ora Lee Malone moved to St. Louis when she was in her early thirties, but by the time she reached the Gateway City, which she helped establish as a postwar hotbed of black working-class struggle, she had already accumulated battle scars through participation in civil rights and labor campaigns in the Deep South. In St. Louis, Malone fashioned a civil rights campaign through her Amalgamated Clothing and Textile Workers Union local, assuming leadership roles to ensure that organized labor lived up to its democratic ideals. Also a deep supporter of black voting rights and the exercise of the franchise, especially in local and state elections, she worked to inform black communities of the issues and decision making that would affect their lives. She spearheaded efforts to establish feminist politics at the local level by founding various women's rights, labor, and political groups. Malone's arc of intersectional political struggle and leadership is not discussed within many historical narratives of black economic self-determination, but it should be. Her politics of economic dignity had a profound influence on black economic activism as it challenged which stories and economic experiences should serve as the basis for claims to citizenship and liberation. Disrupting the politics of the "head-table sitters," as she called them, or civil rights and political leaders who preferred podiums to roundtables, speeches to community organizing, and hierarchy to democratic leadership, Malone's black labor feminism presented an alternative model of black economic liberation.[10]

Black working-class women's struggle for justice and dignity was generative labor, not just contributory; it produced constitutive material for urban agendas of economic justice, black freedom, and social equality. These women's socioeconomic status, images, work experiences, and community engagement became the means by which activists articulated the social misery of the marginalized and crafted prescriptions for social change. Black working-class women's labor generated the prestige and power garnered by black middle-class reformers and entrepreneurs. For example, beauticians gave black business leader Annie Turnbo Malone's beauty and hair care products credibility; they engaged in the very productive and consuming practices that made her business empire possible. The St. Louis Urban League found its footing during the early years of its existence because of black female job seekers' patronage. Black working-class women's labor politics made it possible for black professional and civically engaged women to express their black labor and working-class feminist politics, women like the social workers who staffed the Women's Division of the St. Louis Urban League; teachers like Marian Oldham, who led the battle for jobs as a member of the Congress of Racial Equality (CORE); and lawyers like Frankie Muse Freeman, who advocated for the rights of public-housing tenants. Out of the crucible of the fight for employment, black working women involved in the March on Washington Movement (MOWM) spearheaded one of St. Louis's earliest civil rights organizations, the Citizens Civil Rights Committee, which organized sit-in campaigns in the 1940s to desegregate downtown lunch counters. Garment workers in the wartime and postwartime eras infused antiracism and gender equity into progressive unions. Women's working-class politics constituted black liberation agendas when they battled for economic dignity. The synergy between the movement for civil rights and the movement for workers' rights often formed at the nexus of the overlapping struggles that black working-class women constructed.[11]

This study uses racialized gender as a category of analysis to recover the transformative possibilities and outcomes of black women's working-class politics and to identify and examine the boundaries of movements for black freedom and economic justice. The explosive forces of social movement organization during the 1930s through the 1950s helped raise the visibility of black women's economic activism, but black women workers battled against a tendency on the part of the middle class to attribute their politicization to sources external to women themselves or fail to imagine them as political actors in their own right. White working-class women, on the other hand, tended to resist black women's presence in organized labor. That black women's economic politics were situationally central and often constituted broader struggles for economic justice indicated both political possibility and political marginality. While identifying and examining the instances in which social contexts opened for black working-class women to assert their politics, I also analyze moments when women activists lacked control over the uses of their own stories and activism. These moments, too, shed light on how a lack of recognition for black working women's roles as political critics further exposes the silences, limits, and constructions of political cultures that reinforce inequality. The nature and form of misapprehensions about black working women's political subjectivity or the inability to read black working-class women as political subjects varied based upon the kind of work women performed. Examining black women's "authoring" of urban politics exposes varied mechanisms through which inequality is perpetuated, beyond unfair laws or unequal service provision.[12]

This "Southern-Northern City"

St. Louis's geographic, economic, demographic, and political landscape uniquely shaped black working-class women's economic experiences and incubated their economic politics. A border city—northern rust belt industrial, southern polite racist, midwestern urban frontier—where black women workers simultaneously experienced an amalgam of regionally specific economic realities, twentieth-century St. Louis was a veritable crossroads. The city's industrial landscape accentuated women's employment. St. Louis lacked a large-scale single industry that dominated the local economy and gendered larger cities of the urban Midwest as sites of male production. Meatpacking and automobile manufacturing plants and steel foundries or other "manly" production facilities were not in abundance as in, say, Chicago, Pittsburgh, and Detroit; St. Louis's economy was, instead, diverse and retail-driven. Ernest Calloway, an astute observer of local urban politics and a labor and civil rights leader, wrote, "Because of the light industrial structure of St. Louis, many have found that the city—job-wise—is a 'woman's town.'" This suggests in a very meaningful way that it is easier for a Negro female to find employment in St. Louis than a Negro male. Thus many negro males have moved on to Detroit, Chicago, Cleveland, and other heavy industry centers."[13]

Promoted as a site for the availability of inexpensive women's labor, St. Louis had a "feminized" economy. Civic boosters advertised the city as a desirable location for capital expenditure because women workers were abundant and affordable. A study published by the Industrial Bureau of the St. Louis Chamber of Commerce noted that "the character and type of female workers here are reported to be excellent, and those employed frequently perform operations which in other cities are done almost wholly by males, such as the packing and weighing of moderately heavy materials and many other jobs requiring accuracy and care." The chamber shared that St. Louis's larger industries typically employed women at a rate of 90 percent during "normal times," whereas in other unnamed cities, employers used not more than 75 percent of the female workforce. St. Louis industrial managers had an advantage, the bureau reported, because women's industrial output was "equally well performed [as men's] and at a lower cost." Around the beginning of the 1930s, St. Louis ranked seventh among cites with the largest manufacturing systems. Between the post–World War I era and the Great Depression, the St. Louis economy grew, reflecting a national trend; "light" industrial sectors in which women worked, such as clothing and food processing, grew considerably. To put it another way, the industries in which women worked played an important role in the growth of the St. Louis economy, even as that growth had slowed since the late nineteenth century. In St. Louis, 28 percent of the total number of workers over the age of ten were women; nationally, the figure was 22 percent. St. Louis was not the only city in which industry relied on female production, but this trend became a defining characteristic in black women's economic development.[14]

Marginality marked working-class women's economic experience in St. Louis's paid labor market, but that marginality had a determining racial component. Black working-class women, as in other cities across the United States, worked in the most menial positions in the city, earning extremely meager wages. Since the early twentieth century, black women had made "very little industrial progress," because the most desirable factory work was "practically out of their reach." One observer predicted,

"The negro woman's field for some time to come will be domestic and personal service." Black wage-earning women were largely restricted to domestic service work. Of the total number of women workers in St. Louis's domestic and personal service industry in 1930, roughly 44 percent were black, a figure disproportionate to the percentage of black women in the total population of St. Louis. At the opening of the 1930s, nearly 80 percent of black women in the paid labor market were domestics; 13 percent worked in manufacturing, confined to highly exploitative sectors of food processing, laundries, cigar, and tobacco factories; and a mere 2 percent were in clerical occupations. "No race of female wage earners works under greater difficulties or in such restricted fields," said one student of the black urban experience. Black women worked longer, more often, and for less money than their white counterparts. The menial quality of such work notwithstanding, women's wages eased, to a degree, the financial burdens of their families. For married women, social scientist William A. Crossland noted, "the colored woman . . . is an important factor in supplementing the family income"; "the colored man would often find himself financially stranded if it were not for the additional income earned by his wife." While marriage for white women "will solve all financial difficulties for her," freeing her from the burden of work outside the home and from the responsibility of housework, a black woman's "financial problems are increased by marriage; she must labor that the home may be maintained." "The Negro woman wage-earner is probably the most consistent and persistent worker in the St. Louis labor market," Ira De A. Reid observed. "Neither maidenhood, wifehood nor the widow's weeds tend to eliminate for her the necessity of work."[15]

Compounding the reality of black women's confinement to the lowest rungs of the paid labor market was the fact of their demographic command. Just as for other cities, black women led black migration to St. Louis. In the very early twentieth century, the number of black women matched and later outpaced the number of black men, especially those of working age, who migrated to the city. By 1930, black women outnumbered black men in the age bracket in which both groups were of working age. A similar trend continued through the decade and into the second half of the twentieth century. Black women workers formed the majority of the black population across the period under study, making them hypervisible as subjects of "surplus" worker discourses and indicators of black familial deviancy and racial backwardness in social science studies. Outpaced by the skyrocketing percentage of black newcomers to more desirable Great Migration destinations like New York, Philadelphia, Chicago, and Detroit, the rate of increase in St. Louis's black population, from 6 percent to 11 percent by 1930, nonetheless indicated the potential for a political shift in which black working-class women played a crucial role.[16]

St. Louis was a crucible for the emergence of black working-class women's situational centrality within most of the impactful and decisive episodes of the city's black freedom and economic justice struggle. In some instances, black working-class women occupied positions of political leadership. Critically teasing out black women's labors for economic justice suggests that border cities' unique urban politics possibly facilitated this alternative model.[17] Situational centrality, however, did not always translate to women's political leadership. In other cases, black working-class women confronted discourses and practices that rendered their political subjectivity unintelligible. Whether black working-class women emerged as formal leaders was a matter of context; in either case, however, their economic politics were pivots around which the social justice struggle turned.

Early civil rights struggles, those mounted roughly from the early 1930s through the late 1940s, were not only "increasingly urban, [and] proletarian" but were also, often, and consequentially, women-led. Black women's working-class activisms creatively merged the movement for worker rights and the movement for civil rights. Their economic politics played a critical role in the formation of what constituted "workplace-oriented civil rights militancy," including the growth of the Communist Party at the local level; the emergence of racial-justice-oriented unionism, principally through the work of the Congress of Industrial Organizations (CIO); the rising influence of "protest politics" through the March on Washington Movement and organizations like the Brotherhood of Sleeping Car Porters; the growing labor militancy of mainstream civil rights organizations such as the Urban League and the National Association for the Advancement of Colored People (NAACP); mass unionization; New Deal labor legislation and reform; antidiscrimination executive policies that created measures like the weakly enforced yet symbolically significant

Executive Order 8802, the Federal Employment Practices Committee (FEPC), and wartime industrial, interracial unionism. Some of the most important episodes in the city's racial and economic justice movement of the 1930s and 1940s featured black women workers, making them critical actors in US labor and working-class history.[18]

In the postwar period, black working-class women extended the battles for economic justice. In critical ways, the terrain of struggle shifted to include public-housing battles, as tenants and welfare-rights activists merged the fight for employment with the struggle for decent living quarters. Some black working-class women emerged as leaders of the union movement and in doing so fomented liberal coalitions between women's rights, worker rights, and civil rights organizations. Key black middle-class or professional women activists served as primary allies as they mobilized in the tradition of black social workers involved with the Urban League movement.

That some of the most important episodes in the racial and economic justice movement in St. Louis featured black women workers; that so many activists and organizers of the left-liberal coalition behind the city's labor and black freedom struggles deeply engaged black women workers' economic politics; and that locals' understanding of St. Louis's "traditionally southern" qualities came by way of thinking about black women's labor were all reflected in the Gateway City's sociopolitical positioning. Black working-class women were crucial agents in the formation of what historian Clarence Lang, in applying the Gramscian analytic of a "historic bloc," identifies as "the counterhegemonic politics of subaltern groups" to name the changing contours of the black freedom struggle in St. Louis from the mid-1930s to the mid-1970s. "Workers' agendas," he writes, "formed the core of a 'historic bloc'" by which "the mass nature of black popular struggles favored the laboring majority." Lang finds that "black workers decisively led, forming the nucleus of a black cross-class coalition of resistance" as they acted "as representatives of the popular will." I would add to his formulation the argument that African American women's economic politics played a crucial, defining role in the formation of this "historic bloc," principally because of women's persuasive appeals to the right of human dignity. The struggles waged by domestics, pecan shellers, the underemployed and unemployed, clerks, defense plant workers, garment factory employees, public-housing tenants, and welfare recipients, together with the black professional women who served as their allies and advocates, devised the working-class-oriented method of black freedom making that distinguished the St. Louis movement. In their focus on economic justice, in particular, women's appeals indelibly marked the formation of a black political agenda designed to gain access to power, respect, and self-emancipation. The politics of place—particularly St. Louis's status as a crossroads—helped make this marking possible.[19]

The Gateway City provided space for black middle-class women activists, in particular, to make unique strides. Against the backdrop of sweeping urban transformation, civil rights and Black Power struggles outside the St. Louis metropolitan area captivated the nation. Montgomery, Little Rock, Birmingham, Chicago, New York, Philadelphia, Oakland, San Francisco, and Los Angeles staged some of the most dramatic and far-reaching campaigns and conflicts in twentieth-century social movement history. From boycotts to marches and from rent strikes to rebellions, confrontations in these locations marked national debates about race in America. By contrast, St. Louis tended to contribute to national conversations about urban decay and entrenched racial segregation, not militant civil rights protests. St. Louis usually fell under the radar, an outcome that was not completely unintentional. Local politicians, business leaders, and reporters practiced "polite racism," trying, with relative success, to conceal black dissidence to preserve the city's reputation as an urban center above the fray of racial conflict. Even the religious-charismatic male model of leadership did not dominate, although black churches extended their facilities to protestors, and black pastors and church leaders held leadership roles in the movement. St. Louis had its secular black male militant figures, too, although none came close to reaching the power and visibility of figures such as Huey P. Newton, Stokely Carmichael, or Fred Hampton. Regional distinctions were a matter of degrees of influence. Civil rights leadership in St. Louis tended to be diffuse and decentralized, making it possible for black women to emerge as leaders who worked alongside black men. St. Louis was home to a relatively small black population, from which an even smaller set of activists emerged. The black labor feminists who staffed the St. Louis Urban League's Women's Division, including activist Pearl Maddox, a leader in the MOWM protests and founder of one of St. Louis's earliest civil rights organizations; St. Louis NAACP president Evelyn H. Roberts; Missouri NAACP president Margaret Bush; Frankie M. Freeman, one of the city's most important civil rights lawyers; and Marian Oldham, a leader of St. Louis CORE, ranked with Ernest Calloway's "30 Most Influential Opinion Makers in the St. Louis Negro Community." Operating along the margins in a city where power brokers hid racial upheavals, actively worked to silence contrarian positions, and often misconstrued demands for racial justice, freedom-struggle participants experimented. This is not to say that women did not confront sexism or that they overcame it. Rather, it is to bring attention to the fact that geopolitical forces worked differently from city to city. St. Louis's urban politics had spaces of political possibility for black women to emerge not only as invisible "bridge leaders" but also as visible, formal architects of black freedom agendas.[20]

We tend to understand the historical significance of St. Louis in terms of its contributions to national debates about race, housing, and residential segregation, as a microcosm that powerfully illustrates the systemic nature of the nation's racial quagmire. Less well known is the history of black working-class women's political work in the city, particularly the aspect in which they labored for economic dignity. Advancing struggles for justice, power, respect, and economic self-determination, women activists shaped St. Louis's twentieth-century black freedom and labor movement in two key ways: by helping orchestrate and constitute a social justice struggle that bridged black freedom and economic justice, and by exposing St. Louis as a battleground for economic justice issues, especially those pertaining to inequities in employment and housing. Appraising the significance of St. Louis history to national narratives of race and income inequality from the vantage point of black women's activism suggests that the city carries significant explanatory power for how we conceptualize urban history and social justice movements.[21]

The struggle for economic dignity, for work free of the vestiges of slavery and subject to the highest regulatory standards, connected black working-class women's politics, but there were also difference and divergence in terms of context, tactics, and strategy. There were salient distinctions among black working-class women, such as in socioeconomic status and class identity. Gradations can be found within black working-class women's labor politics. When black women workers self-organized to form a collective relationship with employers, whether with a union or not, they did so based on the type of work they performed, their family makeup, and the location of their work, neighborhood, and community, among other factors. Even perceptions about black women's economic experiences shaped the possibility of cross-class racial coalition building or interracial organizing. Within the black female working class were shades of social status giving shape to real effects.

The following chapters, organized thematically, chronicle groups of black women workers and their attempts to change the conditions of their work. It is not my intent to comprehensively treat black women's working-class struggles, but instead to offer illustrative case studies of significant historical value.

Chapter 1, "We Strike and Win," interrogates the Funsten Nut Strike of 1933, in which nut shellers shut down production to protest poor working conditions and wage cuts. Most nut shellers in St. Louis and East St. Louis worked for the Funsten Nut Company, the largest nut-shelling business in the metropolitan region. In May 1933 a marginal group of nut pickers positioned themselves at the center of Depression-era politics through a highly publicized, Communist-organized strike against nut-shelling factories across the metropolitan region. Among the most influential labor battles of its era, the Funsten Nut Strike carved out a space for black women workers in the growing and increasingly powerful radical labor movement and reinvigorated the local and regional Communist Party. The strike, and the unemployed movement with which it was deeply connected, marked the beginnings of the radical labor movement in St. Louis because of the economic activism of black women.

Chapter 2, "Their Side of the Case," maps the labor activism of St. Louis's largest segment of black working-class women as they mounted a labor reform program that anticipated and challenged New Deal labor legislation. With key black women staffers who led the St. Louis Urban League's Women's Division and progressive Jewish clubwomen who developed important ties to black communities, domestic workers designed and enforced standardization and rationalization policies to make dignity tangible in their contractual agreements. Black professional women led their division as household workers expanded the St. Louis Urban League's goal of fashioning an industrious, model black working class to include resistance. Redefining domestic labor with some success, the two groups intended to assign to it standards similar to those that marked industrial work. A largely female constituency marked the Urban League as a women's organization during its "radical" phase, which extended into the late 1940s. During this era, domestic workers transformed the league into their advocacy institution. As they made moves to "industrialize" household labor, they laid the groundwork for black women's economic battles during the World War II period. Through political activism, nut shellers and domestic workers built a powerful case for black women workers' economic and political indispensability to the emerging black freedom and local worker rights movement. In centering their own survival, they provided a means for community organizations to adopt politically efficacious ways to make themselves relevant to working-class communities at the forefront of a social revolution.

Chapter 3 examines the short-lived though influential Colored Clerks' Circle (CCC), a black youth organization that used boycotts and picket lines to win jobs at drugstores in black communities. Formed in 1937, the CCC combined black self-determination, notions of economic nationalism, and consumer power to address the unemployment crisis plaguing black young people. While the organization had men holding leadership positions, the overwhelming majority of the group's membership was women, and there were more women than men on the organization's executive board. Through community pressure, members won jobs for black women in particular, making an effective case for the right of a group to have some control over the employment landscape of their community. Young activists' Don't Buy Where You Can't Work campaign raised trenchant generational and class-based critiques of black adults who were reluctant to engage in militant and confrontational mass protest methods or who rejected such methods outright. Instead of conceptualizing black economic power through the figure of the black housewife, a method employed by the St. Louis Housewives' League in the early 1930s, the CCC politically actualized young black women as facilitators of racial leadership and racial progress. Moreover, CCC members argued that community change became evident and meaningful when young black women found dignity through employment.

Chapter 4, "This All-Out Struggle for Freedom," argues that black women's largely unsuccessful attempts to abandon domestic employment for jobs in the lucrative local defense industry became a central mobilizing issue around which organizers of the March on Washington Movement waged their wartime black freedom struggle. Women aired personal stories of employment discrimination before committees, filed affidavits against large industrial plants, joined picket lines, shared their grievances through letter writing, gave public addresses at large mass meetings, and formed their own civil rights organizations. The narrative that black working-class women activists astutely and persuasively articulated—namely, that of the beleaguered black woman worker excluded from participation in patriotic service—provided an effective assault on discrimination, exposing the jagged lines of the wartime American democratic practice. Women's labor activism proved indispensable to the making of one of the largest and most active March on Washington Movement chapters in the country.

Chapter 5, "Beneath Our Dignity," analyzes the rocky years of black working-class women's entry into the needle trades, boot and shoe, and laundry factories and their unions during the 1940s. It argues that these women exposed the fault lines of the American racial liberalism espoused by civil rights and union progressives who worked to establish "interracial good-will" in unionism and the industrial workforce. Women's resistance on the shop floor and in the union hall, demanding respect and fairness, disrupted and fundamentally altered community leaders' programs. The women were less interested in breaking the color barrier than in earning fair wages, establishing fair standards, organizing work hours around other commitments, and working and organizing in a hospitable climate. Focusing on black women's work with the ILGWU, this chapter examines their work and union experiences and examines the union's labor education program to consider why conflicts over historical memory; black women workers' long demands for dignity, autonomy, and respect; and social reformers' interracial experiments produced intense battles indicative of wartime upheavals and the Cold War tensions that followed.

Chapter 6, "Jobs and Homes . . . Freedom," uncovers women's postwar battles over housing and labor. It shows how black working-class women's struggles for economic dignity following World War II pointed to a cluster of trenchant urban problems that St. Louis began encountering in the prewar period and later experienced in much more concentrated fashion. The chapter tells the story of urban renewal, public housing, the unemployment crisis, and union organizing by focusing on the lives of public-housing tenants and the activism of Ora Lee Malone, a leading labor organizer. Finally, in examining the professional work of three prominent black middle-class women, DeVerne L. Calloway in politics, Frankie Muse Freeman in law, and Marian Oldham in community organizing, the chapter shows how the plight and activism of black working-class women inspired a generation of black middle-class women reformers to push progressive agendas that centered black women's dignity.

The idea for this research originated in a series of conversations with Ora Lee Malone. Born in the early twentieth century in Mississippi, Malone moved to St. Louis in the early 1950s and later fashioned a cutting-edge activist ethos that centered on economic justice for poor and working-class women and men, especially workers of color. She grounded the story of her forays into postwar trade union activism within a rich and largely untold story of black working-class women's quest for decent employment in the urban Midwest across much of the twentieth century. As Malone's recollections pointed out, and as archival sources confirmed, black women's labor activism in the latter half of the twentieth century did not emerge in a vacuum. Her working-class politics, made possible in part via the Gateway City and its urban political landscape, turned this student of twentieth-century social movements back in time to find threads connecting 1960s activists' struggles to those that preceded them by a generation. The roots of 1960s struggles waged by black working-class women lay in the 1930s and 1940s, when black women, politicized by strikes, wage cuts, worsening work conditions, and increasing job opportunities, inserted themselves into a growing labor movement. It was a telling fact that as Malone and her colleagues planned their 1973 women's labor conference, they discussed the nut pickers, one of whom was related to Malone through marriage. The women's movement activists drew inspiration and organizing tactics from communist Carrie Smith and others who asserted their right to survive.[22]

Thus, what began as a biography of Ora Lee Malone, a figure whose St. Louis career did not begin until the mid-1950s, ended up as a project investigating the generation that preceded her. Malone died at age 93, having lived a long life of engaged struggle that was less a departure from and more an extension of black women workers' dynamic labor organizing in the Gateway City during the first half of the twentieth century.

1

"We Strike and Win"

Food Factory Workers and Labor Radicalism

The nut shellers who toiled in one of the five factories owned and operated by the R. E. Funsten Nut Company entered the shop floor on Monday, May 15, 1933, as they always had, but this day did not follow the normal routine. That morning, Carrie Smith, an eighteen-year veteran at the company, initiated a strike at the plant, informing her colleagues that workers at Funsten's shop on Easton Avenue had planned to strike at 7:30 a.m. and that colleagues in her own shop would do so thirty minutes later. The plan was to whistle when the time had come. Smith announced, "The heavy stuff's here! Get your hats and coats and let's go"; the first part of the phrase was code for workers to stop production. Smith confronted a foreman on her way out to make sure that her colleagues would have no problems with exiting the shop floor. The strikers marched to a nearby park, where they elected Smith chairman and chose ten additional participants to serve on the strike committee. Smith and a colleague confronted their boss, talking for two hours. When they failed to get an agreement to raise wages, the two representatives joined the strikers and made plans to meet with Mayor Bernard F. Dickmann the following morning.[1]

Tapping the organizational apparatuses of community institutions and radical labor unions, black women domestic and industrial workers fashioned a militant worker rights struggle forged out of their particular economic experiences. An outgrowth and extension of the Communist Party's unemployed rights movement, the Funsten Nut Strike marked black women's attempt to recoup losses in pay, put an end to the mistreatment they suffered on a regular basis, and implicate the state in the marginalizing effects of industrial capitalism. Women workers reached their tipping point when, between 1931 and 1933, they succumbed to a series of five wage cuts. With backing from the Communist Party and its Food Workers Industrial Union, a majority of African American women and a minority of immigrant ethnic women waged a workplace struggle that turned into a general eight-day work stoppage with more than one thousand participating. Through militant mass action, nut shellers claimed that as members of the industrial working class, they deserved a living wage. Existing analyses of the strike point out how the insurgency marked a fresh brand of worker self-organization, reflective of early 1930s radical trade unionism, which galvanized communities and connected workers' living concerns to the workplace. Others establish black working-class women's radical economic politics within the scope of a broader working-class movement for racial justice in the border South. This strike was a pivotal moment in the history of Gateway City labor radicalism, in which questions of black women's survival found center stage.[2]

The nut pickers' strike was St. Louis's most significant economic rights battle during the early 1930s. Newspapers in and outside of the Gateway City covered the episode, prominent local leaders weighed in or became involved, and the Communist Party USA (CPUSA) used the strike as a moment to mark the urban Midwest as a new hotbed of radical labor politics spearheaded by black working women. The nut pickers' strike was among the most important labor battles of its time for three main reasons.

Most importantly, the strike established black working-class women as central actors in the battle for workers' rights. Black working-class women formed the majority of the leadership and the rank and file; they were the face of the struggle. They effectively politicized their status as marginal wage workers at the intersection of struggles for economic, racial, and gender justice. At heart, their struggle carved out space for black working-class women within industrial labor, which was viewed by most people as the exclusive or near-exclusive domain of white men. Relatedly, the strike brought visibility to black working-class women's economic experiences and raised their visibility as political subjects. Carrie Smith and Cora Lewis, along with a thousand others who joined them, drew attention to their status as workers whose wages made black women's survival possible. Their labor benefited their families and communities, and it bridged workplace and community along with aiding the struggle for economic justice and racial equality.

Second, the strike helped strengthen the organizational infrastructure of radical unionism and set the stage for an emerging wave of progressive and radical workers' rights struggles as workers in the electric and automobile industries and workers in garment industries, for example, followed suit by engaging in their own work stoppages. Black working-class women's campaign for better wages performed essential work for progressive and radical organizations that operated at the local level. The strike extended the influence of the radical left's unemployed rights' struggle into the arena of industrial work, connecting industrial workers and the unemployed within the same political framework. It also helped the CPUSA maintain its influence within the labor movement and extend its credibility and distinctiveness through adoption of an antiracist platform that made space for black working-class women's political leadership. In addition to assisting the local left, strikers and members of the newly formed union connected liberal social reformers, radicals, and municipal leaders, forcing them to consider the causes and contexts of working women's economic experiences. The community-based approach deployed by the nut pickers, along with their commitment to build solidarity across the color line and among those who performed so-called unskilled labor, laid the groundwork for the emergence of progressive unionism, most powerfully practiced by union members of the nascent Congress of Industrial Organizations. Unionists found relative success by adopting the practices of the nut pickers. Black working-class women's social activism broadened and deepened the economic justice struggle in St. Louis.

Finally, the nut pickers' story, a mix of poverty tales and labor's public expression of its deep disgust, captured the promise and limits that the 1930s brought to the ordinary worker. The labor struggle exemplified the political culmination of worker discontent and disaffection that came to define 1930s politics. It provided St. Louisans with its "instance right at home." "Some future social historian, writing on the country's plight in 1933," an editorialist for the *St. Louis Post-Dispatch* opined, "may well view as a significant phenomenon of our times that 1200 adult woman workers in St. Louis went on strike against a wage scale of 50 cents and less a day, and won terms that were expected to double their pay." The nut pickers' case became symbolic of the conditions that had come to define industrial capitalism and a model of the power of workers' self-organization. Women like Cora Lewis and Carrie Smith symbolized the beleaguered American worker across race and gender.[3]

Nut shellers, the more militant faction of nut pickers' working-class sisters, were a marginal group among those deemed the leaders of black politics, who ranged from heads of social service agencies and advocacy groups to black clergy and black municipal officials. Unlike domestic workers, nut pickers were beyond the scope of legible black female political subjectivity within certain influential and powerful arenas in their own racial community; their story suggests that the ability of this particular subgroup of black working-class women to gain access to political subjectivity depended on the possibility of seizing coalition-building opportunities with groups outside their racial circle. Nut pickers confronted marginalization and political misapprehension. Out of their social marginality, they forged interracial working-class solidarities with the CPUSA, which had also encountered social marginalization among established political and social leaders because of its radicalism. A range of figures with a stake in the strike's outcome carried misguided notions. Some believed that the nut pickers were dupes of the CPUSA, not an uncommon accusation used to delegitimate black progressive and radical politics; others thought they were outside of the respectable black female working class; while still others, including the nut pickers' staunchest supporters, believed that black working women lacked political savvy and finesse. The labor struggles of nut pickers, in particular, expose the gap between black working-class women's marginalization and misapprehension and their own conceptualization of their politics. The gap suggests that among black working-class women, nut pickers uniquely labored to dispute ideas about who embodied the cutting edge of working-class struggle.

"A Shadow of Racism in It": The Nut-Picking Industry

The black women who toiled in the nut shelling factories that were scattered across the St. Louis metropolitan region labored under segregated arrangements and in deplorable conditions. Trapped in a factory management system that privileged employees of a lighter hue, black women worked longer hours, earned less money, and performed more arduous work than the immigrant women of Polish descent who joined them. Black women earned just three to four cents per pound of shelled nuts, compared to the four to six cents that immigrant women earned—a 30 percent to 40 percent difference. In the basements where they worked, black women nut pickers separated nutmeats from their shells, an act requiring dexterity and causing physical strain; by contrast, immigrant women performed the preferred work of sorting and weighing half and whole pieces. Managers created a racial division of labor and even segregated starting and quitting times. "There was a shadow of racism in it," wrote Jennie C. Buckner of the St. Louis Urban League. "The dirty work was parceled out in the Negro community." Such divisions belied the fact that despite their different experiences, all women working in the industry were precarious laborers working under exploitative conditions. All toiled in poorly ventilated rooms, and no health standards were in place. Unpredictable harvesting seasons created chronic turnover and exacerbated the employment cycle during market slumps. After the stock market crash, for example, some factory floors were "practically idle." The combined weight of such negative attributes meant that anyone working in the field labored in a socially stigmatized, submarginal sector of the local economy.[4]

The bleak situation was that black working-class women were caught in a labor market that confined them to the dirtiest, lowest-paying, least desirable, least healthful, and most dangerous jobs in the city. For black women laboring in St. Louis during the 1930s, industrial employment offered very little compensation. Black women in the local nut-shelling industry were among the poorest workwomen in the city; approximately one-third of them were on the city's relief rolls and some received funds from the Provident Association, a private charity that bore considerable responsibility for administering relief during the Depression's early years. Black women made up the majority of African Americans on relief rolls, and black female manufacturing workers constituted the largest group on relief of any category. A Women's Bureau Department of Labor report added the Gateway City to a list of other major cities like

Chicago, Houston, Philadelphia, and Cleveland, where more than 40 percent of black women workers were jobless. Even despite Funsten Nut Company's growth in sales over the course of the early twentieth century and its expansion to multiple plants, nut shellers' wages were so meager that they significantly lowered statewide median wages—a fact not lost on organizers and statisticians. If "all the large group of low paid women in the nut-shelling plants was excluded in the St. Louis figures," claimed Ruth I. Voris of the Women's Bureau of the U.S. Department of Labor, then Missouri's median wage values for women workers would have been noticeably higher. During the 1920s nut pickers earned a median income of only $4.60 per week, which was half of what laundry workers made and some dollars short of tobacco and bag workers' earnings. In some cases, even domestic workers earned more than nut pickers. Ordinarily, however, "because of the larger wages paid in the factories, that is, Nut, Bag, Rag, etc., Negro applicants in this lower bracket constantly refuse offers of Domestic work," one Urban League study reported. Though black women workers in the nut-shelling industry composed only a small fraction of the total number of black women workers in St. Louis's paid labor economy, they composed the majority of the meager 7 percent of black women workers in industrial employment.[5]

Gendered Cartographies: Nut Factory Blues

Before the strike of 1933, the figure of the black female nut picker had already amassed cultural capital as the leading subject in St. Louis blues musicians Charley Jordan and "Hi" Henry Brown's 1932 Vocalion Records tune "Nut Factory Blues." Among a rising tide of black musicians who found commercial success through piercing analysis of the pain and possibility of black working-class life in the urban United States, these two blues artists contributed to the project of remaking the terrain of American popular culture by exploring quotidian worlds. As Amiri Baraka observes, urban blues reflected "the Northern Negro and the Southern Negro," a binary suggesting that the "'space' that the city provided was not only horizontal; it could make strata, and disparities grew within the group itself." Indeed, "Nut Factory Blues" exposed class fissures within black communities but also traversed more complicated and less explored ground as it mined the terrain of black working-class communal life through the prism of gender. In their construction of the black woman factory worker, Jordan and Brown suggest that the interplay between urban space, race, gender, labor, sexual relations, domestic violence, and household production becomes discernible. Bluesmen of the classical era crafted narratives of black women as economic actors—workers, producers, breadwinners—in effect making black women's working-class subjectivity speak for and to broad processes.[6]

In "Nut Factory Blues," space and place are prominent themes. "Down," the descriptive term that bluesmen often use, immediately identifies demarcations within urban space, drawing the listener's attention to its hierarchical dimensions. The bluesmen use the word to identify some of the mechanisms by which the city's underbelly is exposed and examined. In the first stanza, the listener is located in the city's downtown district, on Morgan and Sixteenth Streets. The intersection sliced through the fourth-largest neighborhood of five designated "black" districts, an area home to approximately nine thousand African Americans. Brown and Jordan juxtapose black working women and industrial capitalists to highlight the economic discrepancies between the two and to call attention to the ways that urban life facilitated "meetings" or transactions between individuals who otherwise lived separate lives. Their juxtaposition represented the stark gulf separating black women workers and those with power over women's economic lives. It also marked the economic and physical intimacies these two groups shared precisely because of the ways power relations demanded economic exchange under coercive and subordinating terms. Conspicuous disconnection and inconspicuous intimacy coexisted at the points where these groups intersected. The second stanza takes the listener to an enclosed space below ground; the basement of a cold, damp, and dimly lit industrial factory. In locating black women here, Brown and Jordan point to the fact that managerial systems operated according to rigid, racial lines. As Baraka suggests, the bluesmen unveil carvings in city space and urban landscapes that corresponded with zones of class hierarchy, urban inequality, and labor exploitation.[7]

Jordan and Brown complicate their progressively fine-toothed cartography in the final line of the second stanza, where they invite the listener to ponder a kind of a gender distortion of mainstream black economic aspiration. While the song positions black women industrial workers at the bottom of the paid labor market, it nonetheless emphasizes that, at the very least, black women have standing within it. Black men, by contrast, lack standing within the world of industrial production. "Nut Factory Blues" starkly juxtaposes the black female industrial *worker* and the black unemployed *husband,* thus distorting the widely accepted formula of the family wage ideal by its offering of a consuming man and a producing woman. In Jordan and Brown's reversal, black men bear gender while women hold economic status. In assigning black men to familial status, the bluesmen made a rhetorical move similar to that of intellectuals—especially social scientists, social workers, and justice seekers—when they situated black economic misery at the local and national levels within the larger context of a global financial crisis. For such commentators, the racial tint of class oppression found legibility through what they identified as the economic emasculation of black men and, concomitantly, the relatively higher labor force participation rates of black women when compared to the rates of white working women in the formal economy. This is to say that black women's presence in the paid labor force, particularly in the industrial employment sector, indicated and indicted the economic inequality plaguing black working-class communities. It seems to be the case that the bluesmen were less interested in promoting a male breadwinner and dependent wife ideal as a solution than they were in exposing gender tensions, but whether one aimed to promote or expose the "problem," in both cases the trope of the black working woman acted as a synecdoche in that through her the economic pain and social misery of the black nonworking husband, and by problematic extension, the black family, found articulation. Far from existing solely within spaces deemed formal, respectable, and professional, such critical exploration also found a home in the social worlds that black popular culture made.[8]

The spatial distinctions depicted in the second stanza of "Nut Factory Blues" offer a foundation from which to explore gender conflicts in black working-class households and communities. The bluesmen suggest a causal relationship between socio-spatial locations in the local economy and gender tension. Read together, the third and fourth stanzas show that conflict erupted in the liminal space between work and leisure as women received their pay and prepared themselves for the time they would spend away from the factory floor. In these scenes, black women workers encounter an additional coercive and exploitative exchange, this time with their husbands at the point of remuneration and the moments that immediately followed. We are told that women's failure to bring their pay home and turn their checks over to their husbands resulted in two possible outcomes: abandonment or physical abuse. In its frank discussion of domestic violence and the contextualizing of such within the scope of black men's and women's varied relationship to "the economic," "Nut Factory Blues" joined a tradition of social commentary in black popular cultures that mimicked blueswomen's 1920s productions advancing a feminist consciousness through frank speech, penetrating critique, and bold personal testimony. Artists broke the silence around intraracial gender conflict and the abuse of black women by black men, favoring open expression instead of dissemblance and encouraging public conversation about that which others in the racial community dared not speak of. Jordan and Brown reveal power relationships within some black households and refute the matriarchy thesis as they depict black working-class women as those living under a violent economic patriarchy.[9]

The final stanza pans out to black working-class life in downtown St. Louis. Black women factory workers lived, worked, and played in and around vice districts, the song suggests. The bluesmen point to Franklin Avenue, a street teeming with activity, where "jelly beans," or pimps, street hustlers, dandies, those who engaged in the semiunderground sex-work market, or those who transgressed gender and sexual codes stood "to and fro," conducting business transactions that mirrored the transactional interchanges between black women workers and industrialists depicted in an earlier verse. "Nut Factory Blues" places nut shellers within the frame occupied by sex workers to highlight the similarities that existed between them. Both worked, to varying degrees, within the hub of St. Louis's "interzones," to borrow Kevin Mumford's term, where sexual-economic crossings were routine and indicative of the ways shifting power relations made and remade urban landscapes.[10]

Perhaps the song's final point, posed in the form of a question, best captures the fundamental meaning of "Nut Factory Blues." The query "Which way did my good girl go?" suggests the nature of the impact of black working-class women's economic forays. As women engaged and enacted economic questions, their moves reverberated within and among the worlds they touched: workplace, neighborhood, community, institutional life, and family. That actual nut shellers chose open, organized, resistance a year after Vocalion Records released "Nut Factory Blues"; that they engaged in antiracist labor organizing; and that they did so to emphasize their connection to and location within family and community only further validated the nut pickers of Jordan and Brown's imagined black working-class subjects.[11]

"The New Wave of Strike Struggles"

Black working-class women played an important role in Communist Party–inspired radical organizing before the Funsten Nut Strike. Black working-class women joined the party either as formal members or as supporters who participated in demonstrations that drew thousands. After organizers moved their meeting to the premises of a family undergoing eviction, for example, about forty persons, "among them quite a few Negro workers . . . and some women," joined the CPUSA's Unemployed Council, the branch of the party dedicated to the abolition of unemployment. Magnolia Boyington, a black unemployed woman who was refused aid from the private charity Provident Association, lost her life in a demonstration after police unleashed tear gas on protestors. Unemployed Council (UC) members planned a "mass funeral demonstration" and raised money for the burial. About half of those demonstrating at the uprising on July 11, 1932, were black people, newspaper accounts reported. Black women were among those arrested during the July uprising and charged with inciting a riot. Black women supported the Trade Union Unity League (TUUL), a union organization designed to cultivate working-class unity among the unemployed and industrial workers across racial and ethnic lines and establish radical unions to effectively compete with the American Federation of Labor (AFL). Together, the UC and the TUUL joined a national radical left movement. Black working-class women participated in a UC protest against an eviction where approximately eight hundred protestors gathered to listen to speeches and observe or join a smaller group who transported the families back inside the house on Biddle Street. As members of an emerging social struggle, black women demanded state-sponsored protections for workers. They also called for worker control of relief allocation, unemployment insurance, corporate taxation, the abolition of vagrancy laws, free medical care for the unemployed, and state loans to improve the infrastructure of working-class neighborhoods. As participants of TUUL- and UC-organized protests, black working-class women joined a wave of labor radicalism sweeping the country, a movement in which workers sought radical economic redistribution and social restructuring.[12]

Having taken part in unemployed rights demonstrations in the city, black working-class women were poised to participate in subsequent radical worker rights struggles. Nut shellers' precarious economic positioning, their oscillation between unemployed and employed status, and their exclusion from labor unions and civil rights organizations made them a plausible if not obvious group to extend the radical struggle for worker rights. The next major local struggle emerged from community and family life and from the shop floor, where black and immigrant working women gathered six days a week. The UC movement ushered in a working-class politic built around living concerns and interracial solidarity, and the spring shake-up that occurred a year later in 1933 extended the struggle to defend the rights of workers—this time with black women at the center.

By the spring of 1933, Funsten managers had instituted a series of wage cuts across four years. For two months, black working women and Communist Party organizers discussed the possibility and terms of a work stoppage. When their numbers reached approximately twenty, women began to "organize ourselves into a union that will help us get better wages and conditions and keep them when we do get them." They demanded a ten-cent-per-pound increase in pay for processing whole nuts and a four-cent increase for processing pieces, an equitable wage scale, and union recognition. Strikers and their supporters established an arbitration committee that functioned as a centralized body representing each shop. Committee members presented their demands to Funsten managers and waited in vain for a response. After three weeks passed with no word, activists made plans to walk off the job if, after presenting their demands a second time, the company still refused to comply. Matters proceeded as the group expected, so at approximately 7:30 a.m. on Monday,

May 15, several hundred women workers walked out of their shops and held a mass meeting. They encouraged white women to participate and even conducted home visits to persuade those who had abandoned the effort to rejoin. On the first day of the strike, one striker recounted, "The white girls stayed inside," but more joined the effort the following morning despite being threatened by a "floorlady." Demonstrations, picket lines, and marches were mainstay activities, with participants casting the local battle in terms of a national battle against racial divisions within the working class, racial injustice, corruption in the criminal justice system, and class oppression. Gatherers "brought in the Scottsboro case," or the Communist effort to free nine Alabama black male youths accused of raping two white women, and raised placards that read "Free Scottsboro Boys," "Animals in the Zoo Are Well Fed While We Starve," and "Fight for the Freedom of Labor—Demand Unemployment Insurance."[13]

Nut pickers employed religiosity, establishing compatibility between militant labor organizing, communism, and Afro-Christianity. Alongside bats, bricks, arrests, and calls for an empowered working class were call-and-response communications accented by the undulating intensities of political speeches and prayers. According to reports, striking women punctuated Carrie Smith's "sermon" to those gathered outside City Hall with a "chorus of 'Amen'" and brought Bibles to picket lines, where they invoked divine help for their cause. Women prayed, "Oh Lord, give us strength to win our demands. . . . We made the first step, oh Lord, you should make the second step and help us to win the strike." By these means, the group anticipated protests of the mid-twentieth-century black freedom struggles that employed Afro-Christianity or a religious witness that merged the teachings of Jesus, retributive justice administered through a godlike figure, and a liberation politics attuned to and starting from black segregated communities. Yet the key factor distinguishing the nut pickers' struggle from that of later civil rights protest was a lack of the black church as an institutional base, even though Cora Lewis and Carrie Smith held membership in black churches. In this ethnic and multiracial working-class struggle that centered on black women workers, black churches remained on the fringe.[14]

Black working-class women's labor activism combined Afro-Christianity and the Communist Party's unique blend of working-class radicalism. For party organizers, however, the two were fundamentally incompatible. They used the women's religiosity as a point of departure, a foil to dramatize women's political conversion. Bill Gebert, a CPUSA national committee member and a writer for the CPUSA's *The Communist: A Magazine of the Theory and Practice of Marxism-Leninism,* wrote, "What a change took place among these women who practically without exception were religious!" Gebert, a Chicago-based organizer at the time of the Funsten Nut Strike, recalled a "Negro woman, who at the first meeting . . . prayed to the lord to win the strike." "When the pastor in the church refused to take a collection for the strikers, [she] came back . . . and reported that from now on the union is her church and now she is a member of the Communist Party." In the party's formation, religiosity was an obstacle to overcome on the path to authentic working-class political consciousness: "It is important to note," this writer explained, "that the women in the shops were without exception religious and had no experience in the working class movement." The "change that took place," made possible by their alleged renunciation of religious belief and practice, politicized them. Antireligiosity, the line went, made possible the ability to make speeches, attend meetings, and walk picket lines with such fierce militancy. Communist Party leaders failed to see that nut pickers were evaluating their allegiance to and support of black church leadership, not rejecting their faith. In their embrace of the party as an organizing and advocacy group, strikers were challenging the failure of black pastors and congregations to support their labor movement with time, money, and meeting space.[15]

Beyond the Communist Party's critique of black women's political use of religion, however, lay a more fundamental problem: the conceptualization of black women's politicization as a process external to themselves. Communist propaganda focused upon the party's so-called power to turn black women into bona fide working-class organizers. Building a case for their organization on a platform of the perceived shortcomings of "Negro reformist" groups or duped Black Nationalist organizations that mistakenly privileged racial allegiance over class solidarity, Communist organizers identified their party as the entity responsible for black women's alleged political transformation.

Party organizers and supporters immediately rallied behind the black women strikers. After nut pickers took their struggle from their homes to the streets, print literature announced the news, urging AFL members and those of the "Railroad Brotherhoods" to form relief committees to provide food, money, and clothing "so that hunger will not drive these women back to slavery conditions and starvation wages." Sympathizers responded positively. Organizations in nearby states donated funds to the Strikers Relief Committee. Writers urged communities to join nut pickers' picket lines and to form lines of their own. "It is your strike; as well as their own," the message went. "Follow the steps of these nut pickers" and "call a meeting of the workers in your factory; discuss the conditions, formulate demands, and prepare to strike, like these workers, against oppressive conditions."[16]

Like UC activists, striking women claimed public space to assert and make visible their economic enmeshment in family household production and communal life. Nut pickers transformed Funsten factories and the city streets around them into a political stage for the latest drama of the besieged American worker. Striker Carrie Smith demanded, "We want to be paid on the basis of 10 cents a pound for half nuts, and 4 cents a pound for pieces. This would give us an average wage of about $6 or $7 a week. We think we are entitled to live as well as other folks live, and should be entitled to a wage that will provide us with ample food and clothing." Drawing upon family and community solidarity, black women workers and their husbands, children, and extended kin gathered outside the main factory plant at 5:00 a.m. each morning. Communist Party organizers and students noted black working-class women's preference for what Rosemary Feurer terms "community unionism."[17]

Nut pickers disrupted hegemonic representations of a model household when they grounded their claims for economic protection in assertions about the primacy of their economic caretaking and financial influence. Nut pickers pointed to their role as economic producers and breadwinners. Exemplary black families, strikers argued, organized households around mutually dependent relations of care between men and women. The striking women asserted that the extent to which one carried responsibility for securing a suitable standard of living for one's family and community, not a breadwinner's gender, should determine one's access to a living wage and economic security. Seamstress and striking nutpicker Marcelean Owens, likely the breadwinner in a household comprising her parents and son, argued for more than a wage increase; she wanted recognition as a critical economic contributor. Choosing a seasonal nut-shelling job to supplement her income, the thirty-year-old woman was among those arrested during the first series of demonstrations. Similarly, striker Ardenia Bryant, a ten-year veteran employee, supported her invalid husband with a meager salary and public assistance. Communist Party organizer Cora Lewis, a widow and mother of several children, employed an ethic of familial economic caretaking as a political strategy. Lewis told Mayor Bernard F. Dickmann that her youngest child was in reform school. She explained, "Working for Funsten, five days and one half and one hour over the half day in a week with such low wages, I was unable to support the boy." Because Lewis failed to earn a sufficient wage, her child "tried to support himself . . . with whatsoever was in sight." A target of law enforcement because of her political leadership, Lewis was later arrested and her son was taken to the House of Detention, where officials sentenced him indefinitely to the Bell Fountain Reform School. To protest the harassment and use the moment to advocate for working-class black women, Lewis appealed to maternalism, a political maneuver that had long been a relatively effective means by which women made public claims to greater security, access to public life, and political representation. Lewis's black working-class maternalism, however, extended beyond black professional-class discourses about "juvenile delinquency," motherhood, and working-class life. By contrast, Lewis critiqued the arguments of those who asserted that black working-class women's relatively high labor-force participation rates were the primary cause for "juvenile delinquency," or children and youth who rejected the disciplining and policing forces of work, school, church, family, and community. On the contrary, Lewis argued, "low wages," not work itself, prevented black working-class women from adequately caring for their children. Nut shellers like Lewis expanded and complicated conventional understandings of women's work and responsibility to encompass political agitation. Juvenile delinquency indicated financial struggle, not moral deficiency or a lack of personal responsibility. Activists asserted that good motherhood depended on imagining a political subjectivity for black working-class women that acknowledged their critical economic caretaking.[18]

Implicating the state as partially responsible for escalating tensions between labor and capital and for ensuring women decent wages was a core component of the women's struggle. Strikers cast the state as their protector and advocate and as partially responsible for their survival in times of economic collapse and in instances when managers practiced discrimination or refused to comply with state-issued mandates. For instance, before an audience of strikers, sympathizers, police officers, and reporters—all gathered outside City Hall—Carrie Smith informed Mayor Dickmann that with "low wages" of less than two dollars per week, black women's survival was at risk. Smith argued that nut pickers deserved the same rights as other workers and that although the relatively small group were on the fringe of the industrial working class, they, too, were "entitled" to basic living needs. Smith's statement went beyond oft-cited grievances of industrial workers to critique the low wages that unskilled industrial workers earned and the racial and gender hierarchies central to industrial capitalism. She called for industrial work to fulfill its promise as a desirable alternative to domestic and agricultural work. It was likely that the irony of working in industrial agriculture and lacking financial resources to feed oneself and one's family and community was not lost on Smith and her comrades. Their battle was as much about food justice as it was about anything else, asserting that those who cultivate and process the food that sustains life should also have access to it.[19]

Following a full day of negotiations, Mayor Dickmann and a few "Negro politicians" accompanied the six-member committee of striking women back to Communist Party headquarters in a procession that displayed in physical form the extent to which black working-class women had moved their economic narrative to a prominent place in municipal politics. The approximately one thousand activists who assembled at the Labor Lyceum had been anxiously waiting to hear updates on the latest round of negotiations. Once the group returned, the striking women deliberated and voted unanimously to accept an agreement that doubled their pay and made nearly 50 percent of workers eligible to receive financial relief. With the latter stipulation, Dickmann affirmed the nut pickers' argument concerning the role of government in citizens' economic lives.[20]

After nut pickers agreed to a second offer, wages increased. In addition, on-the-job harassment became less of a problem than before: "We have no more terror from the foreman[;] he quit, and a new one was hired," strike leader Cora Lewis recounted. Nearly two thousand women joined one of the eleven Food Workers Industrial Union locals that activists organized in St. Louis, and a small fraction became Communist Party and Young Communist League members. Each plant formed its own poststrike committee and designated the "best fighters on the picket line" as captains. The women unionists established rules of governance, elected party organizers to connect committees to rank-and-file members, and established a central board comprising representatives from all local shops. Women organized integrated baseball leagues, picnics, and other recreational activities to build camaraderie and provide a social outlet. Morale seemed at an all-time high. "The girls are loyal to the union, and meet regularly with us," noted one union member. Although the Funsten Company did not formally recognize the Nut Pickers' Union (reports are conflicting), activists found it beneficial to maintain community and solidarity even after winning significant victories. Out of the institutional apparatus sustained by the Communist Party and supportive community entities, black women developed a culture of working-class resistance and radicalism.[21]

Women sustained that culture even as the majority of them chose not to become official party members. Perhaps it was the party's failure to make room for black working-class women militants' religiosity that accounted for women's lukewarm response, or the sense that women were already embedded within communities of their own choosing. Nut pickers seemed attracted to the party based on rhetoric and its concrete action in local contexts instead of on official party positions or edicts issued from abroad. "Under no circumstances must we [party members] already feel that all the workers in the nut factories have been won ideologically to the extent that no further work is necessary," one Chicago-based organizer warned. Many striking women more than likely integrated some aspects of communism into their political views, especially positions emphasizing labor radicalism, the strike method and militant protest, and interracial solidarity.[22]

Even though most women chose not to join the party, black working-class women became the high-profile face of militant activism; their strategies served as a model for other workers and union organizers. For instance, rank-and-file AFL workers in St. Louis and Chicago commented that they needed "leadership like the nut-pickers" in their own ranks. In the leftist publication *Working Woman,* organizers Carrie Smith and Cora Lewis gave their own recounting of the strike. Before their recollections a description read, "The working women should follow the example of these militant and courageous working-class leaders, and have faith in their own abilities to struggle, fight and organize." *Working Woman* editors framed the St. Louis nut pickers' strike as an example of what "can and should be followed [by working women] in every section of the country in struggle against the slavery imposed upon the women through the National Industrial Recovery Act." In response to the regulations of codes and prices required by the 1933 act, industrialists across the country drove down wages, which had a negative impact on the earnings of workers at the bottom of the wage scale, many of whom were women, black women in particular. CPUSA leaders praised black women for their working-class organization, citing "the strike of the nut pickers" as the episode that "aroused the masses of St. Louis like no other strike in years" and won "the full sympathy and solidarity of the St. Louis working class." The St. Louis story "shows what potentialities exist in the ranks of the working class," said national party organizer Bill Gebert. "Many comrades who are isolated from the masses are afraid to develop struggles because they fear there would be no leadership," he went on. But "these comrades ought to have been on the picket lines and at the meetings of these Negro women of St. Louis, to have heard their speeches, to have seen them in action and to have seen their leadership. One would think that these Negro women had been for years trained in the working class movement." Nut pickers helped extend the Communist movement among women across race and ethnicity by disrupting a tradition of St. Louis–based unionism that privileged white workers, male and female.[23]

Observers lauded black working-class women for their efforts. Their campaign was destined to have "a far reaching effect on the present scale of wages paid the laboring class and will do more to bring the enactment of laws similar to the [minimum wage] one recently passed by the New York legislature which will prohibit the paying of 'starvation wages,'" wrote *St. Louis Argus* editorialist Floyd J. Collins. "Regardless of the fact that Communist propaganda instigated this strike," Collins wrote on the strike's meaning, "these Negro women should be revered for their loyalty to a just cause." Striking nut pickers took on "a historical role in the new wave of strike struggles." A National Urban League report written by Urban League staffer Ira De A. Reid pointed out that the nut pickers' strike was one of only two "ground-gainers" for black workers during the period. The action extended beyond black women workers, however: "The majority of the strikers are Negro women and their unity and militancy has so inspired the workers of the entire St. Louis district that talk of strike is widespread," the *Daily Worker* noted. Several months after the strike, approximately seven hundred laundry workers in St. Louis, 80 percent of whom were women and nearly half of whom were black, organized the Laundry Workers' Union. Motivated by black women workers in the nut-shelling industry, the union members used the National Recovery Act of 1933, a measure that guaranteed workers' collective bargaining rights, to raise complaints about paltry wages, long hours, and poor working conditions. Other black women followed employed and unemployed workers' call to "do as the nut pickers did" when they struck Funsten Company competitors Central Pecan Company and American Nut Manufacturing Company. Like striking nut pickers, women workers struck against Hoffman Brothers Nut Company and used many of the same tactics that Funsten employees had practiced by calling upon the mediating influence of Mayor Dickmann, rejecting initial offers that failed to reach their designated standards. And like their nut-picking counterparts, striking rag and bag factory workers, many of whom joined Food Workers Industrial Union locals, publicly complained that earnings of one dollar per day did not amount to dignified employment. The Nut Pickers' Union even reverberated outside of relatively marginal industries to reach white women workers in the garment industries. For example, in August, several months after the Funsten strike, two thousand ILGWU members, many of them silk and cotton workers, struck multiple factories in the downtown garment district. Black working-class women turned the Nut Pickers' Union into a platform that extended beyond the scope of their own struggles. Through the union, women had "given leadership" to workers across racial and gender lines, and this fact, CPUSA organizer Ralph Shaw observed, was "the outstanding feature of the strike."[24]

Civil rights organizations and black nationalist groups also sustained critique by black women and party officials. Women strikers themselves were, according to reports, openly critical of the UL: "The Urban League and all other Negro organizations never paid any attention to this indescribably miserable slavery of the Negro women in the city of St. Louis." Indicting civil rights organizations and black nationalist groups, one striker allegedly stated, "The Urban League never sticked [*sic*] with us, nor the Universal Negro Improvement Association nor any other Negro organization or church. The Communist Party is the only one that gives us guidance and leadership." Carrie Smith and coauthor Cora Lewis agreed with party leaders in their article "We Strike and Win," noting that the Urban League "and all the rest of them knew we were sitting in that sweat shop for nothing. None came to our rescue but the Communist Party and I think that I have just as much right to choose who I want in my council as you have in yours. As for the Communist Party, I was with them." Party members' vociferous critique of mainstream black institutions, using the strike to situate the party as the true agent of revolutionary change, represented party propaganda at its best. Even as such critiques advanced party agendas, they reflected some women's views.[25]

The women's movement caught the attention of prominent St. Louisans representing diverse political interests: reformers, activists, politicians, and religious leaders. Especially vocal were leaders like Temple Israel rabbi Ferdinand J. Isserman and John T. Clark, executive secretary of the Urban League—both members of Mayor Dickmann's mediating committee. The two worked to curb the radical dimension of women's protest and reestablish a kind of paternalistic control over black working-class women as they wondered how and why the more militant and much more maligned route had come to occupy such prominent political space.

Along with William Scarlett, Episcopal rector of Christ Church Cathedral, Rabbi Isserman founded and led the St. Louis Social Justice Commission, a progressive, interfaith coalition of white social and religious liberals formed to promote local social justice causes. During the 1930s the group focused on industrial relations. Isserman championed intersecting racial harmony and equality, interfaith coalition building, economic equality, and social liberalism. He framed his pioneering Reform Judaism and progressive political activity within the prophetic Jewish tradition articulated in the Hebrew Bible. Shortly after the strike began, nut pickers and their sympathizers gathered at Isserman's synagogue, Temple Israel House, with the hope that they could persuade the leader to become their advocate. Strikers brought along several unopened pay envelopes worth four days' work and revealed their contents. Two envelopes contained just over two dollars, the others about $1.50 each. One woman reported that for a time she had earned a high weekly wage of eighteen dollars, but wage cuts had reduced her income to a mere fraction of that. Their initial appeal was to little avail, as the Social Justice Commission chose not to become directly involved but instead followed the lead of the mayor, who had appointed Isserman to his mediation committee. In recounting the experience at Temple Israel House, Carrie Smith remembered that the group left the meeting feeling as if it was "the end of the story."[26]

At the time the women likely could not have anticipated Isserman's soon-to-come contrariness with respect to black middle-class leadership. Instead of denouncing the strike's Communist influence, as the mayor, committee members, and mainstream civil rights leaders had, Isserman rejoined, "The nut-pickers' strike was not inspired by Communists but it was led by Communists. The Urban League and other organizations interested in colored people were familiar with this situation." Blaming the very black middle-class leadership who had welcomed him into their protected spaces to address audiences on racial empowerment and interracialism, Isserman accused the advocates of willful neglect: "They (black organizations) lacked . . . the vigorous leadership to bring this condition to light. It is indeed a pity that in our city the only group prepared to speak for eight hundred exploited Negro workers were members of the Communist party." Nevertheless, infusing poor black women's politics with an even greater air of legitimacy, Isserman explained that the strike "was inspired by a wage scale which was un-American, and which did not make possible even the barest subsistence for the workers." The Funsten Company, not the Communist Party with its radical, foreign influences, was the true violator of American tradition, in Isserman's political and religious imagination.[27]

If Rabbi Isserman supported the alliance between black women factory workers and Communist organizers, the local Urban League chapter did the opposite. The organization explained that it did not become involved because black women workers in the nut-picking industry lacked standards—a factor the social service agency could use as a point of leverage in negotiations. UL staff member Jennie Buckner recalled: "The League did not take an active part in this strike. . . . The Negro women working in these storefronts . . . many of them had open sores on their arms and their hands—no health requirements were enforced—and for that reason the league wasn't interested in furthering their cause." What UL staffers also rejected was the confrontational, direct-action politics of the strikers and of Communist Party stewardship. Urban League officials believed "Communists are behind this trouble," attributing women's radicalism to external sources, just as the party had done. The officials continued:

> Radical and militant groups found Negro unemployed workers to be especially desirable for their purposes because these hungry, destitute, and desperate people would follow wherever there was a ray of hope for some kind of relief. We knew the average unemployed Negro worker was ignorant of radical philosophies and that he was not naturally an agitator. We felt that the Negro was being used by something which [he] was not a part of and which he was not in sympathy with. Without making any attack upon their influences, we endeavored to direct the thinking of those who might have been susceptible, as between right and wrong. This was done by personal contacts and influence of our staff with different individuals and groups. How well we succeeded is attested by the fact that there was not a single instance of disorder in our building during the entire year.

The Urban League tapped community leaders to address churches, hoping to encourage religious leaders to steer their members away from radical groups. Some UL staffers, black middle-class women, did outreach work with black women workers at bag and nut factories, and the UL remained abreast of factory conditions, but no real engagement between the nut pickers and the uplift agency seems to have existed. While domestic workers mounted a substantial labor reform movement upon the institutional and organization framework of the UL, nut pickers shared no such relationship with the economic betterment agency that stood at the forefront of many black labor issues during the 1930s. The absence of black churches, the Urban League, and other African American groups from the strike suggests that black women's ability to make themselves intelligible as working-class political actors was linked to their seizure of coalition-building opportunities outside their own racial community.[28]

The sheer number of local leaders weighing in on the nut pickers' strike shows that a group of poor and working-class women managed to position themselves at the center of this "instance right at home" "of wage-slashing and sweat shop conditions" and of the dominant political cultures that came out of the organizing that attempted to alleviate such problems. In this "laboring of American culture" milieu, commentators across the political spectrum spoke of the strike in terms depicting the long, entrenched struggle between labor and capital. For some, the 1933 strike offered a moment not so much to consider race relations as to gain a living wage for workers; others, however, viewed the strike as a graphic, local iteration of the racial problem through the prism of class— a symbol of the disastrous consequences that resulted when racial difference informed labor relations. Still others considered the moment as a kind of intersection of both of these aspects. However one interpreted the event, Christian and Jewish clergy, politicians, academics, social workers, unionists, radical activists, and clubwomen tuned in to the nut pickers' activities. Their collective gaze marked nut pickers' situational centrality within the struggle for economic justice. Windows of political possibility opened, such that this group of black women workers staked a claim in trenchant debates and dramatic economic, social, and political change; but as these more powerful historical actors drew from the nut pickers a larger narrative of social unrest owing to economic negligence and the right to economic dignity, they did so on terms that partially misconstrued nut pickers' activism. The "first major strike by a union in St. Louis," during which the worker rebellions of the Great Depression era brought the issue of economic pain and catastrophe to the very doorsteps of Gateway City residents, even though some mainstream political leaders failed to see black women as acting in and motivated by their own interests.[29]

The nutpickers' victory was short-lived. At the beginning of the nut harvest season in September 1933, the Funsten Nut Company began reducing its labor force on a massive scale. Later, three factories in East St. Louis closed without any prior notice, affecting approximately one thousand women. By 1934 the company closed the majority of its plants and moved its operations farther south. The company had at least one operating shop in St. Louis as late as January 1937, yet the days of its black female majority seemed long gone. As soon as representatives reached a settlement, company president Eugene M. Funsten suggested that his family enterprise would not last long if it remained in St. Louis. Funsten explained, "There has been some improvement in the market recently and we are offering the wage increase to keep going and in the hope that the improvement will continue. Our company has not made a profit for more than two years and is not likely to earn anything until conditions improve materially." Company officials had, in a word, forewarned the public that it would eventually close all of its shops.[30]

Company layoffs did not occur without opposition, however. As they had before, Communist Party organizers tried to mobilize women to fight back. Leaflets reminded union women: "Food Workers of St. Louis, you have one of the best organizations in the United States, and only through yourselves you can keep your Union and earn a living wage scale." Meetings held every Monday evening at the Labor Lyceum were strategy-making sessions. In a last-ditch effort, nut pickers staged a public mock trial indicting the company for poor practice and demanding recompense in the form of full wage restitution and "adequate relief." These efforts produced little response, because organizing against closing factories was much harder than organizing for pay increases. Unable to maintain the energy and resources that organizing required, and lacking any jobs, the movement fizzled. The inability to maintain stamina and the women's precarious economic position eventually made the struggle unsustainable.[31]

The decline of their movement left most nut pickers facing material conditions similar to the ones that had led them to strike in the first place. Just as quickly as numerous records had documented the rise of the nut pickers, a virtual silence about the striking women fell over the city. Although the women workers had won a pay increase, the improvement scarcely fortified their buying power, because of "the topsy-turvy

economics of the period" and because they were "consumers at the bottom of the labor scale." The St. Louis black periodical *Argus* reported,
"Many of the pickers were the sole support of large families and will be
thrown upon the relief agencies. With the constantly soaring prices of
food, clothing, and other necessities of life and the shortage in present
relief funds an additional problem confronts the community." Employers
capitalized on this "situation" by hiring "domestic help to work for food
and lodging with no salary." The groundswell of labor agitation among
black women workers, the closing of an industry that had once employed
local black women in relatively large numbers, and the forced reverse
migration of black women back to domestic work formed the constitu-
ent parts that helped forge the labor militancy fueling the social struggle
among domestic workers not long after the nut pickers' strike.[32]

Organizing did not end after the nut pickers' initial triumph. Their
union waged a second strike during the fall of 1933, this time charging the
Funsten Company with discriminating against union members. Women
also protested mass layoffs and "worsened conditions" in the pecan
industry owing to uneven application of National Recovery Administration codes. Managers frequently fired black women before they would
increase wages or equalize their pay across race. In protest, women activists sent a set of demands to a Pecan Shelling Code hearing where officials discussed standards. Their list included a guaranteed twelve-dollar
minimum weekly wage for all workers and, echoing Unemployed Council movement strategy, a call for an unemployment fund managed by
an employee board of trustees, and unemployment insurance. Indeed,
before the emergence of the Congress of Industrial Organizations and
its practice of interracial unionism, the Nut Pickers' Union, one of the
more well-known labor organizations with predominantly black women
as members, anticipated the strategies and ideologies of working-class
activists who just a few years later used industrial trade unionism to dramatically increase the number of black workers in organized labor.[33]

Like many other labor demonstrations of the time, violence and
police repression were the strike's main features. On the first day, police
arrested black women demonstrators on peace disturbance charges.
Arresting black women was a mainstay of police practices in the late nineteenth and early twentieth centuries, and during the early 1930s black

women were more frequently arrested than their male counterparts, with the rate of charges far out of proportion to their level of representation in the population. Peace disturbances formed the bulk of cases filed against black women. As the work stoppage progressed, strikers began to use physical means to prevent strikebreakers from entering their new workplace. Police officers transported strikebreakers in patrol cars and taxicabs to avoid the verbal and physical threats of nut-factory strikers, who, according to reports, hurled bricks and brandished bats. Striking nut pickers were even involved in the intraunion conflicts that black women's radical labor politics exposed. For example, Cora Lewis sustained a physical attack when local Amalgamated Meat Cutters and Butcher Workmen (AFL) members demanded the names of certain Communist Party rank-and-file members. Physical altercations brought to the surface deep underlying tensions among workers, managers, state officials, and those in law enforcement. That black women were involved in such cases in such high numbers suggests that they were targets of state-generated violence. Physical violence reflected not only their targeting by law enforcement officials, but also their means of resistance against an economic violence that threatened their survival.[34]

St. Louis nut pickers were part of a larger cohort of working-class women of color in the nut-shelling industry who made their mark on Depression-era labor militancy. Their prioritizing of a community-based strategy shaped subsequent organizing efforts and work stoppages. Five years after the Funsten Nut Strike, Mexican American women in San Antonio led a strike of more than ten thousand pecan shellers because a series of wage cuts had further exacerbated the horrible conditions under which Mexican American working women lived and worked in barrios located on the city's west side.

Markets in St. Louis and San Antonio controlled the lion's share of the pecan industry during the 1930s, with San Antonio controlling the greater percentage. Because pecans were grown in the South, and particularly near San Antonio, the city was a hub, and Texas controlled more than 40 percent of the nut industry. Company owner Julius Seligman, the "Pecan King" of San Antonio and owner of Southern Pecan Shelling Company, came to control such a large share because he used only "hand picking" when he opened his shop in 1926, eschewing mechanization and forcing other companies to follow suit, and he exploited Mexican American women workers, who earned even less, on average, than nut shellers in Missouri. After losing his battle with workers, R. E. Funsten moved his company to San Antonio. According to a government-issued study, Texas pecan shellers made less than what an agricultural field laborer made on average. For Seligman and Funsten, the combination of "low capital investment" and an "extremely low wage structure" resulted in a highly profitable business and one of the more egregious examples of labor exploitation. According to one estimate, Southern Pecan produced about 15 million pounds of shelled pecans per year, resulting in profits that exceeded $1 million.[35]

Composing approximately 90 percent of San Antonio's pecan shellers, Mexican American women, like their black counterparts in St. Louis, worked long hours for low wages in crowded shops that had poor ventilation, if any. Workers in Southern Pecan shops suffered at high rates from tuberculosis and other respiratory illnesses. Working women picked up additional odd jobs in agricultural work, and roughly half of all pecan shellers in San Antonio received some form of public assistance. An estimated three-fourths of Mexican American workers did not have electricity, while nearly nine-tenths lacked indoor plumbing. These workers lived in the worst conditions, were malnourished, and often suffered from a disproportionately high death rate.[36]

Formed in the same year that the St. Louis nut pickers struck the Funsten Nut Company, the first Pecan Shellers Union of San Antonio failed to gain traction after Seligman organized a company union. The union revived in 1937 as the Texas Pecan Shelling Workers' Union. This time, the CPUSA and the United Cannery, Agricultural, Packing and Allied Workers of America Union (UCAPAWA), a new CIO union founded in 1937, were the main organizations helping the effort. The UCAPAWA provided "a temporary charter" for the union, with the stipulation that the union would expand to organize all agricultural workers. In late January 1938, Southern Pecan contractors slashed wages. In response, approximately twelve thousand workers stopped production. Much larger in scope than the Funsten Nut Strike, the pecan shellers' strike lasted for about three months. More than one thousand activists were arrested, police used tear gas and violence against the protestors, and the police and fire departments resorted to riot protocol. Strike leader Emma Tenayuca, who joined the Young Communist League in 1935 and the CPUSA a year later, and served as chair of the Texas Committee of the Communist Party, was an outspoken political strategist who battled political targets on multiple sides. Critics from the Catholic Church and labor unions red-baited the protestors. Strikers' hard-fought battle ended when they settled with Southern Pecan, winning back their original wage, which was increased after the implementation of the Fair Labor Standards Act, and won union recognition. Just as Funsten moved his company after his defeat, Seligman mechanized production and fired ten thousand workers. The "largest labor strike in San Antonio history and the most massive community-based strike waged by the nation's Mexican population in the 1930s" had Mexican and Mexican American women at its center. Their transnational working-class struggle, particularly that which Tenayuca envisioned, articulated, and engineered, "operated at the crossroads of gender, class, race-ethnic, and national boundaries." The wage increase was an important victory, but the strike's significance was much greater. Through a grassroots, community-based approach, women's working-class activist leadership demonstrated workers' power by mobilizing a community of laborers on the extreme margins of low-wage industry.[37]

While the evidence does not show that striking women from St. Louis were in communication with their San Antonio counterparts, the strikes carried important connections. First, the two episodes made clear that working-class women of color "authored" radical unionism. Black and Mexican American Communist women were at the helm; they were strategists and unapologetic about their radical politics. In St. Louis, as Clarence Lang observes, "black freedom workers helped build the local CIO; the organization's activities had grown organically from the foundation laid by the nutpickers strike." The 1938 pecan shellers' strike grew out of the formation of the UCAPAWA. Second, their struggles emphasized workers' organization across racial and ethnic divisions. They were not built on a narrow worker rights model focused on wages and conditions but on one that insisted upon integrating the quest for racial and gender equality with the fight for food and economic justice, democratic control, antiauthoritarianism, and freedom of political expression.[38]

Black working-class women's struggle to transform their work in a local nut-shelling industry carried profound implications for the course and trajectory of radical unionism in St. Louis. Carrie Smith and Cora Lewis's version of radical unionism highlighted black working-class women's political leadership. Their politics exploded myths about who constituted the industrial working class and which groups of workers were best poised to lead struggles for dignity and self-determination. The working women brought a sense of their political efficacy—honed through community work—to the struggle, and they shaped the practices of the local CPUSA as much as the organization shaped them. They were visible leaders in the movement to establish radical unionism. They also inspired other workers to join the movement for workers' power by conducting strikes and joining unions. From the hundreds of women in St. Louis's rag, bag, and garment factories to participants in the Chicago needle trades strike, to workers and organizers of St. Louis's electric industry, the nut pickers' battle helped generate a wave of worker unrest—much of it committed to community-based or grassroots organizing and an expansive definition of economic justice. The black working-class women who toiled as nut shellers fomented a solidarity strike of several thousand of the city's most vulnerable industrial workers. Through the prism of their labor experiences and workplace resistance, black women nut pickers raised questions about the broader public sphere's responsibility for black women's survival. Through organizing they won some immediate and important gains and—a more lasting effect—helped forge a fresh synergy between the labor and freedom movements.

Black working-class women's political labors proved useful not only to leftist politics but also to a broader segment of St. Louis residents, including reformers, writers, and ordinary citizens. Most shared the belief that the nut pickers' case powerfully exemplified "the epoch of wage-slashing and sweat shop conditions" and the expectation that business would survive while "consumers . . . earned too little to supply their own needs." Most agreed that nut pickers' economic experience warranted some kind of intervention. While observers diverged sharply in assessments of the nut pickers' radicalism, most agreed that collective action was one of the core contributors to the working women's victory. The "first major strike by a union in St. Louis" brought into sharp relief the Depression's impact in local form and its implications for American workers. It is historically significant that black working-class women's economic experiences and labor activism became shorthand for the economic experiences and labor activism of the working class. This reversal of the typical trend, in which black women workers were invisible within constructions of the "working-class" and "labor," distinguished the nut pickers' labor activism from that of other groups of black working-class women in St. Louis.[39]

Domestic workers, far more deeply ensconced within overlapping circles of black professional St. Louis, used the St. Louis Urban League's Women's Division, not the CPUSA, to form a collective relationship with their employers. Black women household workers' struggle for economic dignity signified not so much the plight of the American worker across race and ethnicity but rather black workers' struggle to overcome the vestiges of slavery. Working in private households or in commercial properties, domestic workers selected political tactics that made sense for their social and economic location. With backing from numerous relatively influential black leaders and sympathetic white liberals, domestics used negotiation and persuasion as their tactics of choice.

2

"Their Side of the Case"

Domestic Workers and New Deal Labor Reform

Only one month after nut pickers organized picket lines, domestic workers engaged in their own collective action. As Americans absorbed the shock of economic depression and newly elected President Franklin D. Roosevelt launched his ambitious New Deal program in 1933, nearly one thousand domestic workers in St. Louis gathered at the Phillis Wheatley YWCA in September 1933 for the mass meeting organized and sponsored by the St. Louis Urban League. Their gathering was the culmination of years of grassroots organizing. It featured stories of exploitation and abuse as well as creative methods of navigating challenges. Women spoke of how little they earned and how difficult it was to take care of their families, while others suggested ways to improve working conditions. Collaborating with the Women's Division of the St. Louis Urban League, which was led by African American women, domestic workers used resources at their disposal to join the workers' rights movement of the Depression era. The record does not indicate that the domestic workers who were involved with the mass meeting were in communication with the striking nut pickers, yet it is likely that domestic workers were aware of and influenced by the Funsten Nut Company strikers. Contributing to working-class struggle during the 1930s, a period during which workers' collective actions influenced the course of national politics, domestic workers challenged ideas about their unfitness for working-class consciousness, labor militancy, and self-organization.[1]

Largely denied membership in organized labor and access to basic labor protections, black domestic workers of St. Louis employed the local chapter of the Urban League's Women's Division to carve out a space for themselves in a growing, predominantly white male labor movement and in the multiple coalitions that configured the New Deal. Domestics used household employment reform codes to lay the groundwork for dignity to manifest in their labor and contractual agreements. From the Household Workers Mass Meeting of 1933 to the close of the St. Louis Urban League's first phase in the late 1940s, black working-class women joined forces with progressive black women who led the Urban League's Women's Division to reform domestic employment through negotiation, enforcement, collective action, and everyday resistance. As a result of their shared work, UL employees showed an increased commitment to reforming household work, and working women had greater political leverage, support, and moral legitimacy when they resisted employer power. Their combined efforts resulted in subtle yet significant shifts in league practice.[2]

Histories of twentieth-century social movements have carefully depicted the emergence of an early working-class civil rights struggle, but the role of black working-class women's labor activism, especially that of the disproportionate number who toiled as domestics, has yet to be fully explored. Examining the 1930s in particular as a moment of activism in which domestic workers demanded to be treated like all other workers, even if the New Deal excluded them, uncovers the vital political work of this often-overlooked group. Exploring worker organization through this lens also shows that domestics' pitched battles contributed to activists' and community leaders' thinking about waged work, class relations, financial security, and economic dignity. The 1930s marked a critical turning point in the history of domestic labor activism, as working-class women built worker rights and civil rights struggles that transformed national debates by centering concerns about racial and economic equality. By advancing their own versions of meaningful work, domestics and their sympathizers exposed the limits of the New Deal and the systemic race- and gender-based negligence that defined the modern welfare state. While capital investment, government subsidies, public policy, probusiness political interests, and many white workers' racial attitudes constructed and supported labor markets and arrangements that designated black and brown female hands as those fit only to clean, cook, and care for others' needs, domestics drew attention to instances of "flagrant exploitation." These women were not simply highlighting the limits of Roosevelt's program of state-based protections; they were critiquing the racialized and gendered logics that elevated only certain laboring bodies to deserving status.[3]

As New Deal liberalism constructed a negligent and antagonistic welfare state vis-à-vis black working-class women, domestics used the resources that were available to them to push local organizations to assume the burden of support and advocacy for their economic well-being. To challenge employer abuse and power, underscore the financial contributions they made to their immediate and extended households, and seek to gain measures that respected their social commitments, St. Louis domestics transformed their local UL into a worker organization. Managed by a slate of progressive black clubwomen who headed its Women's Division, the St. Louis Urban League, as an interracial and interclass organization, provided its predominantly female clientele with the necessary resources to build a worker collectivity designed to resist household labor's idiosyncrasies. Domestics manipulated the local social service agency to make it more closely resemble their ideal advocate and partner, creating a customized service provider–client relationship. Black working-class women's travails created, and in many ways forced, a space of response and potential alliance by black middle-class women reformers of the UL Women's Division. Their middle-class reform work constituted labor—paid and unpaid—made possible by working-class women's economic need and activist engagement. Through such work, black working-class women contributed substantially to the making of the league's "radicalized" phase during the 1930s. Investigating how domestic workers pushed the UL to serve as their vehicle for better working conditions and labor standards highlights the creativity and unorthodox approaches that marginalized workers—those deemed least likely to organize and those on the fringes of organized labor—used to wield authority over their employers with the resources available to them. The decentralized nature of their work, coupled with the marginality they endured, spawned creative responses and effective models of worker organization.[4]

The Political Economy of Domestic Work

As in most cities at the time, St. Louis's labor market for women workers had a sharp division along race and gender lines, with native white women earning the highest wages and working under relatively better working conditions. The overwhelming majority of black women in St. Louis, as across the nation, worked as maids in private homes and hotels, as elevator tenders, and as waitresses. Of the total number of women workers in St. Louis's domestic and personal service industry in 1930, roughly 44 percent were black, 50 percent were native white, and only 7 percent were "foreign-born white." The concentration of black women in the domestic and personal service sector, which was vastly disproportionate to their representation in the total population, and their high rates of labor-force participation formed the basis for black women workers to address some of the most pressing labor relations issues of the day.[5]

Becoming even more like slavery during the Depression, domestic labor reflected the very worst aspects of economic collapse. The Depression brought worsening conditions to an already embattled employment field, intensifying the main grievance that domestics across the United States long had aired: employers refused to set clear expectations, wages, and boundaries. There was a decline in job offers for "live-out" work, the arrangement whereby a domestic worker returned to her own home after workday's end instead of remaining on the employer's premises. As early as the final months of 1930, as many as 50 percent of domestic jobs compensated the worker in the form of room and board only, according to one employment bureau. Before the stock market crash, employers made live-in arrangements during the winter, but a July 1931 UL report found that such a configuration became year-round practice as the Depression wore on. "There is yet the tendency to reduce wages," read Jennie C. Buckner and Marie C. Wilburn's monthly report. "Many household employers want girl to stay on the place nights. This custom is usually enforced more in winter than in summer seasons, but now it is given as one way to reduce expenses and save time." Live-out arrangements meant greater expenses paid on the employers' part, since most domestic workers could not afford transportation. Live-in arrangements, by contrast, required carfare but at a reduced rate and in many cases excluded cash as a form of payment. Because employers themselves financed live-out arrangements by covering transportation costs, this "perk" was among the first to go. The cheapest method, the live-in arrangement, was typically unaccommodating, as it was common for workers to sleep on a cot in a kitchen, a living room, a child's bedroom, a cramped room where all servants slept, or "a basement room unfit for human occupancy." Some employers used not only room and board but also clothing as a form of payment: one asked the St. Louis UL for a domestic worker who was willing to accept "$5.00 per week—no carfare and not to be paid in cash but clothing from her ready-to-wear store." Clothing was hardly sufficient as compensation, and the family wage ideal was largely unattainable for most families regardless of race or ethnicity.[6]

Severe wage cuts reduced workers' options. "In many instances pay for general work has reduced fifty percent," read a mid-1931 report. The following year wages plummeted further, with the typical pay dropping to one dollar per day. African American women under age twenty-one had few opportunities; employers preferred experienced workers because they could now afford them. Instead of reducing wages, some families shrank their workforce, forcing domestics to do "double work for same pay." Attempting to avoid leaving their employees jobless or implementing a hiring freeze, a small minority of employers reduced hours and wages to keep their current workforce in place and continued to hire new workers. In a rare instance, a company employing elevator operators cut wages by 50 percent, reduced the ten-hour day to five hours, and doubled its workforce. Most employers, however, reduced or eliminated jobs, slashing wages and compensating experienced workers at a rate significantly less than the value of their labor.[7]

Black Working-Class Women and the Women's Division of the St. Louis Urban League

In these circumstances, it is not surprising that domestic workers deployed the language of familial need, claimed breadwinner status, and prioritized worker autonomy in their correspondence to uplift agencies like the St. Louis Urban League, which provided assistance to black migrants. On the heels of the Great Depression, twenty-six-year-old Henryetta Makins informed Urban League social workers that she was "not afraid to work." The widow requested a housekeeping position that honored her wish to "keep my child as near as possible." Less than a year after Makins wrote to the St. Louis Urban League, twenty-year-old Jane Story, who supported not only herself but also her mother, a sibling, and another relative, sought employment assistance and complained, "Wages are not enough to support one—save four." Appealing to and complicating Clark's plan for "increasing the number of opportunities for the heads of Negro families to earn an adequate and regular livelihood," she wrote herself within the boundaries of Clark's racial uplift strategy, pressing the secretary to recognize African American women workers as heads of households who deserved advocacy. Luella Webster wrote to explain her efforts to trek northward, specifying that she wanted work that would honor her "desire to go home at night" and an employer who would "pay me enough," while Ellen Hockett requested employment to support her mother and also give her time to attend Sumner High, the first secondary school constructed for black students west of the Mississippi River. Of all the migrant women who constructed meanings of "African American working womanhood," Mary Young, a newly single mother of five living in Mississippi, perhaps best captured black working-class women's longings when insisted that her northern trek must afford "something after working," or a steady, stable, and respectable income sizable enough to make ends meet. With the possible father of her children remarried and working at a grain and feed company in St. Louis, the "light brown, nice looking, very fine person, [who] finished [a] hair dressing trade," perhaps looked to rekindle her partnership for romantic and financial reasons since the meager money her former lover sent home was not nearly enough to cover household expenses and take care of their children. In their letters, women writers such as Makins, Story, Webster, Hockett, and Young exploded the myth of the family wage model of a dependent wife and children and a wage-earning husband by casting themselves as critical financial caretakers whose impact was comparable to that of wage-earning men. For them, migration to the urban Midwest held the promise of live-out work and recognition of their status as workers.[8]

Black women domestic workers who aligned themselves with the UL did not gravitate toward community institutions naturally; they did so deliberately. Few, if any, early-twentieth-century community organizations in St. Louis were more systematically focused on black working-class issues. While the league wished to offer a comprehensive set of programs in the early 1930s, "because the question of making a living has been the worst problem Negroes have met and is growing more critical—we consider as our special task—attempting to increase and improve the working opportunities for Negroes." They located job opportunities to give black newcomers a sense of whether a move to the city was feasible. A social service agency with an interracial board of directors, the St. Louis Urban League was a comprehensive resource for black workers, as were league chapters throughout the country. Rising onto the scene a year following the notorious East St. Louis race riot of 1917, the well-staffed local chapter maintained a wide-reaching network, including white community leaders and a comprehensive database of economic, residential, and social information about black residents. It comes as little surprise that union membership for black male workers was one of the league's priorities, since its leader earned a nationally recognized prolabor reputation as former director of the Pittsburgh Urban League. Shortly after starting his post in St. Louis, Clark created three independent black unions, all under the auspices of the American Federation of Labor. He also helped organize building service, hotel, and building trade workers. Under Clark's leadership, the St. Louis UL promoted racial progress by seeking to build a solidly employed black working class through discipline and respectability. The agency took upon itself the Herculean task of inserting black workers into the labor force, serving as a quasi-union for workers denied access to white labor organizations, forming partnerships with the few unions that permitted blacks to join, and challenging discriminatory laws and customs in hiring and state economic policies.[9]

The St. Louis Urban League's employment bureau became one of the largest and most comprehensive placement agencies for African American workwomen in the St. Louis area. As the hub of the UL's industrial program, women clients legitimated the organization's service to the local community. Across 1933, league workers estimated that nearly one hundred thousand residents—male and female—visited the league's headquarters, with two-thirds of that number seeking employment. The women's division of the Urban League Industrial Department saw the most traffic, since women formed the majority of black workers who perused job notices, completed applications, and underwent preliminary interviews. "During the depression 30's fully 90% of the [job] placements were in the [domestic and personal service] field," read a survey of St.

Louis UL services from the year of its founding to the early 1940s. African American women had more jobs available to them than did men, but women, too, faced an employment shortage because so many of them sought work. The UL office felt the brunt of this economic and demographic shift. A backlog of thousands of unemployed and underemployed women faced consecutive months with no job prospects in sight because of the large number of women job seekers, shrinking job openings, and white employers who were either reluctant to hire black women or simply refused to do so. Between 1929 and 1933 the abundance of temporary work, the overwhelming number of prospective employees, and the poor quality of job assignments meant that for any given month, only between one hundred and two hundred African American women were new applicants, while those who reapplied for jobs typically numbered between eight hundred and twelve hundred. On the whole, the St. Louis Urban League placement agency had more women applying for jobs than men. With a municipal employment agency that operated under the assumption that, according to black women applicants, "white girls could be had very reasonably and were much more desirable in homes," the UL Industrial Department rose to prominence. Swamped daily with requests from white employers for black workers and demands from African American women for employment worthy of respect, the league devoted considerable time and energy to its Women's Division. After the summer of 1933, these efforts intensified when the UL industrial committee agreed to take over the employment bureau of the Phillis Wheatley YWCA; budget constraints had threatened the YWCA program. In the worst years of the Great Depression, the uplift agency found itself deeply enmeshed in the lives of the predominant group of black workingwomen in the city.[10]

The indefatigable efforts of the black women staffers who led the Urban League Women's Division, including Jennie C. Buckner, Zenobia S. Johnson, Marie C. Wilburn, and Valla D. Abbington, account for why so many of the more than 85 percent of black women working "in the domestic line" selected the St. Louis UL as a primary resource. From the late 1920s through the early 1940s, Buckner, Johnson, Wilburn, and Abbington all led the "women and girls" wing of the UL Industrial Department, which began handling women clients after March 15, 1929. Establishing an employment wing as early as 1919, UL staffers housed its female clientele under a separate department ten years later. The women staffers' meticulous reports reflected deep commitment to and concern for domestics' well-being; they scrupulously attended to black women's labors, locating avenues to express their own labor feminist and antiracist inclinations. Working primarily with black working-class women in industrial employment, Abbington was a fierce advocate. Her February 1945 report stated, "The Negro woman is perhaps discriminated against more than any other worker," and continued, "From this angle it looks as if the job of the moment is to give more employment assistance to women."[11]

In addition to confinement to low-wage work, the rampant sexual abuse of black women by white men, often facilitated by the domestic work arrangement, made the "protection of women" a priority for Johnson, Wilburn, and Buckner. In the 1930 report "Orders from Bachelors," they detailed sexual harassment, rape, and solicitation for sex work, revealing an active sex-work industry with clients and providers dependent on employment bureaus for referrals and hiring. Black and white men requested and likely demanded sex behind the mask of the domestic help order. As in the case of the solicitor of "a girl to entertain," orders were "plainly given, so that it is possible to see what the motive is." Other "[requests] are more crafty, and give the usual order." More veiled notices typically requested cleaning and cooking services with a wage of the "usual price," or about three dollars per day. With this sort of announcement, the UL required three or four referrals to "extract the real story" by "read[ing] between the lines." For example, staffers referred four women to a job advertising a seven-dollars-per-week wage to manage a two-person home. On their first day, the four met a white man who "impose[d] himself" and welcomed "couples to drop in from the street." Two other women accepted an order for a "nice looking girl" between the ages of eighteen and twenty-five. Upon their arrival, the "employer" offered the women makeup, perfume, a house shared by "transients," and money should they "entertain the men callers." The employer of recently married twenty-three-year-old Gertrude Simmons "carried her into the living room to talk about the work and immediately began to make overtures to her, putting hands over her body." "Orders from Bachelors" reveals the political commitments of UL women staffers and their impact on league practice. Fighting for the "protection of black womanhood," Buckner and others argued, or organizing for black women workers' "bodily integrity and personal dignity," was indispensable to the UL mission to fortify the economic prospects of black workers.[12]

Collective Organization and Household Labor Reform

The UL Women's Division took a militant turn as the Great Depression worsened: "Evidences of the flagrant exploitation of domestics" who had "no chance of protecting themselves" compelled the group "to take whatever steps we saw fit to help correct this situation." Just months after President Roosevelt signed the National Industrial Recovery Act (NIRA) into law in June 1933, the St. Louis UL hosted a mass meeting for household workers. The NIRA marked Roosevelt's early attempt to recover industry through regulating wages, prices, production codes, and business and labor practices. Section 7a, the act's best-known part, recognized collective bargaining as a right of the industrial workforce. The act created National Recovery Administration to implement and oversee the new measure. Though not included, nonindustrial workers and their allies across the country wrote themselves into the new protection and tailored it to fit their work situations. Applying the NIRA to African American workers in general and domestic workers in particular, the UL organized a September 1933 mass meeting. Having advertised at motion picture houses, in churches, and through local newspapers, organizers discovered that "apparently our meeting is attracting quite a little attention and the prospects are that we will have a good discussion."[13]

Between five hundred and one thousand domestics and their sympathizers packed the YWCA September 21, 1933. Preparing his staff for potential insubordination on the part of participants, Clark confided to League of Women Voters leader Edna Gellhorn just one day before, "We are trying to use every precaution to see that the meeting does not get out of hand." With Afro-Christian overtones and narratives of racial ascent, gatherers opened the meeting with the singing of James Weldon Johnson's "Lift Every Voice and Sing"; prayer was led by a Central Methodist Episcopal pastor and opening remarks were given by UL staffer Zenobia S. Johnson. The meeting was "to arrive at some code for Negro general household workers, in order that they might be better benefitted by the policies of the N.R.A." Aiding the effort was the Emergency Advisory Council, a national UL initiative that worked to "understand the complicated Federal Relief machinery and interpret to Negroes [its] meaning." Program leaders urged staffers to find and create opportunities for black workers, issue formal complaints where appropriate, and seek representation on committees that were tasked with implementing New Deal policies. The St. Louis Emergency Advisory Council chapter, like other chapters across the country, organized to improve the standards under which domestic workers and other members of the black working class labored. They hoped to do so by challenging businesses and industries that practiced "many old traditionally southern customs" that barred black workers from employment or treated them unfairly.[14]

In organizing the mass meeting, black working-class women exploited a New Deal ethic of government responsibility by applying Roosevelt's program to domestic workers despite their exclusion from labor standards. In doing so, they facilitated women's entry into the ranks of the thousands of workers who responded to the NIRA's passage by fomenting increasing workplace struggles at the local level. The September 1933 mass meeting marked a watershed in the history of domestic worker organizing in St. Louis, setting the stage for changes in local UL employment policy and for expanded militant advocacy by black women clients. Even the phrase "mass meeting" reflects the league's politicization. Unwittingly, the NIRA helped facilitate a social revolution in household employment.

Domestic workers used the UL-sponsored program to mirror industrial workers in their increasingly public, militant, and collective claims to economic dignity. Negotiation and appeal to local opinion were the women workers' main tactics. At the mass meeting, attendees made singular contributions, citing multiple indignities and offering suggestions for improvements. Stressing the point that domestics should earn enough to both "live comfortably" and "be able to set aside some money for old age," one speaker suggested a wage scale equivalent to pre-Depression levels. Inverting the traditional logic of the family wage system, a domestic worker stressed the importance of securing an adequate wage to support husbands, children, and extended kin when she estimated that about one in every five domestic workers was the breadwinner of her household. Another, echoing the experiences of many, complained about how a worker earned only $1.50 for three full days of work, and her employer consistently stopped the clock to force her to do overtime without pay. After some discussion, attendees agreed that local employment agencies should adopt uniform minimum wage scales. "Using her own personal example of success," one commentator urged women to negotiate directly with employers. Another suggested that the public ought to cover reduced carfare for day workers. Before the attendees parted ways, they voted to grant "authority" to UL staff "to take whatever steps we saw fit to help correct this situation." Although the affair was billed as a gathering for "well trained women experts in the field of Household Economies [who] discussed at these meetings household management and argued for higher standards in wages and service," the move toward standardization was by no means a middle-class phenomenon. Instead, black working-class women had a direct hand in shaping its course.[15]

The 1933 mass meeting was the culmination of years of grassroots organizing. Local conferences became a primary means by which domestics inserted the ignored field of household labor into New Deal conversations at local, state, and national levels. At a 1930 conference sponsored by St. Louis social welfare organizations—the Phillis Wheatley branch of the YWCA, the Federation of Colored Women's Clubs, and the League of Women Voters—domestic workers "bravely and intelligently" "state[d] their side of the case," wrote T. Arnold Hill, the national UL director of industrial relations. Following a morning session on "the household employment situation in St. Louis," with leaders at various employment placement centers speaking on the subject, the afternoon session featured domestic worker Florence Eldridge, who addressed the topic "Dignifying and Standardizing Household Employment." Other domestics had a chance to speak during a session in which they aired their grievances. Keeping tabs on black workers' activities throughout the United States, Hill featured African American women in the spring of 1930 when he reported his observations of how "Negroes have been in rebellion against domestic service—at least in spirit" in *Opportunity,* the UL's national organ. St. Louis household workers offered their "point of view," he wrote, when they directed their comments to employers who charged black women workers with "technical inefficiency" and "social unfitness."[16]

Critiques such as these, common during the period, reveal the means by which African American women resisted employer authority. "Technical inefficiency" and "social unfitness" were code words for slowdowns, thefts, sabotage, and absenteeism—tactics domestics devised to wrest some control over their time and bodies. Speaking after household employers gave their perspectives, working-class women responded with a litany of abuses they suffered at the hands of housewives. Employers failed to disclose the amount of washing for the day, added responsibilities to agreements, required employees to care for relatives overnight without overtime, and turned back the hands of clocks to prolong work hours. As their testimonies revealed, women cleaned furnaces, built fires, baled ashes, and washed second-, third-, and fourth-story windows from the outside. "Mothers and fathers who have come up through this system abhor the thought of their children following in their footsteps," Hill wrote. And as far as their own labor was concerned, mothers "have objected to the implication of servility as a racial trait" and "have not wished to perpetuate the system of low wages and long hours which prevailed in the industry." As the UL turned to negotiation to manage employer-employee relations, it became clear that the 1930 conference served as a model for beginning the process toward implementing standards in domestic work.[17]

St. Louis household labor reformers modeled their efforts on national campaigns that gained momentum in the early 1930s. The "Suggested Minimum Standards for the Full-Time General House Worker," established at a 1931 national conference of the National Committee on Employer-Employee Relationships in the Home, was the product of an organized effort on the part of middle-class clubwomen, reformers, social scientists, and organizers of state-based labor groups who pioneered the "recent re-discovery of household workers by those who are interested in the welfare of wage-earning women." Led by University of Chicago home economics professor Hazel Kyrk, the committee drew up what the *Literary Digest* called a "Magna Carta." The document called for uniform wages, hours, and working conditions through mutual agreement and cooperation between placement agencies and employer and employee organizations. The 1931 report required that live-in domestics work a maximum of fifty-four hours per week, while live-out employees should not exceed a workweek of forty-eight hours. Overtime pay based on an hourly rate, one free day per week, a one-week vacation with pay, a private living space and bathroom, accident insurance, and an employment contract were policies that could address other immediate concerns. Systems that differentiated between skilled and unskilled workers, reference letters from former employers, and tests to measure competency rounded out the list. An early-twentieth-century example of a labor feminist politics sensitive to racial discrimination, the standards stipulated equal pay for black and white workers.[18]

Reformers analyzed the root cause of overlooking domestic work in national labor efforts. The sheer numbers of women in the field alone warranted intervention, not to mention that the field was known as a site for some of the worst forms of labor exploitation. At the 1931 conference, "it was fully recognized that no machinery existed for establishing and maintaining standards either in the form of organizations of employers and employees or of placement bureaus, and that the hope of making desired standards real depended on such machinery." Reformers understood industrial work as logical, rational, and thus naturally subjected to "scientific" processes. By contrast, household work appeared to be individualistic, decentralized, and "personal" and so posed unique challenges. "Should the problem of household employment be approached as many employers insist as one of right personal relations or of right economic relations?," advocates questioned. Kyrk answered by underscoring the anachronistic image, rejected by actual workers, of the domestic as part of "the family group with the status of the old-time servant whose duties [included] loyalty, unstinted service and consideration only of the family's need." Standardization, the program by which reformers would modernize household labor, aimed not only to regulate hours, earnings, and conditions but also to give the lie to the notion that "any woman can do housework." Stripping domestic work of the personal dimension, reformers insisted that domestic work required skills learned by training, just as industrial work did. This recasting was to strengthen the case for reform.[19]

We should not mistake inclusion of an antidiscrimination clause in the 1931 suggested minimum standards for sustained interest in and long-term commitment to black working-class women. It would not have existed but for the pioneering black women social scientists and radical labor activists struggling nationally and locally who prioritized black working-class women's economic lives. What distinguished black professional women's efforts to prioritize the lives of black working-class women was sustained attentiveness to those largely overlooked in majority-white organizations and committees. Johnson, Wilburn, Buckner, and Abbington were local iterations of nationally known figures such as Ella Baker, Marvel Cooke, and Dorothy Height, who drew attention to twentieth-century "slave markets." The codes that domestic workers and staffers of the Women's Division crafted took shape in the conversations at the 1930 Women's Conference on Household Employment and in the context of the national household labor reform movement.[20]

After the 1933 mass meeting, UL staffers quickly mobilized resources and contacts. Clark formed the Committee on Household Service Problems, which leaders later renamed the Committee on Household Employment Relations. This internal UL committee of staffers and friends of the organization included Edna Gellhorn, Zenobia S. Johnson, Fannie Cook, and Jennie C. Bucker. In addition, three subcommittees were developed to investigate organizing domestic workers with the AFL, connect with the Employment Executives Organization "so that they could discuss and work out a minimum wage that would be satisfactory to the group and to the employers," and organize "round table discussions among groups of employers of household labor." The group also committed to publicizing the effort, "so that better standards could be had in this area, whether or not these workers were covered under a code."[21]

The St. Louis UL's erstwhile concerns about upsetting employers seemed to take a backseat when it came to wages, the issue that most consumed staffers' time and energy. "Quite a discussion as to hours and wages ensued," read the minutes of a UL meeting following the 1933 conference. A month after the meeting, staffers required employers who used their employment bureau to pay a minimum wage of $1.50 plus carfare for day work and $5.00 and carfare weekly. Staffers took their new requirement to UL board members, urging them "to adopt such a recommendation and put it in practice at once" such that placement officers would no longer send "out persons from the League on jobs paying less than the standards that were temporarily suggested." The Urban League Industrial Department persuaded the executive committee of the need to standardize the wage scale and presented a strong case to the UL board for the same. By the end of October 1933, the new standard was in place, though it amounted to only half of the typical pre-Depression rate and only half of what workers had suggested. Remembered as "the first minimum standard in St. Louis for wages for household service," the move stabilized the Industrial Department's wage scale after a round of severe fluctuations.[22]

The emergence of the Urban League's employment bureau in the 1930s and its power to enforce standards because of domestic worker organizing constituted a radical moment for the uplift organization. Despite a decline in placements, which came "naturally, when we quoted our minimum wages to prospective employers, [and as a result] a number of job-possibilities were lost and workers were sought from other sources," the UL enforced the new standard. It widened the league's outreach. In early 1934, for example, through a household conference in Webster Groves, a suburb with a sizable black population, the employment office tapped a new pool of employers willing to abide by the new standard. Some domestic workers, however, cared little about the new wage stipulation, because they were desperate for work and were "willing to work for less than what we [the UL] were asking for them." By the end of 1934, UL staffers reported an increase in the number of placements paying higher than the standard. Their efforts bore fruit: "We emphasized sending out experienced, efficient help in cases where higher wages were being sought." The staff even encouraged other employment agencies to follow suit. For instance, in 1938 the UL persuaded the State Employment Service to accept the standard, but after a change in its administration "this agreement was ignored and emphasis put on numbers placed rather than standards and race welfare." By 1939 it could be reported that the "[standard] rates hold now and as far as possible are adhered to." So important were wages that the UL changed one important detail. From initially considering live-in work a special case, after some discussion, the UL reasoned that live-in workers must be included, because most domestic workers consistently rejected lower offers, and a substantial number of these substandard work offers went unfulfilled. Under staff member Charles Collier, a local leader in the National Negro Congress, the UL therefore demanded five dollars per week for live-ins.[23]

The militancy of the UL Women's Division, and that of Collier, was well represented in post–September 1933 efforts. At the 1933 September mass meeting, Johnson framed the purpose of the gathering as applying the New Deal to household work, but only a few months after the meeting, staff emphasized the goal of giving power to domestics to shape UL operations. Women's Division staffers' insistence on enforcing a higher wage scale came as a result of domestic workers' testimony. "The action [of formalizing the wage scale]," a UL report found, "resulted from the expressions that the workers themselves were given an opportunity to make at a mass meeting sponsored by the Industrial Department for the purpose of learning the sentiment and reactions of the workers." The women staffers accorded black working-class women the authority to devise solutions to their own problems, a tactic also used by national civil rights worker Ella Baker, whose political organizing notably grew in the crucible of Depression-era economic activism. As an incident in late 1933 involving factory workers underscored, the UL's labor militancy assumed the form of support for worker input and, to some extent, workers' control. After an entire workforce of twenty-four women lost their jobs at a paint company, UL staffers decided that "further action on this matter depends on what the girls themselves decide to do in protest against this unfairness, with whatever cooperation the UL can give them."[24]

In cases regarding employer power over workplace relations and structure, UL staff typically advocated accommodation, while workers often pushed for outright defiance. In some cases, what were "petty faults" to UL staff members were serious infractions to wage-earning women. In their readiness to implement their own sense of the value of their labor and apply aggressive approaches to securing changes that accorded dignity and respect, African American women posed challenges to employers, to UL staffers, and even to other labor groups. For example, six maids working at the Roosevelt Hotel found themselves outside of the UL's good graces as they implemented their version of labor dignity. The women refused to accept a rotating schedule whereby a few would work during select weeks and have at least one free Sunday. Unsatisfied, the women demanded all Sundays off for all maids and, after their request was refused, walked off the job. They tried to keep a day reserved for important religious and community work as well as rest and rejuvenation, but their collective resistance did not translate into support. Collier reported, "The girls were not justified in pursuing such action, and had no redress because the policy of all hotels is to keep a minimum number of employees themselves on duty on Sundays." The UL found the incident an example of how "sometimes Negro employees themselves make unreasonable and unfair demands—and having walked off the job voluntarily under circumstances that were not justified, the League could not very well intervene on behalf of these girls." Similarly, wives of personal service workers and women household employees garnered an equal degree of disdain. Organizers formed a ladies' auxiliary in June 1935 to create "some real strength" within the ranks of the janitors group, also creating "a nucleus of the formation of an organization of household workers." Women members angered workers and UL officials alike when they envisioned "a program not only as an auxiliary of the janitors' organization but also as an organization of women employed in the building service field."[25]

Examples of women workers creating their own labor reform program suggest that while employers could and often did circumvent standards, and UL Industrial Department leaders selected which aspects to enforce, domestics carried an enhanced measure of power by virtue of the newly established code to devise and implement their own reform program. Women workers certainly challenged employer authority prior to the league's intervention, but their resistance assumed greater dimensions during the 1930s as UL Women's Division leaders began responding in a formal capacity to women workers' complaints. The 1933 household mass meeting and shifts in UL policy lent moral legitimacy and institutional backing to women's workplace resistance, even as UL personnel critiqued women workers' politics.

Domestic workers pressured the UL and helped make possible black women staffers' ability to forge an "elastic" organization that stretched wide enough to organize workers with a unique set of labor conditions. Domestic workers and members of the Women's Division created subtle yet important changes in household employment at the local level, generating an opening for black women to engage the urban political landscape through building a case for dignified work through standardization. Together, though not without disagreement and conflict, they forged their own new deal by literally writing black working-class women into protections that were not initially designed to include them. Domestics' push to transform the Urban League into a worker organization holds implications for current policy debates about formalizing an enforcement role for community organizations that are often better connected to and knowledgeable about local labor markets. What is perhaps useful to contemporary domestic-worker organizing campaigns is that with the St. Louis case study, the push to enforcement was a direct outcome of domestic worker agitation, itself a creative response to negligent public policy and limited governmental action.[26]

Wartime Transformations

As the engine of wartime production revved up in the early 1940s, African American women workers took advantage of the change, and staffers of the St. Louis Urban League grew increasingly anxious as a result. Having declared in the late 1930s that "household employment . . . is by no means slipping," the Urban League changed its tune just a few years later. For the first three months of 1941, the league's employment office recorded numerous orders for domestic work that women simply ignored. An Urban League report identified the impact of women's collective refusal when it found that while during the Depression 90 percent of African American women found domestic placements through the league, by the 1940s, "not one out of ten applicants . . . accept[ed] regular employment in domestic service paying (as high as) $15 to $20 a week." "Irate" housewives across the city called the "domestic servant problem" "ridiculous" in their frequent complaints to the league. Housewives "go begging for days in our Employment Office unless we find some old and experienced domestic who had become disillusioned with the atmosphere and exacting routine of factory or other 'defense jobs,'" one league report stated. The UL found itself in the throes of a "mad scramble for the services of much needed help."[27]

For an increasing number of women, factory work was standardization in purer form, since regimented industrial work provided sturdier ground upon which to stand. Former domestics turned industrial workers wanted, as one put it, "to make some of that good money." Other women explained that they were "just tired spending all my life away from my family and people" and that you were "never done working when you live with white folks." Racial uplift organizations and what Tomiko Brown-Nagin calls "pragmatic civil rights groups," like the St. Louis Urban League, experienced a crisis of sorts as improved conditions failed to inspire women to pursue household work. The league blamed the infectious spread of factory fever on "active groups" such as the Communist Party, which "confus[ed] the minds of Negro women." The true culprit, however, was burgeoning labor radicalism and emerging state, municipal, and civic apparatuses that supported working people; in addition, wartime labor demands transformed neighborhood and workplace. Domestic workers actively found their way into these developments. The number of African American women in domestic service decreased from 59.9 percent to 44.6 percent, while the number in industry rose from 6.5 percent to 18.0 percent during World War II. African American women were still the "last hired" and "first fired," but wartime upheaval spurred opportunities for rethinking "African American working womanhood" in a way that touched those who crossed the job line and even those who remained in the "old" field of domestic labor. Domestic workers played an active part in their own economic transformation, posing for their patrons nothing short of a crisis.[28]

The UL responded. The local group hosted a Conference on Household Employment in March 1941, explaining that "it was deemed necessary to again consider the problems of this field of employment because of the possibility of a sharp decrease in the potential number of household employees, since National Defense project and factory work openings were causing not only a lack of interest in house work but a complete refusal on the part of many applicants to consider the household field." A committee of community representatives recommended the creation of a written and signed agreement between a domestic worker and her employer. The written agreement, sent to a small group for review, called for bold changes. Again, the language points to a shift. UL Women's Division staffers no longer referred to "suggested" and "voluntary" measures, but to a signed "written agreement," reflecting their willingness to press employers and enforce their rules. The agreement required employers to specify whether the work was temporary or permanent, the number of work hours per week, the wage rate, and procedures for compensating workers. Employers also had to delineate in precise terms the "explanation of service duties," the number of adults and children in the employer's household, and "the employee's obligations to children, invalids, and pets." The agreement included a space for indicating time off during the week and on Sundays and holidays. It included vacation time and an allotted number of employee absences. A final section required employers to specify start dates and the manner in which the employee would receive her wage. Finally, the agreement required employers to provide advance notice of termination. The subcommittee planned to have the specified written agreement, to be "signed by household employer and employee," win "city-wide approval" by the time of the Household Employment Institute scheduled for October 1941. Staffers designed the document to protect domestic workers from abusive employer practices. In an important move, the Women's Division again followed the lead of domestic workers with the written agreement. This time around, the UL committed itself to enforcing improvements that extended well beyond wages, including the very issues that domestics tried to enforce years earlier without UL support.[29]

It is likely that the league's undated "Tentative Draft of Household Standards in St. Louis" accompanied the committee's written agreement, since the tentative draft called for a "written agreement in duplicate signed by employer and employee." Stipulating that "servant" or "maid" be replaced by the term "household employee" or "household worker," with "duties defined clearly," the tentative draft was a further development of standardization. It sought to expand the rights of women workers and thus draw them back to the household employment field. The draft included starting and quitting times, minimum wage, overtime pay, advance notice of termination, telephone use, "church time," paid sick leave, and rest periods. While the 1941 conference included a session titled "Health Examinations for Household Employees," the tentative draft required employers and their families to undergo a physical examination, as "the employee shall be informed of any contagious or infectious diseases in the family, such as tuberculosis." The suggested rate of the post-1941 household employment conference showed dramatic increases compared to the post-1933 mass meeting rate of $1.50 and carfare per day plus $5.00 per week for live-out workers, and $5.00 per week for live-in employees. Competing with wages for industrial work, the minimum scale for "inexperienced" day workers was now $18.00 per week for the time in which the worker received training, during a period that the UL-designated Committee on Training would arrange. Following completion of a training course, cooks earned a minimum of $20.00–$25.00 per week, and those who performed "downstairs work" received $25.00–$35.00 per week. The standards made room for greater detail: if a worker served breakfast and dinner, she had three afternoon hours "during which time . . . [she] is free to follow her own pursuits." The agreement established a maximum workday of nine hours and a record of hours to be checked and approved by employers. Upon hire, workers had at least "four of the eight national holidays to be completed free," and after one year of work, household employees were to receive one week of paid vacation. Entry-level workers were to earn two hours per week for training sources, and a live-in worker should have a "private room adequately furnished in which she could entertain friends; adequate access to and use of bath; and adequate and nutritious diet" and "the privilege of using either the side or front door."[30]

The voluntary agreement and the tentative draft did not survive the planning process, however. The chairman of an eleven-member steering committee canceled plans to bring the voluntary agreement to a citywide vote during the Institute on Household Employment in October 1941 because of "rumors and newspaper reports of a union of housemaids being formed in the St. Louis area" that surfaced just one month prior to the workshop. "The efforts and sincere interests of a larger number of women were scrapped," Valla Abbington, staffer of the UL Women's Division, lamented in a 1941 annual report. "Had this project been completed, St. Louis would have had a permanent committee on household employment acting as a commission to hear and advise on problems arising in this field of employment and also a written agreement to be signed by both employer and employee. Both would have been a great stabilizer of working conditions."[31]

Indeed, a permanent committee and signed agreement would have culminated the Women's Division's decade-long effort and would have signaled concrete progress. This attempt was the final one before the UL fundamentally changed the way it handled its domestic worker clients. Frustrated, by the end of the 1940s the Urban League of St. Louis transferred all of its domestic and personal service applicants to the Missouri State Employment Service office, combined its men's and women's divisions, and charged applicants an annual registration fee. The women's division was, in effect, no more. League leadership, especially Clark and some members of the industrial department, wanted to "weed out a large number of accruing, unfilled, low-wage" workers and the "considerable number of people who clog up our waiting room space for purposes of sociability, convenient accommodation and for the variety of contacts." Of course, the majority of such persons were black women. There were indeed doubts about the proposed plan. How could the league transfer such a large group of the most marginal workers to a placement service known for accepting standards "far below our wage scale"? How could the league give up the connection between successful placements in domestic service and the opening of new industrial jobs? After all, some of the early placements in garment factories came as a direct result of a preexisting working relationship with an employer who hired black women for domestic jobs. Turning over "the large load of placements of domestic workers" to the Missouri State Employment Service was risky, the league acknowledged, but "a working relationship" needed to develop between the two. Besides, the "files accumulating each month" proved too powerful. The league was placing 90 percent of the workers who came to the office in low-skill jobs, and this work "handicaps a staff of eight persons who spend most of their day in the office in the least productive end of their responsibility," one staffer complained. The old division between domestic and industrial work morphed into four new levels: public utilities / government agencies, heavy industry, manufacturing, and commercial. Not only had the organization managed to defeminize its operations, but it also transformed itself into the public face of "finer Negro" employment. The "twenty years of specialized placement service" in which "the problems in the women's section" assumed central stage had come to an end. M. Leo Bohanon, John T. Clark's successor, celebrated the organizational shift, citing the fact that 80 percent of the Urban League's placements in 1953 were in the skilled, clerical, or other jobs classified as "professional." Comparing this statistic to that of job placement figures in 1948, the last year before staff implemented the shift, Bohanon found that "the dropping of routine placement services and services to applicants and employers concerned only with unskilled labor" proved to be a change worth undertaking. It could be made "without ill-effect" because mainstream employment services had no desire to elevate the status of black workers beyond that of unskilled laborers. In effect, the Urban League had little competition.[32]

What new agenda the incoming leadership would adopt remained uncertain, but the legacy of the Gateway City league's first phase, whereby jobs held central place, had been established. Through the UL Women's Division, black working-class women forged a creative culture of resistance that imagined diverse paths to economic empowerment inclusive of, but not limited to, unionization. They made the New Deal work for them even as it was not intended to do so, and their labor activity set the stage for women's wartime labor activism in defense plants across the city. Subtle yet important changes in domestic work at the local level, wrought by the gritty work of negotiation between employee and employer, social service patron and domestic worker client, cracked open fissures for black women to engage the urban political landscape. This they did by means of a malleable, if at times unwitting, mainline civil rights organization.

The political labors of black working-class women in the household employment sector proved successful into the new decade. As black working-class women in St. Louis continued to work hard to avoid domestic work if they could, the domestic work shortage persisted. Now handling, with other state- and city-based firms, the bulk of employment queries for day workers or those classified as "unskilled" household workers since the St. Louis Urban League had released workers falling under this category in 1948 was the Missouri Division of Employment, which announced that the city needed domestic workers. The stigma long associated with this employment had been lifted, local manager Paul P. Connole maintained; it was "no longer considered work of drudgery or servitude"; women could find "good jobs" as "maids, cooks, housekeepers, and day workers" that paid "exceptionally good wages" and provided "good home-like living conditions" with "private rooms with bath and home privileges," should the arrangement stipulate a living-in arrangement. Employers "were very liberal" these days, providing benefits comparable to what one might find in industrial employment.[33]

In the short run, the radical labor movement and the Urban League's respectable labor militancy reaped more from black women workers' participation than did black women workers themselves. Nut pickers and domestics suffered significant losses, but their participation in the economic justice struggle matured their politics, connected them to key constituencies, and disrupted their political marginality. Before the emergence of the Congress of Industrial Organizations and its practice of interracial unionism, the Nut Pickers' Union and the domestic workers collective outlined the strategies and ideologies of later working-class activists and New Deal architects and implementers.

3

"The Fight against Economic Slavery"

Clerks and Youth Activism in the Don't Buy Where You Can't Work Movement

When a storeowner opened a Woolworth five-and-dime store in a black neighborhood in 1932, members of the St. Louis Housewives' League (HL) staged Don't Buy Where You Can't Work pickets to win sales positions for black young women. The recently formed Housewives' League mobilized black professional women to promote black businesses, sound financial stewardship, and black employment through strategic use of their resources. With chapters scattered across the country in major urban-industrial cities such as New York, Chicago, Pittsburgh, and Detroit, HL organizers aimed to mitigate the effects of acute economic suffering by turning inward to mobilize the material and immaterial resources of their own communities. Women carried critical economic power; their collective efforts could move communities closer to racial self-determination in an era when racial and economic discrimination made organization "a matter of self-preservation and protection," so the argument went. With deep ties to the National Negro Business League, which Booker T. Washington had founded in 1900 to support black entrepreneurship and thereby help black people as a whole, the HL extended black self-help traditions of the late nineteenth century as it joined the black cooperative movement of the 1930s.[1]

Just a few years after the St. Louis HL held its protest, the Colored Clerks' Circle targeted the same Woolworths store and issued a similar demand: jobs for young black women. The CCC took a militant approach by pushing for 80 percent representation of black women workers among the store's employees. Failing to meet the goal, the CCC negotiated terms by which owners agreed to desegregate by 50 percent the combined workforces of their two stores located in black neighborhoods. Employing direct action, boycotts, and picket lines, or mass community pressure, to focus not on building black business but on solving the severe unemployment crisis facing black youth, the Colored Clerks' Circle revised and updated the Housewives' League's program. CCC members advanced a racial agenda centered on the employment of young black women and, in doing so, militated against prescriptions that prioritized economic relief and full employment for the heads of black households, what community members and public policymakers commonly and inaccurately defined as black men. Like activists of the black economic rights movement in Chicago who "used girls' employment struggle to bolster their introduction of economic sanctions and commercial boycotting to Black Belt residents," as Marcia Chatelain shows, the CCC directly linked the fate of young black women's economic prospects to notions of racial survival, progress, and destiny.[2]

The St. Louis Don't Buy Where You Can't Work movement, which primarily consisted of the HL and the CCC, challenged deep-rooted understandings of gendered economic politics in black civil rights activism. Instead of positioning black men's economic experiences as the locus of concern, the two groups placed emphasis on black women's economic resources and employment prospects. To varying degrees, the two organizations merged racial self-determination, economic nationalism, women's domestic and communal roles, and consumer activism. Although one organization emphasized black women's consumption and their roles as wives and mothers, and the other focused on black women's labor outside the home in the paid labor force, both advanced the notion that black women's economic pursuits—their employment and their consumption—were indispensable to racial survival and economic well-being.[3]

The local Don't Buy Where You Can't Work movement in St. Louis reflected a broader, national trend of the emergence of black protest politics and the effective use of mass mobilization and cooperative economic strategies during the Great Depression. Scholars locate the movement's origins in the urban industrial Midwest, where progressive *Chicago Whip* editor and political evangelist Joseph Bibb urged black leaders to join a collective movement to increase the economic strength of black communities. Harlem had its share of willing participants, and not long afterward, local versions of the movement emerged in Philadelphia, Richmond, Cincinnati, Pittsburgh, St. Louis, and other major cities with sizable black populations. The New Negro Alliance of Washington, DC, typified the concerns and activities of most Don't Buy Where You Can't Work organizations, as it "was principally interested in such general problems as obtaining civil rights, setting up racial cooperatives, securing employment for Negroes in the District of Columbia government, and securing jobs in private industry through the use of consumer pressure." Don't Buy Where You Can't Work campaigns often acted as battlegrounds for conflicts over tactics, strategy, and generational leadership. Black youths of the New Negro Alliance, for example, grew increasingly frustrated with the leadership of "older and well-established Negroes," or "the respectable, the well-off, and the stuffed-shirt residents of the city," who not only "dominated" racial politics but had, to the youths' minds, exhibited a "general passivity and complete lack of militancy." Disputes notwithstanding, the organizations that made up the Don't Buy Where You Can't Work movement reflected a cross-section of black communities.[4]

The Housewives' League of St. Louis

From its inception, the St. Louis Housewives' League, which was the first group to establish the Don't Buy Where You Can't Work movement in St. Louis, demonstrated the success of black women's economic activism. One year after Fannie B. Peck founded the Detroit Housewives' League, Sumner High School teacher Edwina Wright organized a meeting at Poro College on March 9, 1931, to establish the St. Louis chapter. Two thousand black women assumed the charge "to do all within their power to build bigger and better businesses in St. Louis." The HL's first forays into activism began in the year of its founding, when a group of black women boycotted the St. Louis Dairy Company, located in a black neighborhood. Women activists targeted the business because managers had not hired and had refused to hire black workers since opening its doors in the late nineteenth century. Among the organization's more successful early campaigns, the HL Dairy Company boycott resulted in the hiring of black men as milk wagon drivers with routes that passed through black residential neighborhoods. As "the first to adopt a democratic employment policy," the company set a standard for white-owned and -operated businesses that were located in black commercial districts. After one year, the HL targeted Woolworths, the Nafziger Baking Company, the White Baking Company, and the Pevely Dairy Company, waging campaigns that won jobs for black youths. Members shared a belief in "the need of building an economic structure" that "brought about an improved economic out-look for Negroes in business, while at the same time bringing about a positive and effective employment practice on the part of large concerns in the St. Louis area who were receiving a larger percent of their daily revenue from the Negro market." Historian Anne Valk notes that the Housewives' Leagues were most effective when they engaged in mass demonstrations and protests, producing "an economic impact that compared favorably with CIO organizing efforts and government hiring of black workers."[5]

The Housewives' League foregrounded black women's economic activity to mobilize black communities. Offering a glimpse into members' political imagination, "The Housewives' League Rally Song" stated that black women's spending held the power to construct "better homes and gardens far as Eden was of old." Sung to the tune of "The Battle Hymn of the Republic," the song adapted the Civil War anthem "John Brown's Body" to portray black women as a political army. Written in 1861 to honor the abolitionist John Brown and sung by Union soldiers, the tune had close ties to the theme of black emancipation. HL members communicated the message that racial freedom came by way of black women's economic militancy in much the same way that Boston-based poet, suffragist, and antislavery proponent Julia Ward Howe's verses, upon which "The Battle Hymn of the Republic" is based, signified nationalist assertion. In the twentieth century, singer, athlete, and activist Paul Robeson and labor activist and writer Ralph Chaplin interpreted the tune, with Chaplin borrowing it to compose the popular labor anthem "Solidarity Forever." When they adapted the tune to fit their struggle, the HL appropriately joined a song tradition that, for David R. Roediger, "brought together the emancipation of slaves, of women, and of wage workers." To improve the physical and aesthetic quality of the home, members would make wise use of their finances to save and engage in refined consumerism, purchasing material objects like "art" and "tome" to access "truest culture." On behalf of "Youth," members would win the fight for fair employment by patronizing "our tradesmen," who would, in turn, hire the daughters, sons, nieces, nephews, and friends of HL members. Targeted consumption would benefit women themselves by affording greater leisure "for things that're better far than gold." Like the *Argus* editorialist who, in lending his support, argued, "If we can get the women organized . . . and get the men behind them, much good can be accomplished in solidifying our interest," "The Housewives' League Rally Song" recognized black women as leaders of their communities.[6]

The varied status of active St. Louis Housewives' League organizers suggests that advancing black middle-class and professional respectability did not necessarily depend on members' standing in the paid workforce. Not all HL members were "housewives" in the sense that they did not hold jobs. Some, usually those married to black professional men, had enough resources to restrict their labor to the home, while others worked to make ends meet. "Café owners, a hat shop proprietor, maids, secretaries, and beauticians, as well as the wives of shop owners, physicians, and insurance agents," all composed the membership during the 1940s. The first two HL presidents, Mrs. W. C. Bridges and Mrs. Ida B. Haskell, were both married to physicians, while Kitty Hall, the third president, worked as a matron at the Eden Theater. National Negro Business League members Beulah Kilgore-Bailey, Mae Layne, and Ethel L. Merriweather, owners of a tearoom, a hat shop, and a restaurant, respectively, represented the ideal member or leader, but such representation tended to mask the organization's occupational diversity.[7]

In promoting their cause through the dual prism of black male political leadership and employment, the St. Louis Housewives' League replicated the approaches of certain Don't Buy Where You Can't Work leaders who advanced binary notions of women as consumers and men as producers. HL-organized mass meetings included women-led workshops on household budgeting and featured men as keynote speakers. "The uniting of the buying power of the women for our economic benefit" was the goal to which black communities should aspire, HL organizers told participants who made up a "large and enthusiastic crowd" at Union Memorial Church in March 1931. All speakers save Edwina Wright, the president of the College Women's Association, were men. Cosponsored by the Negro

Business League, the gathering promoted black male leaders' political visions by spotlighting their voices. Chicago-based journalist Joseph Bibb, an early founder of the Don't Buy Where You Can't Work movement, cited racial disparities in the employment sector and black male economic vulnerability in his call for collective action. In stark terms, he designated black women's economic activity as the point at which racial survival and black economic thriving through entrepreneurship intersected. "Now is the time to choose between patronizing Negro business, or standing in the bread lines," he implored. Writer George Schuyler also addressed the group. In similar fashion, *St. Louis Call* editorialist and HL supporter Samuel P. Bills summoned black women's economic power in his local coverage of the Don't Buy Where You Can't Work campaign, suggesting that black women's consumption could address young black male unemployment. Will organizations like the Association of Colored Women's Clubs and the NAACP continue with business as usual or with spending dollars uncritically, "without saying a word about employment?," he queried. Or will the HL fill the vacuum and help the "many Negro boys who can meet every requirement" by making it possible for black young men to secure telegram messenger jobs. As Don't Buy Where You Can't Work or HL spokespersons, Bibb and Bills designated black women's economic activity, their consumption in particular, as their racial community's political weapon of choice. The two voices defined black economic misery as a problem of black male unemployment.[8]

By employing maternalist politics, HL members carved out space for themselves in the crowded world of 1930s black mass politics. There, they advanced a compelling and persuasive assertion about the possibility of black advancement through politically actualized black women, and more, through particular deployment of black women's economic experiences and resources. The HL crafted an explicit black economic feminism that, in keeping with the tradition, promoted the notion that black women held the power to make racial uplift possible. After the HL went through a period of inactivity between 1932 and 1936, Kitty Hall revived the organization as president. Under her leadership, which extended to the immediate postwar period, the group expanded to nearby Alton, Illinois; Kinloch, Missouri; and Prospect Hill in St. Louis County and implemented a consumer education program. The St. Louis Housewives'

League continued its work in the Gateway City into subsequent decades, serving as host for the National Housewives' League three times, in 1956, when the organization for the first time held its national conference in the southern central region; in 1965, when Hannah Williams served as president; and again in 1980. Succeeding Kitty Hall in 1949, Williams piloted social welfare programs through partnership with the Missouri Social Welfare Association, the United Charity Fund, the YMCA, the YWCA, and the NAACP and also established an active youth league.[9]

The Colored Clerks' Circle

The St. Louis HL laid the groundwork for the emergence of youth-oriented groups to advance the cause of black self-determination by modeling how to effectively mobilize a community and devise campaigns that produced tangible results and improvements. Having conducted numerous campaigns that won jobs for young people, black women organizers "readied" their communities for later campaigns that would follow a similar model. The HL demonstrated residents' economic power, particularly their power to address the economic needs of their families and communities to shape spaces of commercial activity in their own neighborhoods. The organization also modeled how to garner support through mass meetings, campaigning, and building partnerships with influential black leaders, especially pastors. While the HL and the CCC shared basic principles, there were important differences between the two. The CCC was a black youth organization that shunned accommodation and quietism in favor of direct action, confrontation, public shaming, and boycotts. Like the HL, the CCC employed a strict transactional approach—money for jobs—which involved mobilizing "the power of the purse," but it defined the quest for black economic self-determination as a project to secure decent employment for young black people, especially black women. Both groups solicited the support of black community institutions, but the CCC was much more willing to highlight the distinctions between its methods and that of older, established leaders and organizations. It was also not opposed to publicly critiquing them.

Founded on March 31, 1937, the Colored Clerks' Circle grew out of two overlapping realities: "economic pressure," or the lack of jobs

open to black youths, and "the unwillingness of the solid mass of merchants, who thrive on the business of Negro people to employ qualified Negro clerks and salesmen." In St. Louis, the black unemployment
rate exceeded 50 percent during the Great Depression, and black young
people were among the hardest hit. Working under the assumption that
there was political possibility in applying community pressure to store
merchants whose shops were located in black communities, CCC leaders turned their attention to black commercial districts on Easton Avenue
and Franklin Avenue, for example, where numerous small shops lined
the streets. Because the vast majority of the shops were white-owned and
white-operated and depended on black dollars for survival, CCC leaders surmised, as they took a page out of the Don't Buy Where You Can't
Work movement's playbook, that with pressure they could create job
opportunity. The group set out to cultivate "a city wide demand that
merchants in Negro neighborhoods should return part of the money
spent by Negro housewives back to the Negro community in the form
of clerkship jobs for qualified young Negro men and women." Eschewing a focus on black business, activists defined their fundamental work as
making space for black youth in St. Louis's industrial and entrepreneur-
ial life. In their formulation, community mobilization to win black youth
employment was tantamount to "the fight against economic slavery." To
put it another way, the CCC suggested that black youth employment
and economic dignity would bring about an economic liberation such
that "the Negro may take his place among the leaders of the world."
The CCC's purpose, as defined in its articles of agreement, was to "promote the best interests of the Negro Race by fostering, encouraging and
stimulating good community relationships between Negroes and other
races in the community; to foster, develop, encourage, train and educate
Negroes to qualify for and obtain positions in the economic and industrial activities and businesses; and to develop, foster and maintain ethi-
cal business practices and standards between Negroes and other races;
to pursue generally a program conducive to the welfare of its members
and the attainment of its objectives towards the community and the public generally." These stated goals placed heavy emphasis on community,
race relations, and local business development, but the Colored Clerks'
Circle's day-to-day practice, from the outset, was inwardly focused; it

concentrated on black young people's material well-being and quality of life.[10]

The CCC was a serious civil rights group that rivaled any well-established association in terms of its structure, development, and organization. Many black youths were attracted to an organization that reflected their sense of worth and determination and provided a space where they could meet with other youth in the city who shared similar experiences. Only high school graduates between the ages of eighteen and thirty-five were eligible for membership. To initiate the consideration process, prospective members had to complete an application and submit strong letters of recommendation from "two responsible citizens." The CCC constitution held members to strict standards. Prospective members were required to pay a membership fee and attend three consecutive meetings before entering a probationary period, which lasted three weeks. Only after an individual maintained good standing for an additional four weeks following the probationary period could she become a regular member. A designated membership committee had to examine a prospective member's application and performance within the organization for two weeks before presenting a candidate's membership to the general body for a vote. Membership Committee members kept a watchful eye on those who endured the grueling admissions process; the Membership Committee was tasked with recording attendance at each meeting and judging "the validity of excuses offered by members for absence from regular meetings." Members were held to strict standards, including the outlined sanctions for absences, nonparticipation, and the failure to pay dues.[11]

Ostensibly an organization catering to broader community interests, the Colored Clerks' Circle actually functioned as a female-led organization for formally educated black working-class women. Women held executive office positions. Josie Hawthorne, for example, handled communications as secretary; along with president Frank M. Jones, she served as the face of the organization. Hawthorne attended a youth conference in Illinois as a CCC delegate, and her colleagues appointed her adviser to a new CCC program whereby members would attend black churches on a monthly, rotational basis to drum up support for their organization. Armelda Delany was vice president. Zenobia Shoulders Johnson, an Urban League staff member and a strong supporter of black working-class women, served on the CCC advisory board, made up of black community leaders who helped to build and guide the organization in its early stages of development. The CCC rank and file "grew almost overnight" as leaders successfully recruited new members and mirrored the organization's penchant for women's leadership. Membership rolls not only reveal that women far outnumbered men, but they also show that a sizable number of members were neighbors who lived just a few blocks from one another or on the same or nearby streets. Women numerically dominated the group to such an extent that, after two years of successful operation, the leadership chose to close the organization to women because "the membership [was] entirely too large especially where ladies were concerned. Therefore, it was necessary to close the membership to ladies in order that those who were members would stand a chance of securing positions." After only one year, organizers founded a second CCC, Colored Clerks' Circle No. 2, to address its growing numbers and serve black youth who lived east of Grand Avenue and those in the midtown section of the city.[12]

The Colored Clerks' Circle embraced confrontational methods, effectively employing community pressure and direct action to create space in the labor market for black young women. Organizers distinguished their group as a black organization with an economic activist program that used direct action and targeted political pressure to realize its goals. Before conducting boycotts and pickets, members first conducted surveys to assess a workforce's racial composition; they also conducted outreach to pastors and community leaders to win their support. In the organization's founding month, activists targeted a five-and-dime store with negative publicity and economic sanction, which resulted in the hiring of the first two black women in the city to work as the store's clerks. The CCC picketed at least 150 stores within its first year and won more than two hundred jobs for its members in the first three years of its existence. Jobs were won for black women at small-scale retail establishments, including Gerken's Hat Shoppe, Matier Shoe Store, Walgreen's Drug Store, and Velvet Freeze, an ice cream shop. Managers of Nafziger Baking Company buckled under CCC pressure and soon hired young black women as "Taystee Bread" door-to-door demonstrators and as "Taystee Hostesses" to distribute samples to Saturday morning grocery shoppers. Nafziger

Company became a leader in industrial integration when it opened a plant in a black neighborhood and promised to further increase its black workforce. Young women such as A. Wiglet, Adele Smiley, and Vivian Crenshaw of Jacobs Ladies Ready to Wear Store; Evelyn Woods; Helen Holloway; Paris Jones (also chairperson of the CCC's Youth Group committee); and Woolworths clerk Ruby Cochrell were just some of the beneficiaries. In 1938 the CCC engaged in "thirty days of walking in the sun and rain on the picket lines," conducted mass meetings, and distributed handbills, winning jobs for black workers in all Kroger establishments located in black neighborhoods. As a job placement agency for its members, the circle established the rule that "no partiality should be shown in securing employment for Circle members" and "the person best qualified for the position should be presented to the merchant desiring to employ a new clerk."[13]

The struggle for worker rights not only involved creating space for young black women workers but also encompassed offering training opportunities, critiquing degrading jobs, monitoring the experiences of the newly hired, and intervening where appropriate. In contrast to the HL's program, the CCC offered classes in consumer education and in sales to make its members more competitive. The Woolworths employees who had secured positions nonetheless counted on the CCC to protest segregated arrangements that reserved a lounge and a radio for white female employees and provided "a small room in the basement" with just one restroom for black female workers. Enterprise Cleaners learned of the youth organization after activists called for a citywide boycott, urging black residents to stop using the business and to cancel their accounts. "It is our policy to carry our facts directly to the public when we are involved in a situation for dignified employment for Negroes," the CCC circular read. For seven years, the CCC and the Urban League tried unsuccessfully to break the color line at Enterprise. For the latest campaign, the CCC demanded that company managers hire drivers, plant workers, and one female office assistant at the weekly wage of fourteen dollars per week. Winning such demands at Scott Cleaners, the CCC replicated its methods for other businesses. Prying open space for black young people involved securing jobs that reflected their worth and value, so despite the fact that Enterprise managers had hired a "Negro dressed in an insulting red monkey suit to attract Negro business" and a "Negro motorcycle driver" to ride through black neighborhoods to promote the company, the CCC still marked the company as a practitioner of racial segregation and discrimination. "Do not be misled by these persons," their letter warned community members, in reference to the two black employees, "Enterprise is still unfair." With economic dignity as its focus, the CCC attempted to fully address the multiple and overlapping issues of the crisis in black youth unemployment.[14]

It would have been easy to misname the CCC, designating it as an independent community-based union because of the group's methods and its commitment to supporting black workers and diversifying workforces. Indeed, CCC campaigns so powerfully reflected unionist principles, especially those of the left-led CIO variety, that members felt compelled to clarify their standing. "We are not union," their literature read, "yet we would be foolish not to subscribe to the union principle for jobs, better pay, a guarantee of stable and permanent employment." The organization urged its supporters, "Don't walk through a Circle picket line." While the black youth organization initially rejected the idea of building an open coalition with "the dangerous union obstacle," it later reneged. "Today we fight side by side with the Union (Negro and White) who recognize our sincerity—often people must suffer together to recognize mutual needs." In August 1937 the group applied for membership in the Negro Trade Union League, a successor to the Negro Workers' Council, a St. Louis Urban League program designed to establish a black independent labor organization as an alternative to the AFL, which barred black workers. Representing a "broad swath of the black working-class public," the Negro Trade Union League won jobs for workers and advocated on their behalf. Although that organization was not an established union, it made effective use of collective bargaining techniques. Some commentators even called CCC members "disciples" of A. Philip Randolph because they, like the socialist, built a movement based upon the principle that "through workers' organizations," activists could direct "the Negro masses the way toward economic freedom."[15]

CCC activists linked the fight for a decent life through fair employment and equal economic opportunity to the struggle for educational and recreational freedom. For example, it is likely that CCC activists were also members of the Negro Youth Forum, which picketed the Strand Theater, a "white-owned, but Negro patronized" movie house, to win motion-picture-operator positions for black workers. That same year, the CCC also protested the 1938 Supreme Court decision in *State of Missouri ex rel. Gaines v. Canada*, which ordered the state of Missouri to create a separate law school for black professional students to fulfill the mandate of the "separate but equal" clause in the 1896 *Plessy v. Ferguson* decision. The following year, CCC activists took to the streets surrounding Poro College in the Ville, where state officials planned to house the state's black law school. "This protest was made," explained a history of the organization written by members, "because the organization felt that it was a slap in the face to the race as well as being inadequate." Criticizing the Missouri legislature for repurposing a former beauty school into a makeshift law school for black students, youth activists explained, "In 1939, our protest was made in regards to the inadequate, improvised law school given our community. We only asked for equal educational facilities that the Negro youth might be ably prepared to face the world and compete with all people." While most CCC activism targeted job discrimination, it also included picketing theaters that enforced segregated seating. For example, not long after they learned that employees of the Municipal Auditorium would seat black and white attendees separately for an upcoming Benny Goodman concert and dance, circle members distributed handbills urging black youth to boycott. Most of them did; only about fifty blacks attended. The activist-oriented Sidney R. Williams, a member and leader of the St. Louis Urban League's Industrial Department, noted that CCC members "have [led] numerous struggles against Jim Crowism."[16]

CCC participant-activism exemplified but also revised a broader, national trend of an emerging, youth-inspired black protest politics during the interwar period. Across the country, black activists embraced mass action to try to bring about economic self-determination. From the black cooperative movement to the Brotherhood of Sleeping Car Porters, the National Negro Congress and the NAACP to black unionists of the CIO and CPUSA movements, black activism in the 1930s, with young peoples' politics as its engine, largely reflected the merger of class struggle and black political assertion at the time. However, the CCC's work marked a corrective to the prevailing methods of and approaches to making the economic condition of black Americans an issue of political import. While the CCC reflected a broader trend of an emerging black political methodology that prioritized militancy, it did so by disrupting patriarchal narratives of black militancy and black economic misery. Instead of dispatching the experiences of black men to galvanize a community, St. Louis black youth activists mapped out a "new technique of social action for the Negro in America" based around a demand for "jobs—white-collar and skilled jobs, if you please," for black women specifically. In the name of economic security absent gender-based restrictions, CCC organizers forced the hand of white business owners "who fail to agree to take on Negro clerks through ordinary diplomatic channels." Black young women foregrounded their economic concerns as they openly challenged established methods of black dissidence: "Today there is rapidly developing in this country a group of young Negroes with strong social convictions that are far removed from the old and outmoded racial "'line' of a decade or two ago." One way the "outmoded racial 'line' of a decade or two ago" model was updated was to include black women's economic lives in understandings of black self-determination. These changes were widely remarked on by observers. "Mass action reached the younger generation," observed journalist Stanley High in the *Saturday Evening Post*. Economic catastrophe, racial discrimination in hiring, an unemployment crisis, a profound sense of frustration with black politics as usual, and demonstrated political efficacy "shocked them [black youth] into serious thought" and action, said another. "Mass pressure along economic lines" constituted the new political apparatus, which "represents a remarkable deviation from the tactics most widely employed by most of the leaders of the Negro race of ten or twenty years ago," wrote observers of the St. Louis scene. They missed, however, how young black women keenly experienced the dismal reality that threw the chasm between their educational attainment and economic opportunity into sharp relief. Their sense of specific economic vulnerability fueled a political project that revised the politics of black freedom struggle and economic self-determination so that it took in black women's economic well-being.[17]

The St. Louis CCC movement also reflected the expanding influence of black protest politics on the Democratic party and the formation of the New Deal coalition through local, grassroots campaigns. Winning hundreds of jobs for black residents, the CCC movement also won respect. Though the local Republican and Democratic parties supported the group, the latter designated the CCC as a kind of unofficial arm of New Deal politics in the Gateway City. One observer put it this way: "Although it is a non-political organization, the very fact that it is progressive in its nature has resulted in most of them being sympathetic to the New Deal." Local Democrats wisely tapped CCC leaders to build bridges between the party and black unions, because it was clear that such an alliance would help ensure future political victories. The circle's growing credibility among ordinary citizens also helped the organization to gain a foothold in formal politics. "When a special struggle is underway," a local observer noted, "They [CCC members] frequently go to the public at large, and, I might report that because of the confidence the public has in them, the response to these special appeals has been most generous." CCC members typically tapped grassroots communities in their jobs fight and did so by cultivating a shared political consciousness among workers, the radical left, organized labor, and New Deal liberals.[18]

The short and remarkable rise of the Colored Clerks' Circle exposed the fault lines that divided the black leadership class in St. Louis. Just as black religious leaders had failed to fully support nut pickers when they went on strike several years earlier, many black pastors and their congregants failed to publicly support the CCC, choosing instead to offer their churches only as meeting spaces. In a letter to black churches, crafted three years after its founding, the CCC criticized religious adults for failing to support the youth who were forging their own path and making opportunities where there had been none. "Many of you present in this audience have not fully agreed or cooperated with us in our struggles," the letter read, "but we have continued the fight against economic slavery with the hope of educating you to the fact that youth must make their own place in the world today." CCC activists were not simply making a case for their organization's efficacy and credibility; they were also making a larger case for the political leadership of black youth. "In our three years of struggle," the letter went on, "[we] have to our credit two hundred jobs." Pointing out their elders' unwillingness to risk their futures for the sake of a larger cause, the letter states that economic opportunity would have been only a figment of political imagination "had not some-one been willing to make the sacrifice and carry on the fight." Members did not aim "to boast but we feel that we have contributed something to our race as well as the community." Turning the proverbial table on churchgoers, the CCC cast its members and their supporters as true engines of "race progress."[19]

In the letter to black churches, the CCC also shared ways to provide genuine support to the youths who had committed themselves to a worthy cause. "Those Negroes interested in race progress" were the ones who "asked [white store managers] for a colored clerk to serve them" and followed with "tell[ing] a merchant that you are glad that he has hired a colored clerk," they explained. Black youths asked their elders to show up at their meetings, such as an upcoming one at Washington Tabernacle, a prominent black Baptist church active in community affairs, because doing so would "be an incentive and encouragement for us to go farther in our fight towards raising the economic status of the race." The appeal to black churches was based on the assumption that the 1930s job crisis hit black young people particularly hard; it necessitated bold critique, principled advocacy, and political risk on the part of black professional adults, along with an awareness that their economic status, while certainly challenged, was generally better than that of a critical mass of young people facing chronic unemployment. Lest older, middle-class and professional black adults dismiss the CCC struggle as the latest whim of the young, youth activists persuasively argued that the civically minded young could ably engineer racial leadership in their calls for political solidarity across generational and economic divisions: "We are not fighting for the C.C.C.," they opined, "We are fighting for the race."[20]

Threatening the established position of secular, social-service-oriented black organizations like the Urban League, the CCC worked to maintain its independence, which was not an easy task because of the UL's influence over local black labor issues. UL leaders tended to paint young black activists as upstarts who lacked sufficient credibility. St. Louis Urban League staffers Arnold B. Walker and Sydney Williams penned an article for the National Urban League organ *Opportunity* to share their assessment of the new, youth-led movement taking place in their city. While they praised the group's tenacity and inventiveness, they found, "The one lamentable fact is that the mass-pressure method of securing jobs . . . does not seem to have evolved a well-thought-out theory of action." "Too many energetic groups of Negro youths," they argued, "have gone forth to battle armed with no theory at all, but simply a rugged determination to get jobs." After working closely with the CCC for some time, Walker broke formal ties, stepping down from his position as a member of the advisory committee because of the "certain technique used by the Circle in obtaining jobs." Both organizations were at the forefront of black labor issues in the city, and they even shared similar goals in supporting efforts to increase local black employment; but with more established roots in the area, an older staff, and tenuous partnerships with the white business owners that the CCC directly targeted, the Urban League held firmly to the notion that research, education, negotiation, appeal, and cooperation were the most effective strategies for achieving success in the jobs fight. Historian Priscilla Dowden-White finds that "social work–oriented community organizers viewed blacks' efforts to attain fairness in employment, education, health care, and housing as largely a problem involving the education of civic organizers and the broader citizenry as to the rightness of their demands." Perhaps no other black organization of its time better exemplified this approach.[21]

It is remarkable that the CCC pioneered new approaches to building space for black economic self-determination by making black women's employment a priority. "Even though the temperature was three below zero, twenty-five members of the organization held the picket line for twelve hours" outside the National Clothing Store in January 1940. They won a job for Lola Lindsay, who moved to a sales position. Embedded within young activists' argument was that the acute unemployment crisis necessitated not only bold critique of former methods and the introduction of new tactics but also recognition of black women's survival. Instead of centering its mission on strengthening black businesses or even on the consumption practices of black "housewives," CCC activists connected the fight for the economic security of young black women to notions of committed and principled racial advocacy. Conflict with black religious leaders and racial uplift organizations highlighted the disruptive nature of the CCC politics.[22]

CCC protests set the stage for a struggle that soon eclipsed it in scope and influence. The St. Louis March on Washington Movement built upon the groundwork laid and the momentum set by the CCC to intensify the struggle for fair and open employment. "Pressure tactics" remained central, and so, too, did black women's employment. It is tempting to use the life of T. D. McNeal, one of St. Louis's most important black activists, who became the first African American elected to the Missouri senate, to tell the story of struggles for black economic justice from the 1920s through the 1940s. McNeal, after all, was the Gateway City leader who spearheaded the local Brotherhood of Sleeping Car Porters, supported the CCC as he led campaigns during the Great Depression, and led the local MOWM movement of the 1940s, but for the one "leader" of a movement, there were many more, mostly black women whose working-class politics fused various struggles. We know much more about McNeal than we do about Hattie Bobo, for instance, who was a CCC member and an active member of MOWM, but Bobo and many other black women whose stories remain hidden or absent in the historical record carried the black struggle for economic rights. These women drew necessary attention to their economic experiences and in doing so helped mobilize a community to political struggle, a theme that animated Double V politics in the Gateway City.[23]

4

"Riveting the Sinews of Democracy"

Defense Workers and Double V

In the summer of 1944, Modestine Crute Thornton, Pearl Maddox, Myrtle Walker, Gessie Mae Myles, and Annabelle Mayfield testified at a local Fair Employment Practices Commission hearing against several companies with practices that barred them from access to defense employment. Using labor testimony as a political weapon, the five, along with other women who participated in the hearing and the many more who filed formal complaints with the FEPC, shamed their city's war plants. Their narratives fueled the local Double V movement, a black-led racial justice project that advocated for the end of fascism abroad and the birth of racial justice at home. Black working-class women's stories of economic discrimination in particular constituted the ground upon which the St. Louis Double V campaign built a powerful case for fair employment and economic opportunity for all St. Louis residents. In addition to filing formal complaints, women supported and participated in demonstrations and marches and served on leadership committees. The St. Louis Double V struggle for a meaningful economic existence, like many other campaigns of its kind, trafficked in narratives of black women's economic experiences and labor. In speeches, on placards, and in memos, Double V spokespersons amplified black working-class women's stories of economic suffering. Women's labor activism became an integral part of the rising tide of black militancy during the wartime forties, fueling the growth and influence of the St. Louis March on Washington Movement, one of the largest and most active chapters of the organization in the country. Black working women played a central role in labor, black freedom, and metropolitan reform movements in St. Louis, serving as key shapers of tactics and strategies, potent emblems of the social misery of poor and working-class people across race and gender lines, and pivots on which debates about social and economic justice turned.[1]

Black working-class women used the organizational apparatus of the local March on Washington Movement to mount damning evidence against their city's economic landscape and articulate a broad urban political agenda based on the right to decent employment. Through carefully constructed labor testimony and direct-action protest, they used an organization led by charismatic black men to expand the possibilities of economic opportunities for women, advance their economic and political interests, and forge narratives of the black freedom struggle rooted in their own economic lives. In the wartime context of shifting attitudes about black women's work and reconfigurations within local labor markets, MOWM organizers rallied around black working-class women's quest to abandon domestic service and carve out space for themselves in the industrial workforce, making women's articulation of their political subjectivity, racial loyalty, critical patriotism, and entitlement to citizenship defining elements of the black-led movement.

Wartime formulations of black economic self-determination forwarded the notion that black working-class women's economic experiences served as a barometer of racial democracy. Prospective black "Rosies" and black community organizations like the MOWM held overlapping ideas about black working-class women's advancement that involved representing them as potential or aspirational war workers and loyal citizens. The women's stories were narratives of rejection, exclusion, and discrimination—just the sort that worked well for an organization wishing to spotlight companies' noncompliance with an executive order. This chapter examines black women's working-class politics in defense industrial employment and their utility as a political strategy.

Black Rosies

As the national MOWM pushed successfully for the establishment of the FEPC to oversee the implementation of Executive Order 8802, which made unlawful racial, gender, and religious discrimination in federally funded defense industries, local MOWM members mobilized to schedule an FEPC hearing in St. Louis. Two years after issuing Executive Order

8802, Roosevelt implemented Executive Order 9346, which expanded the reach and resources of the FEPC. Although he established the FEPC in an effort to quell the rising tide of black militancy, it actually emboldened African American women and fueled their campaigns for economic justice. In their most powerful demonstration, women used the hearings to expose and shame the companies that refused to hire them. Their labor narratives became vehicles for demonstrating their worthiness, patriotism, suitability for civil rights protest, and right to citizenship.[2]

MOWM-sponsored and MOWM-organized mass meetings staged a core strategy of black women's working-class politics, which played to racial liberalism's success; black women cast themselves as capable and disciplined workers whose economic dignity was central to the realization of progressive, labor–civil rights visions. For example, on the night of August 14, 1942, approximately nine thousand to ten thousand MOWM activists gathered for a four-hour mass meeting at Convention Hall in the St. Louis Municipal Auditorium. Attendees adopted a resolution demanding "equal rights now," after listening to nationally renowned civil rights speakers such as Walter White, A. Philip Randolph, and Milton P. Webster. That night, speaker and local civil rights attorney David M. Grant argued that World War II was a choice opportunity to secure employment rights for black workers, because the moment fueled a redoubled commitment to black freedom. As a contrast to World War I, during which black Americans were "promised equal rights but didn't get them," World War II would witness black insurgency "to make certain now these rights will be his [the Negro's] after this war." Sallie Parham, representative of the National Council of Business and Professional Women of the YWCA, set women squarely within Grant's framework. She began by articulating the extent to which the slogan "We fight to live, work, and die for democracy as equals" addressed the unique experiences and potential contributions of black women, in particular. Black women's "place was to guard 'the destination of the men who serve' to protect us," Parham explained. The job of preservation and protection included legal activism; the struggle to end discrimination in defense industries "where our men and women are to work"; standing proxy for "those men who have gone to fight for democracy"; and staging demonstrations when necessary. Parham ended her speech urging women to "shoulder the problems of the American

Negro in the same way many men are shouldering the guns." In Parham's political vision, an unidentified St. Louis woman worker who had successfully completed a training course in welding from December 1943 to March of 1944 served as a model. Speaking for the aspiring black Rosie the Riveter, Parham positioned black women as arbiters who determined whether American democracy was real or imagined. According to the rhetoric, black women industrial workers were leading America to the realization of its most cherished ideals by connecting their loyalty to family and the race to the nation. Women would demonstrate their centrality to national identity and belonging through the prism of their own labor. Black women's status as precarious workers and marginal labor organizers made these claims hard-hitting and disruptive to the national wartime consensus.[3]

In St. Louis and, indeed, across the country, black women workers could hardly fulfill Parham's mandate, because before they could gain ground in the industrial economic sector, the nation began to plan its transition to peacetime. By May 1943, for example, approximately four thousand black workers out of thirty thousand were employed at Small Arms, an ammunitions plant of the United States Cartridge Company, but officials announced that by the end of the year, approximately one thousand black workers would lose their jobs. Layoffs would subsequently continue, company president B. E. Bassett informed the public, explaining that excess production warranted significant workforce reduction. Black working-class women were hardest hit by the transition to peacetime. Richard Jefferson of the St. Louis UL explained that women were not finding jobs in defense industries and that the organization planned to turn to the textile and garment industry as a means of addressing the shortfall. As predicted, if overstated, men had "no trouble finding new employment" during the summer after managers implemented a string of layoffs in December 1943, "while the women are still searching in most instances or have decided to stay home." The broader peacetime conversion propaganda that women were only "temporary workers" did not work for black women because they had long been forced by economic necessity to work for a wage.[4]

With black women workers most powerfully signifying the black worker's inauspicious encounter with American industry, the St. Louis

MOWM focused more pointedly on black women's lives during the war's final months. *Chicago Defender* correspondent Howard B. Woods announced, "With the country in the midst of post-war planning, militant talk about winning the peace, 17,000 of St. Louis Negro women are jobless with no immediate employment relief in sight." Woods defended black women, calling them "the main solution to the acute manpower shortage," for whom "husbands and older brothers or relatives are in the armed services and with the shifting of responsibilities they are finding it necessary to seek employment." Theodore McNeal told reporters that black women's job situation was "acute"—a fact he learned from the scores of women who sent letters of complaint to the local MOWM office. More than six hundred black working-class men staged a walkout at General Steel Casting Armor in the fall of 1943. The union members complained so bitterly and persistently about the refusal to hire black women, segregated facilities, and discrimination that Urban League representatives "dropped everything else in an effort to settle the grievances." The group of men shamed their union for failing to take a stand and successfully negotiated with the company to win some demands, including, among others, employing black women. Even the local NAACP, also an important player in the jobs fight, filed a complaint against ordnance producer McQuay-Norris Manufacturing Company, citing its predilection for preferential hiring and unwillingness to hire black women. "It is common knowledge that the company employs Negroes only as porters," the statement read, "that it will not train Negroes in its training schools and that it will not employ Negro women. We are urging you to investigate this matter immediately for the plant will soon be fully staffed."[5]

Black working-class women's activism, particularly their moves to build public awareness and concern for their economic plight, fueled the St. Louis MOWM's militancy. "Pointing out that . . . local war plants are daily turning down hundreds of colored women applicants and that the President's Committee on Fair Employment practices is holding hearings in St. Louis in the near future," MOWM director T. D. McNeal argued that "times are over ripe" for black women to secure defense and government jobs. Organizers vowed to ramp up their campaign and "use mass picketing and other pressure methods on war plants now denying colored women work as was done in the case of U.S. Cartridge and other plants here." "Women workers wanted" memos to churches informed the faithful of the "new rules of War Manpower Commission [which] make possible your employment." Advertisements in weeklies invited "young women with factory experience" who "want jobs and are willing to help open up new employment opportunities for women of our race" to schedule an interview at the organization's headquarters. It was an established fact that the decision to apply for an industrial job necessarily signed one up for the fight for fair employment, whether one formally joined the group or not. Therefore, MOWM organizers encouraged as many black women as possible to apply for jobs and record their encounters with discrimination. Activists decried the fact that more than one thousand black women were on temporary unemployment insurance because of cutbacks. Cessation of insurance, the committee warned, required black women to "face the necessity of either going into domestic service at extremely low pay or be subjected to actual want." The struggle involved breaking down barriers to industrial employment and also prying open economic opportunity in the white-collar, professional job sector where secretarial jobs at public utility companies such as Union Electric and Laclede Gas and Light already had white women employees. Through the prism of black women's economic hardship, MOWM spokespersons assessed St. Louis's racial record, indicting their city for its mistreatment of the black working-class. "There is no other city in the nation than St. Louis where employment conditions are as bad for colored girls and women," remarked one. Actually, black women workers across the country confronted conditions similar to those of their sisters in St. Louis, but the comment did highlight the fierce resistance on the part of white company owners and white workers to fully incorporate black women into the industrial working class. Linking the fate of their city to that of American democracy, activists redoubled their efforts to call on "all race-minded individuals and organizations to join in the effort in order that our women may secure a just share of employment." Understanding black women's employment as a category related to black men's employment but separate meant that MOWM leaders challenged the positions of industrial officials like the vice president of Wagner Electric Corporation (a transformer, motor, brakes, and aircraft fitting manufacturer), who argued that "because of the considerable number of

Negro men (13.6 percent of the Company's employees are Negro men) employed no discrimination was involved in the practice of not employing black women." Black organizers rejected claims that suggested that advances for black men equated with improvement for black people as a whole. The MOWM made moves to resist the erasure of black women.[6]

Driving the local MOWM's sense of urgency was the critical mass of black working-class women using labor testimony as a political weapon. Women's stories of economic discrimination fit squarely within a Double V political agenda of exposing the limits of American democracy at home. MOWM leader David Grant armed himself with black working-class women's labor narratives when he traveled to Washington, DC, to address the House of Representatives Committee on Labor hearing on June 6, 1944. When a committee member asked Grant if there were "any of your race that you know of in St. Louis who are unemployed now, who cannot get work," Grant pointed to "the great reservoir of negro women who have shown their ability in mechanical work, who have been discharged in the cut-backs that have taken place." Grant told the committee of the Small Arms Company's failure to hire black women even after the company employed approximately eight thousand white women at one time. Although representatives of the War Manpower Commission and the US Employment Service had recently "screened" approximately twenty-five thousand black women in the city, Grant continued, the vast majority of these applicants were not hired. "A cut-back . . . in the release of women who have shown their aptitude for machine work and for production work," Grant lamented, resulted in women "now walking the streets [looking for employment], even though there is still a need for workers down there." A member of the mayor's Inter-Racial Committee and the St. Louis and Kansas City chapters of the National Council for a Permanent FEPC, Grant promoted the cause for greater accountability at the federal level.[7]

The FEPC hearing in St. Louis, held on August 1, 1944, marked a departure from MOWM methods, in that black working-class women themselves told their own stories before a public audience. Although women's narratives were mediated by organizational leaders and FEPC protocol, the hearing offered the singular opportunity to hear ordinary women frame racial discrimination in terms of their own economic lives.

Literally and figuratively, black women seized the microphone long used in black communities to air grievances, define racial discourses of suffering and overcoming, and prescribe political practices. Situating their laboring bodies within the trope of the loyal citizen, black working-class women were well represented at the hearings, with many of them "reappear[ing] as witnesses against more than one company."[8]

Lillian D. Reynolds; Emilie T. Lee; Albertine Burrill, a 1933 Vashon High School graduate and a former elevator operator at Famous-Barr Department Store; Harriet Katherine Berry, a vocational high school graduate and lathe machine operator; Pearl S. Maddox; and Myrtle Walker were all leading witnesses. The women testified that Amertorp, a producer of serial torpedoes for the US Navy, either refused them outright or encouraged them to complete applications but failed to return their calls. Women who testified against Bussman Company, a fuse producer, explained that they encountered similar obstacles, charging company representatives with failing to give them applications or giving them the excuse that the company had filled all positions. Walker, who completed training in high school in lathe operation, reported that an Amertorp employee "lost all interest" in her application when he discovered she was a black woman.[9]

Black women workers were more than half of the complainants against Carter Carburetor Company. The St. Louis NAACP official sent formal complaints against Carter filed by Isa Whitfield, Vora L. Thompson, and Pearl Maddox in February 1944 to the FEPC office in Kansas City. Whitfield, Thompson, and Maddox together traveled to Carter in early February 1944. "There were about 10 people sitting in the employment office when we arrived," four of whom were white women, Maddox explained in her affidavit. University of Illinois graduate Vora Lee Thompson suggested that the officials exhibited "nervousness" around the three of them, searching for some way to turn them away without refusing them outright. Those testifying included married and single women such as Pearl Maddox, Vora Lee Thompson, Emilee T. Lee, Audrey Smith, Bertha Brown, Margie Foster, Carrie Berry, and Ollie M. Haynes. For the first day of hearings, black women formed the majority of the twenty total witnesses.[10]

Making full use of the opportunity to contribute to civil rights causes, some black middle-class women who had held no jobs prior to the war assumed a working-class subjectivity to join the local Double V movement. For instance, Maddox, who filed a complaint as early as 1943, used patriotic rhetoric to inform the committee, "I had never worked but to help the war effort along I thought I would try to find a job. . . . I had no training, but I knew I could be trained." Sallie Parham, Thelma McNeal, Juanita Blackwell, and Ruth Mattie Wheeler were not only MOWM lead organizers, but also speakers at the hearing. The "almost equally proportioned crowd of Negro and white" packed courtroom 3 of the new federal building to hear Maddox and others expose the practices of the city's largest war plants. Before an interracial board of labor representatives and their attorney, as well as A. Philip Randolph, the two-day session amassed considerable attention.[11]

The one industrial plant that complainants left relatively unscathed was Curtiss-Wright Corporation, an aircraft company located at Lambert–St. Louis field. Company officials agreed to train black women for riveting positions with funding provided by the US Office of Education. According to vice-president and general manager C. W. France, the company began training black women in mid-December 1942, with ten at the plant and an additional fourteen at Washington Technical High School. Black female skilled workers, among them a seamstress, four college graduates, one social service worker, and a swimming instructor, trained for three weeks before beginning on-site training. In the final two weeks of the program, Curtiss-Wright implemented equal pay for women, reports confirmed. The company launched the program after integrating black men onto the production line as of June 1942. Women including Margaret Gerdine, Mayetta Yokeley, Lena Alexander, Elvessie Jones, Marybelle Reddick, Audrey Cook, Hester Edwards, and Stella Cloyd worked in the production of military planes as riveters. Following a trajectory similar to Pearl Maddox's, the former social workers, swimming instructors, seamstresses, and postmistresses proudly wore "slacks and overalls" and "cover[ed] their hair with a turban or net to avoid any serious accidents" for victory's sake. The availability of defense work for women, wartime political discourse and mobilization, and black women's deepening political militancy rendered flexible a class identity. Black women who joined the industrial workforce, as supportive UL staffer Arnold B. Walker put it, "debase[d] the femininity of the dress and powder puff and accentuate[d] the slacks," making it respectable for women from ostensibly middle-class backgrounds to assume working-class status, if only for the war's duration. "'Rose the Riveter' is not fictional or just a song hit," Walker concluded.[12]

Women's formal FEPC complaints revealed a concerted effort on the part of St. Louis's most important defense employers to bar black women workers even when there was a labor demand. Most witnesses either began or ended their detailed statements with some variation of the line, "The company failed to hire me because of my color." Ollie Haynes applied for an operator position at Bell Telephone Company. With "four years of college training," six months of experience as a bullet machine operator, a riveting certificate, and eight years' experience as an elementary school instructor in Tennessee, Haynes was more than qualified for the position. When she arrived at the office, however, staff members "stated they did not hire negro women." Annie Dove Bizzle's experience was representative of what happened to many aspiring defense workers. She filed charges against the US Employment Office because after she read a sign calling for nearly twenty-five thousand "war workers needed immediately," an interviewer informed her that there were no longer any openings in defense work; the only available positions were in "hotel, restaurant, and laundry work." "I did not accept this inasmuch as I wanted defense work," she explained. "I have had some training on machines."[13]

Women's accounts exposed employers' preference for filling positions with white women workers and tendency to use demobilization as an excuse. "There were numerous white women filling out applications in a room, however, the Auxiliary Military Police, who was passing out applications, refused to give us one, although at the same time, he was giving applications to white men and white women," Candace Little complained, helping mount even further evidence against the McQuay-Norris Manufacturing Company. Mary Little likely traveled with Candace, perhaps as her relative, on the same day and had the same experience. Candace Little added to her complaint: "I have a husband, four brothers, and two cousins in the U.S. Army, and are currently located in the European theatre." "White girls crowded the place," Thelma Shuford wrote, but personnel informed the applicant that Bussman Manufacturing Company did not hire black workers even though in a phone conversation "they had told me they needed help." Sumner High School and Stowe Teachers College graduate Modestine Thornton confronted a personnel officer when he refused to give her and a friend, Annabelle Mayfield, employment applications. Thornton recounted, "I then asked Mr. Zeller if, in view of the fact the company was advertising for women employees both in the newspapers that day and outside the office building, we were being refused applications for employment because we were colored." Geneva Coleman worked for the United States Cartridge Company for only seven months, losing her job "because of the reduction in force order." Hoping to land a position at Wagner Electric Corporation, where managers issued newspaper ads "calling for production trainees," Coleman never received a call from the company after completing an application. For nine months she waited in vain for a reply.[14]

Some complainants went straight to the White House with their grievances. Mary Johnson penned a plaintive letter to President Roosevelt in the spring of 1945, asking him for advice when, after following recommended procedures, a job in a defense plant was still beyond her grasp. Johnson informed the author of Executive Orders 8802 and 9346 that she had responded to the mayor's call in the local paper for women to apply for thousands of industrial positions. As instructed, Johnson traveled to the US Employment Service office and was refused an application. After she showed personnel the newspaper clippings, a staff person provided an application but informed Johnson that there were no openings for black women. Demonstrating her entitlement to make claims in the state, Johnson wrote that she had been a St. Louis city resident since 1935, was a registered voter, and had a brother and a cousin who were in the military "serving our country." In a letter to Roosevelt in late December 1944, Hattie Mann told the president, "I am trying to do all I can for my country and I am willing." She informed him that United States Cartridge Company managers had released her from her duties but had retained white women workers. Economic opportunity in the form of wage labor not only allowed one to live decently but also provided the opportunity to buy war bonds and stamps, which Mann purchased on a routine basis. With three brothers and a nephew in the military, Mann argued that black women were untapped resources; they were "able to work for our country" just as black men were, if only given the opportunity. FEPC officials turned Mann's case over to union agent Joseph Squires, who sent her complaint through the procedural protocol outlined in the union's contract with the company.[15]

Thirty-two-year-old Ethel Mattingly, mother of two teenaged children and caretaker of her mother, worked as an attendant at the Jefferson Barracks Station Hospital for about six months before securing an operator position at United States Cartridge Company, where she worked from May to December 1943. In a letter, a similar version of which she mailed to the newly elected Democratic Missouri governor Phil M. Donnelly, she addressed the nation's president in blunt terms, sharing her frustration: "God know this is why wars exist," she wrote, explaining the hardships that black working-class women encountered. "My mens folk are fighting that they women get a right to earn a salary to support their family," employing with this turn of phrase a Double V agenda that not simply linked the war abroad and the fight against racism at home but defined the fight specifically in terms of black women's economic citizenship. "An what I get when I go to these war factory an ask for a job to support my two little children?," raising a rhetorical question. No openings for black women: "I am not white so I get no war job," she explained. Mattingly vouched for the president's program, stating that she was fully behind his efforts to confront racial discrimination, yet she felt that for the measure to meet success, enforcement by the federal government of local administrators was necessary. She openly shared the emotional anguish that joblessness was causing to her family. Annie Dove Bizzle and Arlean Ward composed a jointly authored, succinct petition to the president. "I wonder is it because I am Colored," the two shared as late as February 1945. That spring, Enola Sampa also wondered whether, after unsuccessfully locating a job following her husband's deployment overseas, she, too, was subject to racial discrimination. Having traveled to "all Employment offices" and looking into "all plants," why did she come up short? Mann, Bizzle, Ward, and Sampa also filed formal FEPC complaints.[16]

Published just two years after Gunnar Myrdal's tome *An American Dilemma* shook white liberal America's racial conscience, *Mrs. Palmer's Honey* revised and complicated Myrdal's assessment by establishing that while the Negro problem was fundamentally a white problem, its solution depended on black women workers, in particular, who mobilized for securing "Negro rights." *Mrs. Palmer's Honey,* for example, the third of five novels by the Jewish civil rights activist Fannie Cook, depicts the swelling political capital that black working-class women amassed during the World War II era. Having spent many of her activist days witnessing and helping to shape the social and political ramifications of black women workers' journey from the household to the factory, author Cook had her finger on the pulse of a changing historical moment. The award-winning novel's message was straightforward enough: first, the American democratic experiment, in general, and the interracial, working-class civil rights struggle, in specific, depended on politically actualized black working-class women. Critical to this transformation were the upheavals that World War II brought to the American city. In the coming-of-age story, the novel's main character, Honey Hoop, ultimately succeeds in steering the domestic half of the Double V campaign in fruitful directions by disrupting urban and economic politics-as-usual in the Gateway City.[17]

Honey Hoop's transformation from domestic worker to militant unionist is the axis upon which the story turns. Honey is the eldest of several children who live with their mother in a small house in the city. To survive, the entire household depends on Honey's work ethic, wages, and good working relation with her employer, Mrs. Palmer. A devoted daughter, sibling, and domestic worker, Honey exhibits "neurotic" devotion to the Palmer family until World War II begins. When calls for "Negro Womanpower" hit, Honey abandons her station in search of a new devotion. As one reviewer put it, "when the urgency of war swept her from the pantry to the assemblyline," Honey quickly jumped ship. Excited by the prospect of earning twice as much, Honey locates a job at a defense factory. Before she can enjoy the new pillowcases, sheets, and towels her first paycheck affords, however, Mrs. Palmer, her former employer, requests her services after becoming a widow. Learning of the housewife's emotional loss, and tugged by the emotional bonds she has established, Honey returns to the kitchen. There, she completes nineteen years of service to the Palmer household; then Mrs. Palmer decides to sell her house. Jobless and desperate to find employment, Honey moves in with her brother, Lamb, and his soon-to-be spouse, Glory, and the couple introduces Honey to the world of the CIO and its political arm. Initially reluctant to join the struggle for worker rights, Honey soon warms up to the cause, becoming a lead organizer and campaigner for Roosevelt's reelection. At the beginning of the novel, the reader meets Mrs. Palmer's Honey, but by the end, Honey squarely belongs to the vanguard of the left-wing labor movement.[18]

Mrs. Palmer's Honey's wide reception reflected that during the early to mid 1940s, black women's economic politics became indispensable to national debates about the extent and limits of American citizenship and notions of civic responsibility at the local level. The novel remained at a steady position of fifteen or sixteen on the *New York Times* bestseller list for one month after its publication. Doubleday and Company awarded Fannie Cook's third novel its first ever $2,500 George Washington Carver Prize for "an outstanding work dealing with the American Negro," infamously passing over works by notable authors such as Walter White, Arna Bontemps, Chester Himes, and Ann Petry, whose novel *The Street* achieved a more nuanced portrait of a black urban community and more deeply textured portrayals of black spatial politics and black women's labors.[19] A product of a racial double standard by which most white publishing houses and literary prize committees overlooked black novelists, Cook's novel received praise from reviewers for its cheerfulness, heartwarming and optimistic tone, and tendency to avoid the sordid aspects of Negro life. But some found *Mrs. Palmer's Honey* a melodramatic rendering, "more tract than novel." These critics could have added to their list a limited political trajectory for Honey, since despite all of her accomplishments and her significant metamorphosis, she never loses the burden of the Mammy stereotype; she merely transfers her devotion and "her almost neurotic loyalties to her white employers" to the diverse and committed cadre of "union organizers, students, ministers, [and] workers who were united to re-elect Franklin Roosevelt." Although *Mrs. Palmer's Honey* misapprehends her subject in these particular ways, the novel still accurately conveyed the ways that black women's labors had a meaningful impact on the social and political order of the wartime forties.[20]

Black Women and the Defense Industry in St. Louis

City leaders and industrial managers sprang into action following a national call for defense production. As early as 1940, the St. Louis Cham-

ber of Commerce published a five-volume study of all local manufacturers, which it sent to more than one thousand defense contractors across
the country. In the same year, training programs in several schools and
universities began to offer new courses on a weekly basis. Within a month
after the attack on Pearl Harbor, more than six hundred St. Louis plants
began producing war-related goods, increasing their output by fully 150
percent. Black workers of the second Great Migration, which brought
approximately 5 million African Americans to the North, the West, and
the Midwest, remapped the terrain of urban America as city landscapes
morphed and melded to reflect the imprint of cosmopolitan black working-class cultures. According to an Urban League analysis of St. Louis
census data from the early 1940s, the majority of black workers living in
the city proper and in adjacent areas were employable and desired to land
industrial jobs. Statistics from before the Pearl Harbor attack had predicted that blacks would make up approximately 10 percent of St. Louis's
new defense workforce.[21]

They would not do so without a fight, however. St. Louis had thriving industrial plants, but employers were reluctant to hire black workers.
According to one statistic referring to the eight hundred defense plants
on the St. Louis Chamber of Commerce's list, the workforces of large
companies could potentially swell to twelve thousand employees—with
only one hundred of them black men. A few black workers landed positions at ammunitions manufacturer United States Cartridge during the
war's start, while even fewer worked at other leading companies, such
as McQuay-Norris Manufacturing Company, Atlas Powder Company,
Emerson Electric Company, and McDonnell Aircraft Corporation. Black
women fared worse. As late as 1941, though black wage-earning women
"hoped that the defense boom would afford other opportunities," one
report noted, "the picture remains one of mostly personal service," even
though women passed qualifying examinations for various entry-level
defense positions. Of all the companies, only United States Cartridge
Company made plans to hire black women in the first year. The picture
improved in 1942 when, owing to mounting production demands, thousands of black women began working in defense plants. "Since the outbreak of war the demand for women's services in manufacturing and war
equipment and munitions plants has greatly increased," noted one Urban

League staff person, but even with this boom, only a minority of black women held positions classified as skilled or semiskilled; the vast majority performed menial tasks or those deemed unskilled. While black male workers' path followed a similar pattern of increased hiring and relegation to menial positions, black women's trajectories became particularly significant to the MOWM agenda. Because women remained at the very low end of the hiring process across the war's duration, with many failing to secure defense positions at all, the campaign for fair employment began to feature women's experiences especially as the final years of war approached.[22]

The St. Louis March on Washington Movement targeted St. Louis's largest employer, United States Cartridge Company, to raise public outcry about black women's abysmal labor force participation rates. The company managed Small Arms, one of the largest manufacturers of .50 and .30 caliber ammunition, with multiple buildings spread over four to five square miles. United States Cartridge owners restricted black male workers to unskilled, low-paying, and menial jobs and refused to hire black women altogether. After organizers applied community pressure through meetings and negative publicity, the company announced in April 1942 that it would arrange to hire approximately 3,000 to 4,000 black production workers. By June of the same year, however, after receiving upward of 110,000 applications from black women and men, management hired only about 300 to 600 black workers, all at the unskilled level, out of more than 20,000 total employees. Although United States Cartridge later announced that establishing an all-black production facility was in the "immediate future," organizers proceeded with their scheduled demonstration. Gathering at Tandy Park on June 20, marchers carpooled to Small Arms Company and walked silently in rows for about two hours. The *Pittsburgh Courier,* a leading black weekly with significant coverage of the St. Louis MOWM, hailed the four hundred to six hundred picketers as a "vast arsenal" of "patriotic Negroes" who staged "one of the most spectacular [demonstrations] ever held in the Mound City." Following a protestor carrying the American flag, a "cross-section" of black community leaders carried placards reading "8,000 Women Employed—Not One Negro Woman" and "Twenty Thousand Workers at Small Arms Plant in Production—Not One Negro." MOWM activists demanded the hiring of black women and "immediate compliance" with FEPC regulations and state laws that required employers to provide written explanation for all discharges. Shaming company managers, the demonstration forced R. V. Rickord, the company's industrial relations manager, to declare publicly that the employer would soon hire about 100 black women to work as matrons or porters. Within two weeks the company hired 90 black women, and by the end of 1942, 900 black workers secured Small Arms jobs: 200 men as machine operators, and 400 men and 300 women as production workers. According to an Urban League report, all of the new employees had successfully accommodated themselves to the rigors of factory discipline. A survey revealed that black workers had the lowest rates of absenteeism and tardiness, a 12 percent higher overall production rate, and a 6 percent higher rate of Class A ammunition production than any other group of workers employed for a similar length of time.[23]

The MOWM picketed the Carter Carburetor Company in late August 1942, after the demonstration against United States Cartridge. A year and a half later, the MOWM informed FEPC regional director Roy Englund that though the Carter Carburetor Company was "engaged 100% in war production," it was "still practicing a policy of exclusion from employment where Negro citizens are concerned." After MOWM activists "publicly demonstrated their disapproval of the undemocratic and un-American employment policies," company officials gestured toward redress but failed to take action. Beginning in 1944, a cadre of black women applicants filed formal complaints against the company. Irene Barnett Mason traveled to the office one early afternoon with Edward J. Hamilton, a black male applicant. An administrator called the two of them into a room and soon directed them to return in two hours. Upon returning, Mason informed the office administrator that she had previously worked for United States Cartridge for approximately six months as a gauge reader for seventy-two cents per hour. The company official informed Mason that there were no available positions. When she asked to complete an application to have it filed anyway, the official refused to give her one. Mason's affidavit noted that "there were about a dozen white people sitting in the room," a fraction of whom had, presumably, secured positions. African American high school graduate Helen Patterson completed a course in beauty culture and two years of study at a business college, worked as a power-machine operator at International Shoe Company for eight months, and worked as a nurse's attendant as a member of the Women's Army Corps for the US Army, but despite such experience, Carter Carburetor administrators informed her that the company was no longer accepting applications.[24]

When black women workers confronted company officials about the discrimination pattern, either in the practice of not hiring black women altogether or in forcing them to work under segregated conditions, managers typically blamed white working-class women who resisted black women's presence on industrial shop floors, even in cases in which black men were already a part of the workforce. Pointing to women's staged walkouts and slowing of production lines, business representatives argued that community discrimination, not the particular proclivities of any one shop owner, was the real culprit. As Bussman Manufacturing Company's attorney, George B. Logan, explained, "We plead 'not guilty' to the charge of discrimination. It is community discrimination, beyond our power. Integrating and intermingling of the races in St. Louis simply is contrary to the established social pattern. This is particularly true as to women." The "cure [to the race problem]," he went on, "must come not by force, which will disturb the peace of this community, but by the slow process of education among the younger generation in the schools and churches." Amertorp Corporation's public relations director, Orden C. Oechsli, informed civil rights activists that the company generally followed "the pattern of the community," which favored segregation, because it aligned with municipal custom. Although Amertorp had recently opened its shop floor to black men, the company's managers resisted hiring black women because of white women's fierce opposition, Oechsli explained. Others cited pure logistics as the cause. Carter Carburetor representative James E. Garstang explained that the company had a list of white workers who were potential hires, and until managers processed them, no black women could secure a position. Such case studies illustrate that the perceived threat of the black male–white female encounter in industrial shops was not the only point of significant conflict during wartime. White working-class women, certainly precarious workers in their own right, perceived black working-class women as a threat to their livelihood, as evidenced by their fears that managers would replace them; and white working-class women also perceived black women as a threat to their status, because black female laboring bodies had long signified degraded economic and class standing in St. Louis's highly stratified labor market.[25]

Months after the August hearing, few signs of progress existed. With weak enforcement power, the FEPC could only ask companies to prohibit discrimination but could not require compliance or even apply sanctions. The Women's Division of the Urban League reported that while companies such as McQuay-Norris had screened a number of black women, none had been hired yet. Other companies "share[d] equally in discriminating against Negro workers, especially women." The common practice of accepting applications without the "slightest intention" of hiring remained firmly in place as late as early 1945. For example, the Bussman Manufacturing Company ran weekly ads requesting white women specifically and restricted the few black women hired as managers to inspection jobs despite their qualifications. The FEPC held a second public hearing in early March 1945, where activists brought charges against the General Cable Corporation for discriminating against black women, among other abuses. As organizers predicted, when the company addressed the problem by hiring a small group of black women, more than one hundred white women walked off the job. While the new black women employees retained their jobs, company managers refused to continue the experiment in desegregation. If some women workers met blatant hostility, others faced employers who exclusively assigned domestic responsibilities. Women at a chemical plant, for example, abandoned their posts after their employer ordered them to wash windows on the second floor. It is worth noting that this very same request had infuriated domestic workers in the early 1930s and became the key grievance around which they organized to change the conditions of household employment.[26]

The "normal pattern" of black women's economic precariousness in the paid labor market fundamentally held before and after the war, as immediate postwar reconversions served to highlight the fragility of their economic standing even when defense jobs became available. Beginning in mid-1945 and increasingly thereafter, companies began announcing plans for major layoffs; they released, over time, more than forty thousand workers in the city of St. Louis. Along the margins of defense employment, black workingwomen were hard hit. Amertorp brought production to a screeching halt after July 1945, shortly after managers had hired black women. By December of the same year, Carter Carburetor owners retained only six of the sixty black women managers they had hired during the war's peak years, claiming, "The average peace time operation is too heavy for women." The year 1944 witnessed cutbacks and closings in ordnance and aircraft, with workforce reductions at U.S. Cartridge, for example, reaching fourteen thousand from forty-five thousand; the company cut its black workforce down to fourteen hundred from five thousand. For black working-class women, one observer wrote, "industrial jobs are practically closed to Negro women and Negro men are able to find limited openings"; many were "forced to return to their homes as veterans return to their jobs and the normal pattern is resumed." Bertha Brown was a gauger at United States Cartridge from late May 1932 through mid-December of the same year. "I was laid off," she explained, "at the time of the December cut-back and I am sure that I had more seniority than some white employees who were not laid off." Similarly, Emilee T. Lee worked as a drop tester in segregated Building 202 at the company for approximately seven months before losing her job. She was "sure" that white workers with less seniority than she had held on to their jobs. Another former Building 202 worker, Ollie Haynes, explained, "When I was laid off white people with less seniority" were kept.[27]

Although black women workers did not enter the ranks of the war production workforce on the scale that they had hoped, and although those who managed to enter did not do so along the lines that they had imagined, black working-class women did lay the groundwork for the emergence of postwar social justice struggles rooted in women's long struggle for economic dignity.

Most black working-class women failed to secure lasting economic change during wartime upheavals, but one significant outcome of the Double V movement was the emergence of black women's civil rights leadership. For activist Pearl S. Maddox, 1944 was a busy year. As the nation prepared for the coming peacetime transition, black women's political work revolved around the struggle to hold on to and expand the limited wartime gains made during the war. Pushing for greater economic opportunity, Maddox served in 1944 as a team captain for the annual membership drive of the St. Louis NAACP. As the "Judge Hastie" division leader, so named for William H. Hastie, the Harvard University Law School graduate and first black federal judge, Maddox oversaw the work of twelve teams, each with its own group of ten campaigners. Of the local NAACP's four division leaders, three were women. The St. Louis NAACP ranked among the ten largest chapters in the nation, and its 1944 drive saw the branch reach its then-largest-ever number of registered members. While legal activism formed a core component of the St. Louis NAACP, so too did direct-action demonstrations and campaigns that forced locals to confront racism in education, employment, and municipal politics, these progressive methods and tactics no doubt influenced by black working-class women such as Maddox. Work of this kind by African American working-class women existed not only to hold on to the limited gains made by way of expanded wartime industrial production but also to push for even greater opportunities. This movement was not limited to St. Louis but took place all over the country. The explosion in national NAACP membership during the 1940s, rising almost tenfold during the war, was the direct result of women's grassroots organizing. Activist women forged ties and constructed networks that connected community members around a shared social vision for racial and economic justice. Local NAACP chapters were some of the most active, because of black women's organizing. Primarily through the efforts of African American women, local NAACP chapters, including the one in St. Louis, became some of the most militant organizations in the country. Black working-class women struggled against core problems like segregation and economic injustice, all while challenging a patriarchal leadership model that resisted the idea of women as framers and public representatives of social justice agendas and movements. These pioneers created institutional bases that allowed them to shape and openly critique mainstream civil rights leaders and the positions they put forward. They created and led organizations and headed antibias initiatives in mainstream institutions.[28]

In late 1944 Pearl S. Maddox founded the grassroots Citizens Civil Rights Committee (CCRC), an interracial organization that used cutting-edge, direct-action tactics like sit-ins and pickets—which the *St. Louis Post-Dispatch* called "silent protests"—to challenge segregation. In late

May the CCRC conducted a sit-in at the Grand Leader department store. After failing in her attempt to arrange a meeting with the owners, Maddox, along with two additional black women, NAACP field organizer Birdie Beal Anderson, Myrtle Walker, and one white woman decided to target the store with direct action. The activists selected Grand Leader because its managers and employees were "more friendly toward colored people" and because black residents were regular customers. In July the CCRC expanded its demonstrations to establishments that were less hospitable to black customers. With support from the NAACP, the group targeted the city's "big three" department store chains: Stix-Baer-Fuller, Famous-Barr, and Scruggs-Vandervoort-Barney. Although most St. Louis store owners allowed African Americans to shop in their establishments, they usually barred them from being served at in-house lunch counters. Typical shopping trips for black customers, therefore, involved packing lunch to be eaten uncomfortably in restroom facilities or perhaps outside the store, weather permitting. The CCRC had great success challenging this practice, building upon wartime democratic rhetoric that embarrassed storeowners who wanted to maintain the guise of patriotism and politeness. In a relatively short period of time, department store owners succumbed to community pressure, hoping to avoid public embarrassment and maintain the guise of racial politeness. CCRC women, the majority of whom were African Americans and included college students, housewives, professionals, and office workers, carried placards reading "Justice for all but me" and "Fox holes are democratic, are you?" as they walked picket lines. One demonstrator had five sons in the US Army. The African American *St. Louis Argus* hailed the protests as "thoroughly planned and well executed," praising the "courageous, determined and dignified women" involved. Demonstrators shrewdly employed the politics of Double V to highlight discrepancies between American rhetoric and practice. Maddox was part of the critical mass of civil rights activists in the Midwest, the North, and the upper South who made effective use of the sit-in strategy two decades before the more widely known southern sit-in movement of the early 1960s.[29]

Maddox's CCRC served as a platform for black activist women to establish political independence from organizations led by black men. Through her organization women could express their political leadership and openly critique a male-led model of civil rights activism. The CCRC challenged established civil rights organizations and leaders, including the MOWM. In October 1944, when at a mass meeting local MOWM leader T. D. McNeal mischaracterized the CCRC's desegregation campaign, Maddox responded in an article written for the *St. Louis Argus,* stating, "While Mr. McNeal through the M.O.W. is to be commended for his valiant fight for equal opportunities for all, it should be remembered that there are others who are doing their bit in this fight, but we all do not see things alike. There are others who have honest opinions about how some things should be done for the benefit of the whole." Maddox penned her public response to what she termed McNeal's "'highly colored' and misleading presentation" to clarify the CCRC's position. Maddox's organization actually rejected an offer extended by Scruggs-Vandervoort-Barney because it required that blacks be served in the basement only. While McNeal celebrated the offer as a limited victory, Maddox called it a "jimcrow set up." Drawing a parallel to Bell Telephone Company, which, according to Maddox, answered blacks' call for fair employment "by opening a strictly segregated office," the activist worried that "the set-up . . . could easily become a segregated arrangement." Pushing store owners and black, male-led civil rights organizations alike, Maddox publicly differed with arguably the best-respected civil rights leader in the city. While it is possible that Maddox agreed with such prescriptions, her emphasis was not on reforming individual behavior; she highlighted the need for structural change. That she disagreed in print with McNeal, and that the local black weekly published the rebuttal, indicates the power that black activist women wielded in St. Louis's social movement spaces. Indeed, Maddox was such a threat to St. Louis's prevailing racial and economic order that her bank threatened to take away her home.[30]

It is possible to map a lineage of black working-class women's economic activism that advocated for the rights of black communities but also fought for black women's survival, militating against projects of black economic self-determination that prioritized the economic needs of black men. The CCRC's campaigns were direct descendants of the CCC's Don't Buy Where You Can't Work movement that swept St. Louis during the 1930s. Both campaigns centered on black women's economic experiences, whether through mobilizing black consumer spending to secure jobs for young black women in the CCC's case or through connecting black working-class women's access to living-wage jobs to their freedom to consume and participate in popular leisure activities in the example of the CCRC. Like Maddox's politics in the MOWM and the CCRC, CCC members advanced the notion that black women's economic pursuits were indispensable to racial survival, community organizing, and economic well-being.[31] And like Maddox's political work, CCC organizing suggested how black women's economic experiences as a site for community organizing often reveal intraracial tensions falling along generational, political, and class lines. The St. Louis Congress of Racial Equality (CORE) extended the CCRC's ethos about the centrality of black women's economic experiences into the 1950s and 1960s when members led protests at retail and banking establishments.

While activists such as Sallie Parham, Thelma McNeal, Juanita Blackwell, and Ruth Mattie Wheeler labored for dignity primarily through, within, and against the St. Louis March on Washington Movement, black working-class women in the garment industry performed their political work through, within, and against the unions of St. Louis's garment and apparel industry. Also laboring within the context of the wartime 1940s, they navigated the relatively unchartered, colliding worlds of black women's unionization, interracial unionism, and industrial capitalism. Those women who mobilized with the MOWM were largely aspiring industrial workers, while the garment laborers examined in chapter 5 were actual industrial workers. This difference shaped garment workers' economic politics differently as they navigated numerous challenges to their place in the industrial working class.

Unemployed march, Pine Street, 1931. Black women were active participants in unemployed demonstrations of the early 1930s, which laid the groundwork for the Funsten Nut Strike of 1933. Courtesy of the Missouri History Museum Library and Research Center.

Carter Carburetor protest, March on Washington Movement, 1942. On August 28, 1942, March on Washington Movement members and supporters staged a demonstration, marching from Tandy Park to the Carter Carburetor Corporation. The hundreds who gathered charged the artillery manufacturer with violating Executive Order 8802 by refusing to hire black workers. Black women filed formal complaint against the company, using their economic experiences as a means to bolster the Double V cause. Courtesy of the State Historical Society of Missouri.

March on Washington Committee rally at Municipal Auditorium, August 14, 1942. Nearly ten thousand black activists attended a five-hour mass meeting organized by the March on Washington Movement. Joining A. Philip Randolph, Milton P. Webster, David M. Grant, and Theodore McNeal, Sallie Parham addressed the crowd, making the case for black women's role in the wartime struggle for fair employment and economic opportunity. Courtesy of the State Historical Society of Missouri.

Above and opposite: Pruitt-Igoe residents move into their new apartments, 1954. Many low-income black women were eager to move into new housing developments constructed through federal and state funds during the 1950s. Having previously lived in dilapidated structures with no private facilities, many women initially looked forward to living in the new facility. Courtesy of the State Historical Society of Missouri.

ILGWU chorus practice, accompanied by Kenneth Billups, 1956. By the mid-1950s, the ILGWU's cultural productions were more integrated. Here, the chorus, which includes Barbara Jenkins (Pickett), who often played leading roles, practices with Kenneth Billups, a leading musician and composer in St. Louis. Photo credit: *St. Louis Post-Dispatch*. Repository: Missouri History Museum Library and Research Center.

Three striking tenants of the Newstead-Cook Tenants Organization talk with their attorney, Curtis Crawford, February 20, 1967. In the 1960s, the strike method became a key tactic for black low-income women to leverage their power. Before the 1969 rent strike, black working-class women formed collectives that constituted the organizational apparatus that made the larger, 1969 demonstration possible. Photo credit: *St. Louis Post-Dispatch*. Repository: Missouri History Museum Library and Research Center.

Public housing protestors picket the Federal Housing Agency, 2031 Olive Street, November 8, 1967. The year 1967 witnessed an uptick in black low-income women's protests. Activists targeted the St. Louis Housing Authority to demand better living conditions. This protest was one of several that helped to set the stage for larger demonstrations. Photo credit: *St. Louis Post-Dispatch*. Repository: Missouri History Museum Library and Research Center.

Work and experience pickets at Taylor Avenue and Euclid Avenue, May 3, 1968. Protestors against the War on Poverty job training program took issue with the nature of that training by suggesting that it only served to further relegate black women to jobs in domestic and personal service and black workers to service positions in general. In raising a critique of local job training, black women protestors in the 1960s questioned the motives of the antipoverty program. Photo credit: *St. Louis Post-Dispatch*. Repository: Missouri History Museum Library and Research Center.

Pruitt-Igoe tenants share their grievances with Police Chief Curtis Brostron at the Police Academy, October 16, 1969. The practice of forming a collective relationship with predominantly white, male power brokers (employers, police officers, public housing officials, etc.) as a means of struggle is powerfully evidenced by this photo, which depicts a group of public housing tenants confronting St. Louis City police chief Curtis Brostron. At the meeting, women expressed their desire for more effective, responsive, and measured policing. Photo credit: *St. Louis Post-Dispatch*. Repository: Missouri History Museum Library and Research Center.

Ora Lee Malone. One of St. Louis's most important labor leaders, Ora Lee Malone founded several grassroots organizations and spearheaded critical campaigns for the rights of St. Louis workers. Grounding her working-class politics in struggles for racial justice and women's rights, she challenged those involved in the struggle for social justice to draw connections between the experiences of various marginalized groups. Photo by Wiley Price/*St. Louis American*.

5

"Beneath Our Dignity"

Garment Workers and the Politics of Interracial Unionism

Lillian Jennings, Ardella Harris, Bessie White, Naomi Blackmore, Lillian Reynolds, Geneva Crawford, Vedora Grant, Ida J. Poole, Bernice Wren, and Ernestine Springfield broke ranks with their International Ladies' Garment Workers Union (ILGWU) local during the wartime forties. The St. Louis ILGWU was a progressive trade union that spearheaded creative and groundbreaking efforts to build interracial unionism among urban working women during and following World War II. Asked to play the role of slaves in a theatrical production covering the history of labor in the United States, the ten, as a group, declined the invitation, resisting the portrayal of black women as Mammy caricatures. Along with hundreds of black working-class women who made up the first cadre of their racial group to break the color barrier in St. Louis's garment and apparel industry and its unions, the ten women advanced a critique of liberal unionism that challenged and disrupted both industrial labor and the practice of building class unity across racial lines. As they initiated their collective act of refusal they both revealed the tensions embedded in union cultural programming and also suggested ways to think differently about the civil rights and worker rights movements of the 1940s. The ten dissidents labored in multiple ways: as industrial workers earning a wage for the survival of their families, their communities, and themselves; as political workers deepening interracial, industrial unionism; and as community workers contributing to numerous grassroots initiatives and projects.[1]

The black working-class women who composed the first cadre of black women to integrate the St. Louis garment and apparel industry and its unions during the wartime 1940s did not "champion the labor movement as the principal vehicle through which the lives of the majority of women could be bettered" so much as they developed a powerful and dynamic critical unionism. The cohort to more fully integrate the St. Louis garment and apparel industry and its unions articulated a black labor feminist agenda that made critical interruptions and interventions into industrial labor and liberal racial unionism through resistance and performance. Black garment workers worked to ensure that their employers would provide decent wages, organize work hours around the workers' leisure schedule, speak to them in a respectful tone, and hire them by the same measures used to hire white women. By the same token, these new union members struggled to transform organized labor to fit their own models of appropriate and relevant advocacy. Exposing the racialized and gendered fault lines of shop-floor production, union bureaucracy, racial liberalism, historical memory, and the cultural politics of labor education, black women unionists opposed the historical narratives of worker theater that drew upon Old South nostalgia and failed to account for their particular economic experiences. But they enthusiastically participated in performances and cultural programs that reflected their prolabor sentiment, celebrated their artistry, and strengthened interracial worker solidarity by foregrounding shared political interests. They were simultaneously participants in and critics of labor organizing. Although integration within the mounting civil rights movement of the 1940s was not the most important agenda item for these working people, they nonetheless made critical contributions to larger civil rights and wartime challenges through their multidimensional labor practices.[2]

In addition to critically examining black working-class women's resistance on the shop floor and in the union hall, we can also analyze black women workers' critical unionism by examining their engagement with the ILGWU labor educational program, particularly its worker theater productions. Resisting roles steeped in historical narratives that failed to attend to their unique labor experiences, and enthusiastically participating in shows that celebrated their artistry, women helped forge a "vibrant union culture" even as leaders deemed them unfit industrial workers and poor union members who threatened community progress on the local racial front. Redefining "black working womanhood" by infusing it with cultural and political meaning, black women worker-artists sang, danced, acted, drew, and participated in prolabor expressive culture to build social cohesiveness, foreground shared interests, and refashion working-class identity. They were the local version of the national cultural renaissance of black women artists during the 1940s who, as Farah Jasmine Griffin observes, merged popular front politics, Double V campaigns, and migration to urban centers to make singular contributions to artistic and political life. Black working-class women from Harlem to Chicago, Detroit to Los Angeles, Philadelphia to Memphis, and Birmingham to Atlanta transformed America's cultural landscape. The "particularly fecund period of creativity" of the wartime 1940s was by no means limited to women in New York City; black unionists in the Deep South were also a part of the black working-class cultural renaissance of the Depression thirties and wartime forties. Worker-artists in Birmingham, for example, were active gospel music singers who "performed in a quasi-sacred style and [were] empowered by the unifying ideologies of evangelical Protestantism and democratic unionism," notes Brenda McCallum. Their "pro-labor songs provided an active mode in which Black workers could articulate an emerging consciousness and a new collective identity." Despite having little influence beyond the boundaries of their city, black working-class women in St. Louis nevertheless made important contributions to this "social and artistic movement." The "laboring of American culture," during which the landscape of cultural production shifted by centering working-class sensibilities and aesthetics, achieved its work partially through labor educational programming. As local black working-class women labored in complementary fashion with the radical black women political theorists of the 1930s through the 1950s who constructed a "black left feminism" that challenged constructions of the left as the vanguard of social struggle, they promoted a fresh social and economic analysis that positioned intersectionality as an analytical category and complicated anticapitalist, cooperative economic political visions; black working-class women in cities with less exposure also deepened black freedom movement politics, white left feminist proscriptions and analyses, and struggles for worker rights. Focusing on St. Louis, the headquarters of the ILG-WU's labor education program in the Southwestern District, this chapter argues that at the local level, black working-class women contributed to popular front politics by constructing a dynamic critical unionism that privileged differentiation, discontinuity, and racial particularity within constructions of historical memory and a "usable past" for the twentieth-century labor movement, making possible the creation of alternative, interracial working-class solidarities.[3]

Jane Crow in St. Louis's Needle Trades Industry

One of the leading "ready-to-wear" clothing producers in the nation and the fourth-largest producer of women's apparel, early-twentieth-century St. Louis was home to a garment industry and unions that generally barred black women. If a black woman worker secured employment in the garment industry, she performed menial tasks as a "floor girl" or "matron." On the whole, these positions resembled the labor and working conditions that were commonly associated with domestic work. During the 1930s civil rights groups tried unsuccessfully to locate spaces for black women. There were a few exceptions, including some garment unions that organized black women workers in the fall of 1933 during an AFL-supported strike against "starvation wages, long hours, and unsanitary working conditions." Of the roughly seven hundred union members engaged in the struggle, approximately half were black and 70 percent were women. Though a considerable number of the strike's participants were black women, Urban League director John T. Clark described the event as "entirely a white workers' strike," suggesting that although black women swelled the numbers of the rank and file, they had little power in union governance. While the struggle to desegregate the garment industry originated in the 1930s, it began in earnest a decade later. In 1940 an estimated twenty thousand black women workers in the "local labor market" sought jobs in the growing industry. "With the active support of Negro garment workers, the press and Negro women's organizations," read an Urban League report, "a year-round struggle has been waged against the Jim Crowism that characterizes the needle trades industry in St. Louis, including the trade unions which have jurisdiction over the field."[4]

In St. Louis the racial wall surrounding the garment industry and its unions began to crack under the crushing weight of wartime mobilization and the global spread of ideologies promoting racial tolerance. As one observer put it, "Necessity as a result of the war may break down barriers of prejudice where persuasion has failed." It was the garment industry that most powerfully evidenced black women's shift to industrial employment. In 1941 the first black woman joined the ILGWU, and a year later nearly thirty black women were hired as machine operators. In most cases, if one secured a position as a machine operator, it was in a closed shop, which ordinarily meant that workers became eligible for union membership. By 1943 a handful of black women garment workers swelled to more than 200, with between 150 and 275 in dress manufacturing and another 100 in the production of neckwear and hats. After David Portnoy, one of the largest dress factories in the area, made plans to open an all-black shop in March 1943, several additional shops followed suit and "rushed in at once." By the end of that year, factory managers hired black women as operators, spotters, drapers, foreladies, instructors, finishers, pressers, and trimmers. Experienced operators earned, on average, between thirty and thirty-five dollars each week for forty hours of work per week. Manufacturers established five new all-black factories in 1944, two of which employed approximately 100 women each, raising the total number of clothing factories with black women employees to approximately thirty. In the following year, the garment and needle trades industry led in employment opportunities for black women; by this time approximately 700 were ILGWU members.[5]

Industrial managers and white workers alike were deeply reluctant to embrace black women's presence, because it so fundamentally disrupted the racial and gender division that had organized St. Louis's industrial labor system for most of the twentieth century. For example, garment manufacturer David Portnoy's shop "is a most promising enterprise," read Urban League staffer Valla D. Abbington's report, "except for the facilities made available for the Negro employees." Portnoy's willingness to hire black women workers garnered praise from the social service agency, but the way he treated black women belied the League's enthusiasm. Portnoy forced black women to use the rear entrance and the freight elevator in so-called desegregated shops, while his all-black locations had "practically no exits for the Negro in case of fire." Garment manufacturer L. M. Levy, described by UL staffers as an emotionally volatile employer, managed a shop that "rises and subsides like a body of water." Inside the factory a "negative philosophy [was] preached daily," and black women confronted a routine barrage of insults and threats. When challenged by black women workers, Levy charged that black women had "failed and have failed their own race," squandering what was "an unusual chance to prove their worth and remain in the garment industry." As soon as the war effort drew to a close, black women could "go again to house work and restaurant work of all kinds" and "whites [could] return [to industrial factories]." Militant in their display of racial hostility, working-class white women often staged strikes or quit to register their dissatisfaction. Racial resistance became a central component of white women's labor militancy, especially as it pertained to undermining managerial authority. For instance, 15 percent of white women workers in nonproduction units, all prospective members of Local 516 ILGWU, "practically all refused to sign up [for the union] because they do not wish to become a member of an integrated local." Two months after black women operators and "floor girls" began work at the Ace Uniform Company in early 1945, white workers quit their jobs "at the rate of five a day." Similarly, in just a few months the percentage of black women workers at the Kearns Brothers Dress Company, all of whom were either full members or workers who held temporary union permits with the ILGWU, grew from 60 percent to 87 percent. Kearns managers initially established "an entirely integrated setup . . . with the policy that white and Negro applicants would be accepted and employed indiscriminately," but in a short time white employees registered their complaint through flight. About six months after the Kearns Company integrated its workforce, "the shop has become almost totally filled with Negro operators" because "most of the white operators dropped out one by one." With greater economic mobility, alternative job prospects were possible. There were rare exceptions to the rule, but in general, working-class black women in St. Louis toiled in hostile environments. White industrialists' and the working classes' intransigence made one union organizer comment, "As far as it can be ascertained from our observations, indications are that St. Louis presents more race prejudice of white workers toward Negro workers than demonstrated in any other southern city."[6]

The same pattern existed in organized labor. Garment unions "openly discriminate against Negro women in violation of union principles and union constitution," wrote Valla Abbington, an Urban League field secretary and specialist in black women's employment. Black workers were once excluded altogether from the United Hatters, Cap, and Millinery Workers Union, the Paper and Paper Craft Unions (AFL), the printing trades locals, the Boot and Shoe Workers Union (AFL), and the Upholsterers' Union. The experience of black women who aspired to become members of the United Hatters, Cap, and Millinery Workers provided the raw evidence supporting Abbington's observation. When Seigel Specialty Company's manager laid off his all-black workforce on the "pretense that he was going out of business" (he was actually refusing to pay black women at rates stipulated by union policy), the 51 percent of black women workers who had recently signed union cards turned to labor organizer Henry Fromkin to find new jobs. Only one company, the Funk Brothers Cap Hat Company, a closed shop where employees were members of the Cap Makers Union (Local 17), was "completely sold on the idea" of hiring black women. After holding a "lengthy conference" with company owner Julius Funk, Abbington tried in vain to reach Fromkin to complete the process; each time she called, "his office girl" informed her that he was "out of the city, sick, etc." The Cap Makers "deliberately dodged its responsibility to seek employment for its members," wrote the frustrated field worker. After Abbington brought in a younger veteran organizer to help out, black working-class women finally unionized with the United Hatters after nine months of struggle.[7]

Like industrial managers, some union officials blamed the rank and file for stalling interracial unionism's progress. An official of Local 60 of the Leather Luggage Workers' Union (CIO) explained that he "could move out no further in interracial work relationships than his union membership permitted." He explained that there had never been black workers on production in the shops under the union's jurisdiction, with the exception of two black women who were employed as matrons or cleaners at the Prince Gardner Manufacturing Company, with a workforce totaling more than three hundred workers. When an Urban League staff member offered to host a "conference at which time the entire leather luggage industry might be discussed," unionists "flatly refused" to consider the possibility of racial inclusion. St. Louis was a center for shoe manufacturing; black women had long struggled to secure positions in the industry and the unions that represented its workers. The Boot and Shoe Workers Union (AFL), for example, a group with about two thousand to three thousand members and one of the largest of its kind, with jurisdiction over most St. Louis shoe factories, did not accept black members, according to one representative. A federal contract made it possible for black working-class women to secure temporary employment at the Johansen Brothers Shoe Company. After the war, however, having worked at the company for about two years, the women were summarily fired and told that the union did not accept black workers. Ben Berk, regional director for the Boot and Shoe Union based in St. Louis, continued to avoid the racial question as late as January 1948.[8]

In the cases in which unionists successfully confronted racial tension, black working-class women benefited. After the Leather and Luggage Union Local 60 (CIO) won an election at the Bernard Handbag Manufacturing Company, for example, the first black women to join the union worked at Bernard, manufacturing women's purses at the starting union wage rate of fifty cents per hour. In the closed shop of eighty-five employees, 60 percent were black women and the shop steward was a black woman. While these workers were hired as matrons, managers made plans to hire a second shift of black women workers as machine operators. Other women successfully mobilized to win union recognition. For example, workers at the Doris Dodson Dress Company demanded ILGWU representation from Local 516 vice president Julia Johnson Mayes. Their organizing paid off, resulting in "a new job status with recognition deserving their seniority and importance to the total industry." In time, several hundred black women joined the ranks of a local whose officials had once been strongly opposed to desegregation.[9]

Workplace Dignity and Critical Unionism

Industrial employers' hostility emerged in response to working-class black women's resistance. Employers' frequent complaints and accusations against black women pointed to workers' determination to shape the factory experience and define industrial employment and unionism on their own terms. Managers alleged that black women took home the manufactured clothing that they had produced to wear themselves and to share with their families, "called [the] employer names," and "[wanted to give] orders to whites when whites are accustomed to giving orders to Negroes." Black working-class women were "too slow," "stole clothes and money," "broke employer's perfume bottles," and "refused to follow instructions." Some women did not show up for work, others "laid the employer out" or "fussed with her [the employer] all day," and still more quit after employers asked them to wash windows from the outside. Others worked at their own pace, completed tasks in their own style, set their own hours, and demanded wage rates that exceeded scales set by employers. The culture of resistance was apparently widespread, as the Urban League's field secretary for women found it difficult to fill experienced power-machine operator positions "because the only ones who are available are those who have been fired or quit from other plants." "Absenteeism, lateness, quitting without notice, [and] creating disturbance on the job" were listed by ILGWU representative Grace Bullard as the problems particularly associated with black working-class women.[10]

Black women workers tended to pursue more pragmatic and immediate outcomes than desegregation or the far more ambitious integration of St. Louis's industrial workforce—a pursuit shared by most racial advocacy and civil rights groups. While the Urban League praised David Portnoy's garment company because it was "out in front of practically all others in hiring an entire Negro staff," women workers were far less enthusiastic. They viewed their jobs casually, explaining that they understood their jobs as temporary because they believed that they would eventually lose them to white women once the factory shifted to peacetime production. Some black women workers left their jobs to spend time with husbands who were members of the armed forces; one worker quit because "the pressure under which she has to work . . . was getting to her"; one "decided [she] didn't like the work"; she was "just tired and needed rest"; her "eyes are getting bad"; she "had to work too fast"; she "couldn't make enough money"; others said "they feel they are being exploited, and not being dealt with fairly"; and some could or would no longer tolerate mistreatment by midlevel instructors, supervisors, or trainers or, as in one report on the Portnoy Garment Company's practices, the "methods used by the white forelady in dealing with Negro employees." In a letter to company owner David Portnoy, UL staffer Valla D. Abbington raised the case of Codelia Jeffries, her sister, and the four other employees who quit because "it is impossible to work in constant confusion where they (workers) are told upon the slightest provocation to ring out their time cards." Black women identified Belle McKay Dress Company owner L. M. Levy as an abusive manager and worked as McKay employees for stretches that lasted no longer than two to four weeks. One employee brought her husband to work to confront the employer, who had failed to pay her after Levy found her work unsatisfactory. The two men came close to an altercation.[11]

The employee who brought her husband to the job was one of many black women workers who raised disputes over wages and race-based wage differentials. Employees at Dollie's and Birdie's Hat Shop, for example, quit after working just a few days because they received a weekly wage that was two dollars less than expected. Nine of the fourteen black women workers at Regal Manufacturing Company quit in late 1944 because the company owner paid a higher rate to newly hired white women working as machine operators. Regal's owner added thirteen to eighteen white women to the workforce, and the morning after the move, the black women workers, who had made army hospital bed sheets, screens of cheesecloth for the navy, and sun visors for soldiers "stationed in tropical climates," clocked out one by one, walked to the main office, and demanded their checks, "protesting that they had been discriminated against on the basis of their race." Approximately six months later, on Saturday, June 9, 1945, four thread clippers quit after their manager requested that they work an additional hour to fulfill a shipment. Without notifying their boss, they left, and as the manager called out to them from a window, asking them to return, the women continued on their way, explaining that they "simply had to attend a club meeting." Regal Manufacturing Company managers tried unsuccessfully to persuade the workers to return, explaining that they would receive a raise in time based on the wage scale and timetable. Like Ellie Williams, an employee of the J. H. Mittaman Hat Company who "got into a heated argument" with her boss over a wage dispute, newly hired black women workers emphasized equal pay and, along with this, the right to air grievances and insist on fair treatment.[12]

Ellie Williams and others pushed not only for equal pay but also for the right to exercise some autonomy over their work schedule. When asked "why they did not want to work" overtime, they responded, "[We] worked all day" and "just wanted to go home." Her colleagues "were married and just had to have time to do their washing and ironing." On one Saturday morning, black women employees at the Lewin and Mathes clothing shop began leaving their shift one by one. Although every employee was required to work a full six days per week since the company's production quotas had increased, Saturday was the only day available to purchase groceries and other goods for their families, the women explained. Leaving too late on Saturday meant they would have little choice when selecting food items. After holding a conference, the women voted in favor of a measure that required managers to hire additional workers and open the shop earlier on Saturdays. In addition, managers switched the official payday from Friday to Saturday to give women more time to conduct their affairs and to delegate "other members of the family [to] do their shopping for them on Saturday morning."[13]

Black women's resistance extended to their initial forays into unionism. "Negro Factory Girls Slow to Join Unions," read a headline in an Urban League bulletin. Citing an inverse relationship between the number of new garment factories that opened their doors to black women and the rate at which black women joined their unions, the article mentioned one factory where just one out of twenty employees became an official member. Seventy black women at another shop joined only after they learned that they would otherwise lose their jobs. Employees of the Ruth Adler Dress Company refused unionization after two months of working in a closed shop. The shop chair visited the factory to cajole the women, explaining that upon paying their dues they could earn an increase of ten cents per hour. Despite the attempt, by the end of the year, some black women workers still rejected membership. Finally, "after explaining to them the meaning and protection of union membership," "they consented to pay up their back dues" and attend a meeting. Percy Ginsburg, United Hatters, Cap, and Millinery Workers Local 17 organizer, "stated and restated that many of them [black women] seem to have the mistaken idea that a union book automatically means more pay even when they are not producing a sufficient quota of work to justify an increased rate of pay." Similarly, the women who were among the first black workers to organize with the Leather & Luggage Workers Union Local 60 (CIO) were, according to officials, of the opinion that "there are certain privileges they can take since they join the union and that the company can't fire them." Activists in the labor movement believed that black women needed discipline and responsibility, and while a certain number of them needed to learn unionism's workings, it is also the case that women were advancing their own definitions and were reserving their allegiance until the benefits of unionism were apparent and accessible.[14]

For social architects, black women workers' forays into industrial work and interracial unionism played a critical role. With much to lose because of its abiding interest in producing respectable black industrial workers, the St. Louis Urban League constructed a labor education program of its own, with all the interventions it could muster to make sure the experiment would succeed. The UL's report for March 1944 read, "Unless the Negro employees can be sufficiently impressed with the necessity for being a first class employee we fear that many of the present opportunities will be closed to them during the post war period." Urban League workers arranged meetings with black ministers to preach the gospel of industrial discipline and conducted studies. Field secretaries distributed brochures on "the 16 points on how to hold your job," and officials even brought in NAACP national secretary Daisy Lampkin to help motivate the workers. The Urban League invited local ILGWU official Grace Bullard to discuss ways to manage black women. Union officials announced that they would no longer support undisciplined workers and would require union members to undergo a thorough background check before being granted a new assignment.[15]

In a patronizing and degrading manner, the Urban League sided with managers and union officials' notions of black women's unfitness. Black women workers were "so suspicious, sensitive, and retiring" that a rigorous program "to suppress 'smart alecks,' crude loudness and coarseness, [and attitudes that favored] fewer hours and no days off" was critical, leaders explained. The *St. Louis Urban League Bulletin* announced that the league's duty was to transform even those at the "bottom of the barrel [of] labor" and that it could do so through training and near-constant observation, arbitration, and negotiation. Investigating a recently organized dress shop where "the morale and the output of the shop was at its lowest," staffers found that about 90 percent of the employees "had been hired directly from the street" and not from the Urban League's own referral process. The ten who had been referred by the Urban League quit, according to officials, because "they were unwilling to work with such unruly workers," whom the league described as workers who had caused "many instances of boisterousness and conflicts which showed a lack of discipline, resentfulness of union rule and general hostility." League staff members felt that they were confronting an urgent matter, with the long struggle for an interracial workforce and unionism at stake, but their manner of doing so served to further pathologize black women as deficient industrial workers and union members.[16]

"To Tell the Story of Its Struggles"

The Educational Department of the ILGWU's Southwestern District had already been in operation for about five years when the upheaval over black women's economic forays intensified in the 1940s. In fact, organizers behind the worker theater wing of the St. Louis ILGWU soon assumed the task of reducing the conflict between employers who complained of what they interpreted as black women's insubordination and supposed unsuitability for industrial work, on the one hand, and women workers' dogged attempts to resist factory and union discipline and to define industrial work on their own terms, on the other. When it opened in 1935, the labor education department included only St. Louis, but by the end of the decade, the district stretched as far north as Minneapolis and as far south as San Antonio. Director Doris Preisler, a noted labor leader based in the metropolitan St. Louis area, grew the department so much that by the 1930s it had its own office, committee, and budget, with funds provided by the national ILGWU and locals. Even after the geographical expansion, St. Louis remained the hub. Preisler imagined a working-class academy that would instill "self-confidence," since "a goodly portion of the people who are responsible for the building and functioning of the country do not consider themselves capable of understanding its problems or of coping with them." With National Recovery Act regulations shortening work hours and the workweek, administrators saw their role as one of creating productive activities for workers in need of a reprieve from the monotony of physical labor. Preisler and her team also imagined that labor education would keep unionism healthy. With so many new workers, many of them black women, joining locals in the early 1940s, officials feared that the influx would threaten traditional union culture. St. Louis–based ILGWU locals later began to require new members to complete a three-session orientation course to become formal members. Ideally, educational programs would acculturate new members to the discipline of respectable unionism, assist workers to "acquire the knowledge of advanced industrial methods in order to secure from industry advanced returns for the energy and intelligence [the workers] invest," and infuse a sense of personal and collective power into the rank and file. Rooted in the labor education movement, the start of the ILGWU's program reflected pedagogical models advanced at institutions like the Highlander Research and Education Center, which had been founded by activist Myles Horton as a training ground for labor and civil rights activists.[17]

Worker theater soon became the heart of Doris Preisler's educational program. "It would be fine, we think," Preisler envisioned, "to have a true workers' theater with plays acted by workers before audiences of workers." The department's first major venture was *Surging Forward,* a pageant depicting scenes in labor history, from immigrants laboring with dashed hopes to the Triangle Factory fire, worker organizing, and a celebration of ethnic diversity through folk dance. Adapted by the St. Louis's ILGWU from a New York City–based play, *The Story of the ILGWU: A Radio Play in Six Episodes,* which aired on New York City's WEVD to spread the gospel of unionism through performance, song, and sketch, *Surging Forward* was an ambitious attempt to bring worker theater to a St. Louis audience. Local theater producer Edward L. Butler, who was no stranger to large-scale productions and politically charged theater, wrote the play. Anna Agress, a professional dancer with experience in local community productions, served as director of dance. With musical numbers, dance routines, and a set that impressed audiences, *Surging Forward* addressed "how trade union organization wiped out the sweatshop and replaced it with shops in which shorter hours, living wages, and decent conditions are the rule" by telling the story of "the unfortunates," the working-class European immigrants who found reprieve from the sweatshops of early-twentieth-century urban America only through mass organization. ILGWU members made their own costumes, while unionists in the electrical and stagehand industry served as the backstage crew. Debuting in June 1936 at St. Louis's Municipal Auditorium, the play did not sell out, but members of organized labor and other sympathizers supported it, purchasing blocks of seats selling for forty to fifty cents each. Though costly, worker theater built morale and solidarity among workers, Meyer Perlstein, ILGWU director of the Southwestern District, explained. *Surging Forward* "mark[ed] the first time in the history of St. Louis labor organizations that a body of workers has resorted to the drama to tell the story of its struggles." With a cast of workers and their children totaling between two hundred and three hundred, the play was a spectacular, sixteen-scene, three-act debut, lasting more than two and a half hours. Recruited by director Doris Preisler, who selected prospective participants at locals' meetings, members spent many days after work and on the weekends rehearsing at ILGWU headquarters on North Ninth Street for more than two months; and when show time was just around the corner, they rehearsed nightly. After the play's successful performance in St. Louis, union leaders arranged for a production in nearby Kansas City two months later. One reviewer noted that, from the rehearsal to the stage, *Surging Forward* was "fundamentally a group project in which the importance of the individual is minimized, the emphasis being rather on the uses of mass for effect." The absence of "solo dances," for example, reflected emphasis on collectivity and the argument that it was through collective action that marginalized people—workers—make their mark on history. By means of a focus on collective action through overcoming ethnic differences and a triumphal narrative of union organizing, the production achieved success through historical interpretation and pushed local and regional agitprop to the center of the district's educational programming.[18]

Although the first five years saw little involvement in labor education projects from black women, by the early 1940s, labor education directors extended invitations across the color line. Working-class women, in turn, used the opportunity to expand the culture of resistance they had established in the union hall and on the shop floor to the space of labor education and its stages, even while they supported the work of spreading the gospel of unionism. Writer, director, and ILGWU organizer Rita Oberbeck invited approximately ten black women to participate in a new production planned for the spring of 1943. Together, Lillian Jennings, Ardella Harris, Bessie White, Naomi Blackmore, Lillian Reynolds, Geneva Crawford, Vedora Grand, Ida J. Poole, Bernice Wren, and Ernestine Springfield declined the offer, informing Oberbeck that they refused to play demeaning roles.[19]

The department's fourth major production, *Tomorrow Must Be Ours,* recounted the history of worker struggles in the United States by depicting scenes of Native American life and colonial America, the American Revolution, slavery, the railroad and Pullman strikes, and the jazz era. Based on Henry A. Wallace's 1942 "Century of the Common Man" address, *Tomorrow Must Be Ours* opened with a monologue that declared, "We who fight in the people's cause will never stop until that cause is won. Let no one ask our color or our birthplace—we the people are on the march. . . . Ask not my color or my birthplace just say that I am a man." The play openly dealt with racial prejudice among white workers as it called for interracial working-class unity. While the group of women workers did not specify which roles they found offensive, various scenes could have fallen into this category. It was likely the "plantation scene," depicting "men and women dressed [in] colonial fashion having a garden party" with a "background negro group humming softly," that the women rejected. In act 2, two of the party's white attendees, Sue, the "Southern Belle," and George, the "Gentleman," ponder abolition, mentioning Elijah Lovejoy, who "Wants us to free all our slaves." "What would we do?" the couple wonders. "Besides they're happy—listen to them." At this point, "slave singing wells up," the script directs. George, a "Yankee-school"–educated "Negro sympathizer" angered at the white mob that has lynched a black man, reveals, "They're selling little Georgia tomorrow," to which Sue responds, "Yes, Papa just had to. I begged him not to take her from Mammy Cloe but he just would [not] listen." The conversation continues, and when George mentions "a man named Lincoln in the White House" who is "starting something that will never be forgotten," "slaves" begin to sing again as Abraham Lincoln appears in shadow. As the "Great Emancipator" reads the Emancipation Proclamation, the script instructs, "slaves listen, faces gradually rise—singing becomes more joyous—finally whoop it up." Unaware of how black women's collective memory of slavery deeply informed their labor politics in the twentieth century, particularly how their sense of a racialized past shaped the ways they negotiated their racialized present, Oberbeck was surprised that these women chose to miss out on what she understood as a golden opportunity. Black women's critical unionism was based in part on raising awareness of, and critiquing, the labor continuities between enslavement and industrialism. Working women wished to challenge wage slavery of the wartime 1940s, but to do so in such a way as not to replicate enslaved labor.[20]

A golden opportunity it was, local Urban League officials agreed. According to executive secretary John T. Clark, refusing to participate would further embed ideas about black women's unfitness for industrial labor and derail a long struggle to integrate unions. If women wanted simply to "make a few dollars this Spring" or "to buy yourself an outfit," then it mattered not whether they participated, Clark wrote. If, however, the group "would like to so entrench the value which Negro women can give to the needle-trades," then they should "play that role," and along the way, make sure that black actors had lines in every act and that "the Negro power-machine operator is now a recognized fact." Clark reminded them that the nationally acclaimed "Marian Anderson never fails to sing the Spirituals whenever a program is planned for her." Likewise, to Clark's way of thinking, black women workers exhibited a tendency among black people that inhibited racial progress: "We are such a sensitive race and foolishly sensitive over little things that when we are asked to play any role which we think is beneath our dignity—we rebel." Like the play's director's vision, Clark's myopic focus on integration seemed to blind him to black women's own sense of themselves as workers, their historical memory, and the visions of freedom and autonomy that they brought to unions and to the workplace. There was, of course, a significant distinction between the humming requested of the black women laborers and the spirituals sung by Marian Anderson. Leaving little room for performance and interpretation, humming was a device often used in productions that played upon Old South racial nostalgia's representation of the docile, happy slave. Black shadows humming in the background stripped the performers of the ability to articulate their long-ings, desires, and worldviews. In contrast, when Marian Anderson sang spirituals, her performances infused texts with twentieth-century political life. From her voice, a civil rights movement found expression through articulation of a long, collective historical memory that profoundly reso-nated in the context of the age of Jim Crow. As Shana L. Redmond notes, "spirituals spoke directly to the contemporary political struggles of Afri-can Americans."[21]

Racial nostalgia for the Old South was not limited to the 1943 play. A 1940 celebration of American ideals, *Let Freedom Swing* included num-bers like "By De Side of De Road," also known as "The Sharecropper's Song." Written to honor the 1939 sharecroppers' strike in southeastern Missouri, the song used so-termed black dialect to indicate economic suf-fering and class oppression. "I know de Lawd has heard my cry," the song begins. Speaking to the despair some strikers likely felt as they camped along Highway 60 during the winter season, performers sang,

> Der ain't no place we kin go;
> Nothing to eat and nowhere's to stay.

"The Sharecropper's Song" offers an illustrative example of the problems some progressive unionists encountered when they engaged racial and cultural politics. Even as the tune offered a teachable example of inter-racial worker solidarity that carried resonance because it harked back to populist struggles of the late nineteenth century, it did so by advanc-ing a racial liberalism steeped in Old South nostalgia. *Let Freedom Swing* also included a tune about political boss Thomas Joseph Pendergast, who served a federal prison sentence for tax evasion. Script notes instructed the actor portraying Pendergast to sing in the "Al Jolson–mammy style." One critic found that the actor delivered an "effective song number" as he borrowed the style of the Russian-born blackface performer who found great commercial success in the United States. Efforts by black musicians like Marian Anderson and Paul Robeson illustrate how critical performance was to negotiating black racial representation in popular cul-ture. Black singers performed dialect differently, often using it to achieve political effect or abandoning the language altogether.[22]

Theatrical productions were not the only site for contestations over race, labor, and historical memory. Regional conferences, organized by the ILGWU's labor education program, contained their own controversy. Gatherers at the Southwest Regional Conference in St. Louis in June 1942, for example, received a songbook of popular American folk songs such as "The Band Played On," "Home on the Range," and "She'll Be Coming 'round the Mountain." Organizers included the official songs of the states in the region. Adopted in 1949 by the state legislature, though not without controversy and after officials amended the song to remove the racist language of Old South parlance, "The Missouri Waltz" or "Hush-a-bye, Ma Baby" articulated an Old South longing to craft state identity.

> When I was a Picaninny on ma Mammy's knee
> The darkies were hummin',

one stanza reads. Instead of amending the lyrics, however, the ILGWU program printed the original version. "Carry Me Back to Old Virginny," another folk tune listed in the program, expressed Mammy's longing for the refuge of the plantation household: "I labored so hard for old Massa," in the land where "the old darkey's heart am longed to go." Mammy's body functioned as the portal through which passage to the Old South became both possible and desirable. Such narratives "became a way for Americans to define the character of the nation, the meaning of freedom, and the racial and gender boundaries of the citizenry." Taken together, the narratives defined not only nationhood but also labor and unionism. The labor education department taught messages on multiple levels, since musical text designed for community building off-stage also had didactic import. Black women, too, likely protested against easy narratives of inclusion and solidarity when those narratives required participating in gatherings like regional conferences. Refusal to participate joined tactics like slowdowns and theft in black women's political arsenal.[23]

Theater productions in the mid to late 1940s found greater success, not by resolving conflicts over historical memory, but by placing less emphasis on contested histories. Later productions tended to highlight the cultural contributions of African Americans and made space for a few black women to play leading roles. In this period the numbers of black women performers increased, and efforts to create partnerships with local black cultural leaders succeeded. Performed at the Goldenrod Showboat on the Mississippi River, *Mississippi River Revels* (1949) was a vaudeville show designed to pay tribute to the profound influence of the body of water on the shaping of St. Louis arts and culture. Unlike earlier performances in which integration was difficult to achieve, the fifty-member cast included multiple black women performers who primarily sang in the chorus under the leadership of local black composer Kenneth Billups. It seems that director Rita Oberbeck realized that there could be no proper tribute, or for that matter, success in building racially integrated audiences without saturating the performance with black cultural aesthetics. The Mississippi River long served as inspiration for jazz artists like Louis Armstrong, writers like Langston Hughes, and blues musicians like W. C. Handy. Barbara Jenkins, a kind of ILGWU darling in the dramatics department, was clearly a breakout star whose participation determined the production's success. While she performed in multiple scenes, including a polka routine, and led the tune "Life upon the Wicked Stage" while backed by cancan dancers and the ILGWU chorus, her most important contribution was playing the "wronged woman" in Handy's 1914 breakout tune "St. Louis Blues." Bringing the song to life on the stage, Jenkins likely drew upon Bessie Smith's performance in Handy's 1929 film to convey the sorrow experienced by a woman whose lover had left her for another. "I hate to see that evening sun go down," Jenkins sang, "Cause my baby, he's gone left this town" for "the St. Louis woman with her diamond ring." Oberbeck's casting of Jenkins in a role steeped in black women's blues tradition infused the production with cultural relevancy and authenticity. Serving as cultural ambassador for the union, Jenkins performed with a select ensemble to honor national ILGWU president David Dubinsky during his visit to St. Louis. She performed in a trio, where she stood at the center. While Jenkins was a star, she was not the only participant. In plays directed by Kenneth Billups, such as *Mississippi River Revels,* black women cast members were in the majority. Black women performers donned elaborate costumes, sang in the chorus, and danced to popular tunes. Using song as rebellion, they were redefining black womanhood through working-class subjectivity.[24]

While black women played visible and active roles in theater productions, the record of their full contribution is sparse. Images of women singing, dancing, and participating in community programs tell the story of their increasing levels of involvement across the 1940s. In rare instances, black women worker-artists had their stories told in local papers. For example, the *St. Louis Post-Dispatch* featured the "skilled dress finisher" Martha Ellis, a three-year veteran of the St. Louis's ILGWU education department's evening sketching class, held weekly from October thru May. The newspaper featured Ellis in a photo-story titled "Union Art Students," as among those highly skilled sketch artists.[25]

Doris Preisler and other worker theater directors regularly used black women's talent and hypervisibility to try to establish the ILGWU's reputation as a progressive labor union. "At our meetings you have often asked me what labor unions do to create better race relations," Preisler told members of the St. Louis Race Relations Commission. "One of the best examples of what we do is the inter-racial musical revue." With a nod to earlier conflicts, she added, "The show has had inter-racial direction and the audience of course is inter-racial." The "exceptionally worthwhile project" was clearly the product of hard-fought battles, but the deeper story of black women's resistance and the impact it had on shaping union culture did not reach the public record. An obituary of writer and director Rita Oberbeck stated, "When the St. Louis ILGWU took in the Black people who began working in the garment industry during the war years, it was Rita who made them welcome in the Educational Department and laid the base for their future integration in all Educational Department activities." In this telling, an imagined racial unity shaped this official union history. Still, such imagined solidarity functioned within the work of one of the more progressive and politically creative unions in the city when it came to questions of integration and implementing racial liberalism in a tangible way. In a tribute to her colleague, Doris Preisler rightly noted that Rita Oberbeck was a champion of "industrial democracy, the integration of the races and nationalities and international peace and brotherhood." The ILGWU educational program demonstrated its commitment to building racial consciousness in numerous ways, including arranging for members of the explorers club to visit the Old Courthouse where lawyers had tried Dred Scott's case and inviting Brotherhood of Sleeping Car Porters and March on Washington Movement leader T. D. Neal to address the St. Louis Youth Labor Forum. Yet what black women workers insisted upon in this racial experiment was a more difficult unionism that recognized the uniqueness of their own labor histories. Their early resistance created the conditions for Preisler and Oberbeck to amend their practices around the very issue—racial progressivism—that liberals identified as the ILGWU's distinguishing quality.[26]

The first cohort of black women to break the color barrier in the St. Louis garment industry and its unions had anything but a smooth transition. Determined to mold factory employment, labor discipline, and unionism according to their own models, black women garment workers could barely be comprehended as members of the modern workforce, as the constant barrage of complaints about their unfitness suggest. Employers tended to believe that black women were ill-suited for industrial work, proposing that they were better suited for domestic labor. Union officials were equally suspicious; they suggested that black women could not handle the responsibilities associated with union membership. From another angle, filtered through black uplift discourse, were "shape up" messages from civil rights organizations such as the Urban League. The precise texture of women's marginalization within the various political cultures produced by various progressive struggles for economic and racial justice would not have developed in the ways that it did had it not been for black women. An active part of the process, they carved out a space for themselves in the political discourse and social change activism occasioned by the wartime political moment.

Black working-class women's economic politics, specifically the attempt to make dignity manifest itself in their relations with employers and union officials, and in the social contracts that undergirded the ILGWU's cultural programming, sheds light on the ways gender and race shaped the wartime interracial experiments that gave rise to new thinking about working-class identity and status. The point should also be made that progressive unionists and racial reformers traded in black working-class women's work and labor activism to carve out a space for themselves in the struggle to establish "interracial goodwill" in industrial factories and union halls. Worker theater productions became a primary site for such experimentation and contestation. They by no means resolved the racial and gender tensions present in the social upheavals caused by the reorganization of labor, but they most certainly brought the tensions into sharp relief and so hinted toward implementing revised social and political approaches in the postwar period.

Documenting the wartime 1940s often involves a celebratory rendering of the period, since chroniclers mark the moment as a high point of the labor movement. In many respects, it most certainly was. Union membership nationwide reached its peak, wildcat strikes emboldened the working classes to harness the power of their collective strength, and workers of color and women infused the task of building a robust worker rights movement with a sense of the priority of racial and gender justice concerns, but the story of black working-class women in St. Louis, and across the country, invites us to consider this history more carefully. Women's resistance to "little things," as the Urban League director derisively put it, was in actuality a sustained critique of progressive unionism and racial liberalism. Scholars of black women's working-class history argue that spatial politics are absolutely essential to understanding how women shaped their responses to oppressive economic conditions and power hierarchies. The space of the worker theater stage and the union-sponsored labor education program set the parameters for black women's resistance. Progressive unionists' racial liberalism, along with their creation of a program to empower workers, resist hegemonic ideologies, and challenge corporate power, made possible working-class black women's politically generative use of new resources and opportunities. Notably, women created their own political platform, drawing attention to the deeply embedded tensions within racial inclusion projects of the 1940s. Black working women highlighted salient differences among working-class people, noting, in effect, how class identity is differentiated.

Black working-class women in the St. Louis garment industry were not alone in shaping American racial liberalism through a kind of political assertion with black working women's economic experience at the center. In the 1950s and 1960s, debates over public housing emerged as an important crucible of black working-class women's struggle for economic dignity. The struggle for decent, state-subsidized housing, along with the struggle for adequate public assistance and employment opportunity, fit into a broader political project of laboring for dignity. Black working-class women's struggle surrounding housing and the state also revealed the deep connections between public housing, "community unionism," and low-income black women's living conditions.

6

"Jobs and Homes . . . Freedom"

Working-Class Struggles against Postwar Urban Inequality

St. Louis Argus staff members silenced Sarah Wallace's voice in their story about her living conditions and the squalor that defined the neighborhood and residences of the city's poor and working-class black population. Instead of providing Wallace with a platform from which to speak about her lived reality in her own words and on her own terms, they just presented a vivid description of her living quarters to depict life in St. Louis's most notorious slums. A widow and a welfare recipient, Sarah Wallace was also unemployed and the sole breadwinner of her household, but this critical dimension the writers omitted. Writing in the tradition of some journalists who in the 1950s used sensationalism to raise awareness about the need for urban renewal, the *Argus* writers rendered Wallace mute and her breadwinning status illegible. The fact that she was an economic actor, albeit a marginalized one within the scope of St. Louis's paid labor landscape, failed to make it to the record. Although Wallace's voice did not find a place in the newspaper, voices like hers found expression through the alternative channels that emerging forms of activism opened in post-1945 St. Louis.[1]

Shifting the lens to black working-class women's lives and political labors in a city better known for its postwar failures, this chapter rewrites the history of urban decline. Black working-class women were situated and situated themselves at the center of the overlapping battles that constituted St. Louis's contribution to the debate over the long-term vitality of American cities. Caught between municipal officials who wished to drum up public support for "slum clearance" and black community leaders who had been advocating for years for safe, affordable, and quality

145

housing, black working-class women became the face of urban poverty. They were not only symbols, however; they also reshaped postwar American cities into arenas of struggle for economic dignity. Refusing to accept outsider status or to be cast as victims of the fallen American city, these women threw light on the many challenges they faced as low-income black urbanites and became active participants in challenging the deep structural problems that threatened the Gateway City's postwar progress. The cluster of economic issues that their working-class politics made public anticipated and marked the core elements of the city's decline.[2]

During the 1950s and early 1960s, public housing, urban renewal, economic opportunity through welfare reform and jobs, and trade union leadership emerged as key battlegrounds. In this era, black working-class women measured economic dignity in terms of the quality of life of low-income residents in St. Louis city proper. For public-housing tenants, jobs and homes were interconnected; they made no easy divisions between access to decent public housing and acceptable employment, rent and a living wage, or clean and safe buildings and working conditions that mirrored their self-respect. Housing matters were deeply crucial to black women's economic experience and working-class activism because women determined through their politics that the fight for affordable and decent public housing was a critical component of a workers' rights political agenda. Residents of the city's newly erected housing developments worked to build new communities of solidarity and support that would later make it possible to engage in effective political action. As Ora Lee Malone quickly emerged as a leader of the trade union movement, her political labors echoed public-housing tenants' emphasis on urban life and economic rights. Her political labor matched that of better-known labor and civil rights activists such as Theodore McNeal and David Grant of the MOWM. One might compare Malone's trade union activism to that of the Teamsters' Harold Gibbons and Ernest Calloway, who pioneered "total person unionism," a practice that aimed to address the totality of workers' living concerns. Malone used the platform of her political leadership in organized labor to address a wider set of issues pertaining to black working-class life in the inner city.[3]

As the leadership profiles of public-housing tenants and Ora Lee Malone grew, so too did the visibility of black middle-class women, who

also took on the fight against urban inequality. Working in the tradition of the black women social workers who had led the St. Louis Urban
League's Women's Division during the thirties and forties, Marian
Oldham, a CORE leader; Frankie Freeman, a civil rights lawyer with a
national presence; and DeVerne Lee Calloway, the first African American
woman to win a seat in the Missouri House of Representatives, built their
careers around working to improve black working-class women's quality
of life. Their advocacy for low-income black women, in particular, served
as a means to raise the status of their own credibility as civil rights workers. Black professional women's leadership drew upon and extended the
worker mobilizations led by black women during the thirties and forties.
In St. Louis, workers' issues were front and center in civil rights struggles, with most falling within the scope of the fight for housing and jobs.

  This chapter examines how black low-income women figured into the
politics of urban renewal, the actions that public-housing tenants took to
change the condition of their lives, the trade union activism of a figure
like Ora Lee Malone, and the advocacy work of black professional women
to demonstrate the connections between public housing, unionism, jobs,
and working-class women's living conditions. All are examples of how
black women labored for economic dignity, or how they sought work
and access to expanded economic opportunities, and how their economic
conditions, particularly their housing and living conditions, became constitutive material for discourses of urban poverty.

"We Talk about 'Decay' in St. Louis"

By 1950 St. Louis was a city in free fall. The process of steady decline had
started long before, but even as sociologists, urban planners, and municipal leaders noted the crisis during the interwar period, people still held
a glimmer of optimism. As the grim realities of the postwar economy
gripped the city, however, even the rosiest of observers could not deny
that things had gotten progressively worse over the decades. Having lost
its turn-of-the-century bid to become the railroad center of the Midwest,
St. Louis had relied for years on an outdated river economy that kept it
from emerging as a major regional hub, a failing that became more evident daily. The city's dramatic population decline indicated its shortcom-

ings. The fourth-largest city in the United States in 1900, it had fallen to eighth by 1950. It dropped to twenty-sixth by 1980. While this out-migration characterized many great American cities, including Chicago and New York, the trend began far earlier in St. Louis and thus could not be attributed merely to a failure to sustain postwar economic gains. The city's problems were far deeper than that. In a 1950 series called "Progress or Decay? St. Louis Must Choose," Richard G. Baumhoff of the local *Post-Dispatch* expressed a fear that "St. Louis would take a back seat among American cities." Trenchant problems in race relations, housing, education, and transportation marked the city's peril.[4]

St. Louisans were concerned about their city's notoriety. *Our World* writer David A. Hepburn, an African American journalist for John P. Davis's national lifestyle magazine, published "Shocking St. Louis" for the February 1950 issue. Hepburn called St. Louis a "shank" and a "juicy town" because of its "vice, corruption and high crime rates." To com-pose his exposé, Hepburn spent time at the Homer G. Phillips Hospital over one weekend, where he cited more than one hundred patients under care for "shootings and cuttings." The seedy element's members likely procured their weapons through transactions conducted in nearby East St. Louis, Illinois, Hepburn told readers. Photographer Wilbert Blanche complemented Hepburn's scathing commentary with photos of blood-splattered women and men caught in the crosshairs of urban violence. Blanche captured the wounded James Williams, "his head . . . a mass of blood," being escorted by a police officer after an altercation in a car; seventy-eight-year-old Mary Little being handled by a police officer and three hospital attendants, with twelve stiches from a strike to the head with a metal rod by her husband; a woman "screaming in agony from [a] compound leg fracture" after a cab driver struck her with his vehicle; black youths embroiled in violent retaliation against white youths who themselves had used violence to resist the integration of the Fairgrounds Park swimming pool; pictures of men shot, stabbed, and cut; and sex workers "clandestinely carrying on in [the] tradition of a hot time."[5]

"Slum, squalor and filth is the housing story. Toughest, most menial jobs go to Negro workers," read the title of the section following the first, which covered "the allied diseases of graft, vice, the rackets, gambling and corruption." "You've never seen slums if you haven't seen those of

St. Louis," Hepburn wrote. "The river shanties, the Biddle Street hovels, the shacks in 'the Patch' around Chouteau Street" vied for top billing as the worst slums in the country. Readers learned that while black residents comprised approximately 14 percent of the city's total population, they accounted for half of those in the city's housing. In "Biddle patch" "slums," residents had to shell out the high price of "12.65 a month for two dank rooms in a rickety firetrap without heat, water or toilet." Photos depicted overcrowded, "rat ridden" dilapidated structures and the families inhabiting them. "This city is bulging at the seams and crying for low cost housing, to no avail," Hepburn wrote. While the black population waits for city leadership to fix the housing problem, local officials "cannot make up [their] mind[s] whether it should be entirely jimcrow or not." On a concluding note, Hepburn argued that Jim Crowism, "fear, hunger, unemployment, ghettos, [and] squalor" had created the conditions for the underground economic activity and vice to thrive.[6]

Black male professional St. Louisans were unhappy with Hepburn's read. Henry Winfield Wheeler, described in the *St. Louis Argus* as "this city's 'Mr. Civil Rights,'" said the piece was "a slanderous falsehood embellished by half-truths and gin-soaked . . . mumbo-jumbo." A *St. Louis American* editorial argued that the article was so misguided and inaccurate, the product of not only "a malicious job, but a lazy, inexpert one," that it did not warrant the respect of a rebuttal. Attorney John W. Harvey, president of the Mound City Bar Association, pulled the popular magazine from his office. "If they had said the shocking slums of St. Louis, I could have understood, . . . but to indict an entire city after spot checking it for a few days seems to me to be in journalistic bad taste." Former state legislator J. Claybourne Bush urged every St. Louisan to discontinue support. Sidney R. Redmond, a former Urban League staffer, pulled away from the pack, arguing that the article offered an opportunity for leaders to implement reforms. Redmond said, "Unfortunately much of the article is true. I hope it serves as a challenge and makes us overcome some of our deficiencies. They are as the grains of sand." Urban League industrial secretary Chester A. Stovall found the middle ground, citing two recent Supreme Court decisions with origins in the Gateway City— the 1938 Lloyd Gaines case and *Shelley v. Kraemer* (1948)—as evidence suggesting local progress on the racial front. Wheeler offered a long list of the city's accomplishments: "We challenge them ["the writers of "Shocking St. Louis"] to name a city in America that has in the last ten years made as noble a fight for human, dignity, equally [*sic*] of opportunity and Christian fellowship as St. Louis." Although Wheeler overstated the case, it was true that city leaders had passed measures that supported integrated auditoriums and city buildings, that activists had battled against discrimination in private lunch counters, and that the black voting public had helped to elect residents from their communities to citywide, state, and national political office. Stovall suggested that Hepburn had succumbed to a northeastern bias among the upwardly mobile black professionals "who probably a few years ago migrated from the deep South into the new found freedom of New York and could not see our trends of progress in St. Louis." Whether black St. Louisans lived harsher lives than their counterparts was a question open for debate, but that the central city's concentrated poverty was a deep problem and that leaders across the color line needed to demonstrate substantive progress through clearing black low-income neighborhoods was a widely held belief.[7]

To convey the urgency of the matter, writers, thinkers, and policymakers portrayed black low-income women as the face of urban blight and poverty. "St. Louis, like any other Big Town is rotting in its core," asserted *Argus* writer Odell W. Morris. While Morris identified city inhabitants as "Negroes and poor whites," he, along with *Argus* staff photographer William B. Franklin, visually represented urban deterioration with a large photograph of a black woman and her children and three additional pictures of dilapidated homes. Sarah Wallace, a widow and a welfare recipient with four children, "typifies the plight of thousands in stricken area," the caption read. The family lived in cramped, two-room living quarters with no electricity, using a kerosene lamp instead. Without access to child care and as the sole breadwinner of her family, Wallace had to remain home, because only one of her children was of school age. Another photo of "ramshackle outside privies" had the caption, "Woman on back porch was determined to get in on the act [by standing within the frame of the photograph]—one man ducked camera." Black children were also a focus. Photos and captions depicted and described a young boy "dumping food scraps into uncovered garbage can," and others showed "children play[ing] cowboy in pool of stagnant water," "a dead dog which children had been dragging around while playing," and "a group of children playing on the roof of a rickety shed" who "swarmed to the edge when the photographer and the reporter appeared." Depicting urban poverty through portrayals of unemployed black women and ostensibly abandoned black children became the main currency of arguments for the erection of public-housing units. "A tour of the area . . . revealed people desperately in need of housing and in many cases, of food and clothing." "Sharecroppers of the Machine Age," low-income black women were symbols pointing to the need to turn "the wheels of politics and common sense." With federal funds and private capital commitments, St. Louis mayor Joseph Darst green-lighted the razing of Wallace's home, which sat in the DeSoto-Carr region, bordered by Franklin and Cass and Eighteenth and Jefferson Streets; the mayor promised to fix the problem of overcrowding and unsanitary conditions.[8]

"Mother, Five Children Face Street Eviction," read a front-page *Argus* headline. This time, the newspaper featured Mary Smith, a Carr Square public-housing resident, who had recently broken her leg on the way to a court hearing. Smith, mother of five children, faced eviction by the SLHA, who charged her with "fraudulent claims" and alleged that she had lied about her husband's employment status by failing to report that he had a full-time job at an electric plant. Under Housing Authority policies, Carr Square residents submitted monthly rent payments based on a family's total income. Smith explained that her husband's economic status was unpredictable and unreliable since his employment fluctuated and that, for a time, she was the sole breadwinner who made ends meet from the fifty-four dollars she received from Aid to Dependent Children and the thirty dollars a month her husband provided. Like Sarah Wallace, Mary Smith was looking for a new place with a lower rent scale and better conditions, but St. Louis's severe housing shortage meant that both were trapped. Photography, too, was a crucial component of telling the woman's story. With a forlorn expression, Mary Smith, wheelchair-bound with a fractured leg and a dislocated foot, stared longingly into the camera lens while her five children, standing, surrounded her with eyes fixed on their mother. Sarah Wallace held a similar pose for an *Argus* photographer.[9]

The deplorable living conditions of residents like Sarah Wallace were the result of choices that municipal leaders had made. Overcrowding stemmed from city officials' failure to accommodate black migrants. The racial makeup of St. Louis shifted during this period; its black population swelled when southerners relocated to cities across the nation to take advantage of wartime industrial jobs as part of the second Great Migration. Before this wave, drawn to the city after the 1904 World's Fair were "maids, cooks, porters, all of whom stayed," and between World War I and World War II, "rough farm-hands from Arkansas, Mississippi, Georgia and Tennessee" moved to the city hoping to make more money by securing jobs in "the steel mills, textile factories, packinghouses and leatherworks." This black migration was as much labor migration as it was anything else. Whites, meanwhile, fled to newly created suburbs that were financed by state and federal subsidies. The outward migration of capital left the cities with a decreased tax base just when the World War II economy was grinding to a halt. Segregated from almost all of these emerging suburban communities, many African Americans found homes in the city's just-built public-housing projects clustered in areas north of downtown that were increasingly holding a sizable percentage of city residents. Substandard housing plagued St. Louis's eastern, northern, and central districts, where blacks were contained and isolated by policies such as restrictive covenants, redlining, and zoning laws. These areas also suffered from high unemployment rates and segregated schools.[10]

Thus, when local advocates envisioned and implemented urban renewal schemes in hopes of stemming the tide of decline wracking St. Louis, they targeted African American neighborhoods. Far from the panacea that municipal planners imagined, however, urban renewal drastically worsened systemic problems. Programs supposedly designed to revitalize the city instead removed low-income black people from zones targeted for commercial development. At their heart was an unstated belief by city leaders that for St. Louis to rebound, it would have to limit the mobility and access of poor and working-class people of color. The urban renewal movement exposed rather than ameliorated the antagonistic relationship between city politicians and African American residents, as blacks were removed from prime locations without their consent. One plan, for example, displaced by the end of the 1950s approximately twenty thousand residents, more than 90 percent black, from centrally located Mill Creek Valley, just west of Union Station and bounded by Twentieth

Street, Olive Street, Grand Avenue, and Mill Creek Valley, when city officials deemed the community blighted. In mid-February 1959, demolition on the 465-acre area began. Mayor Raymond Tucker and other officials looked on as workers for the R. E. Harder Contracting Company, which received a $125,000 contract from the city to demolish 275 buildings in ninety days, took a "headache ball" to the tenement at 3818 Laclede Avenue. "The result would be an impressive belt of rejuvenation through the heart of the city along thoroughfares traversed daily by thousands of people on the way to work and by visitors arriving at Union Station," *St. Louis Post-Dispatch* journalist Harry Wilensky explained. Redevelopment through erection of commercial and industrial properties was a kind of reconstruction that "logically lends itself" to the area, and "should serve to reinforce and stabilize the central business district," Tucker surmised. Because of the concentration of black residents in the soon-to-be razed area, Tucker appointed an impressive array of black community leaders to sit on an advisory committee, including Valla D. Abbington of the St. Louis Urban League, the only woman. The destruction of Mill Creek Valley meant that African American families lost homes, businesses, and community institutions; an area that once had been a hub for working-class life was destroyed by this forced dispersal. Mill Creek Valley had long been an area where low-income black women and their families and friends found ways to make a life despite crushing poverty.[11]

One would be hard pressed to find one resident who disagreed with the notion that major public intervention was necessary. A study found that nearly 90 percent of the mostly black residents living in the area, which extended over more than three hundred acres, had no private flush toilets or baths, and just over 50 percent had no running water. Nearly 90 percent of the residents were tenants, more than 75 percent were renters, and the vast majority of them qualified for public housing. Overcrowding and dilapidation produced hazardous conditions for low-income black Mound City residents. Across the city, not just in Mill Creek, black residents' homes were death traps. In early 1950, for example, an explosion killed four, including a two-year-old child and a ten-year-old child, and injured seven of the thirty-two persons crammed into a building designed to house four families. The "ancient structure" "stands as grim testimony to the evils of Jim Crow housing and the vicious pattern of the ghetto system in St. Louis," read a *St. Louis American* caption. The "two-story building" was "a shocking indictment of our economic system."[12]

Low-income black women welcomed municipal projects to improve living conditions in the city's central corridor, but not without concern for what would happen to them once modernization was under way. Although Mayor Tucker promised Mill Creek Valley residents that they would be among the first to enter the newly constructed public housing, and that in the meantime the city would provide access to affordable temporary housing, many of the neighborhood's black residents, whose families had lived in Mill Creek Valley for generations, were skeptical. One writer put it in these terms: "The visions that have floated through the city this week of towering, modern residences with beautiful parks and playgrounds, set off by underpasses and elevated expressways, have been received by Negro citizens with something less than the bubbling enthusiasm of those who dreamed them up." While the *Post-Dispatch* failed to cover black residents' concerns about urban renewal, the *St. Louis Argus* and the *St. Louis American,* the city's two black newspapers, provided thorough coverage in this respect. A study conducted by journalists for the *Argus* found that residents worried about their futures and were more likely to understand urban renewal as "Negro removal" instead of beautification. Resident Frances Williams told researchers, for example, "We need new building in the area. So long as they're making plans for the people in the area, I think it's a good plan." Another resident, Eugene Thomas, echoed the sentiment of many women when he said that he was in favor "so long as 'poor people are taken into consideration.'" St. Louis leaders had already established a municipal pattern that equated urban reform with black dispersal and displacement, yet a most recent example drove home the need for black skepticism. "Recently," penned one editorialist, "St. Louis leaders became greatly elated at the prospect of city beautification" with the building of Aloe Plaza, which replaced poorly built properties occupied by low-income black tenants. In this case, "there were speeches, radio talks, pictures, news stories, pamphlets, all trumpeting the merits of this urban redevelopment," but when black citizens demanded demolition and construction jobs, members of the Urban Redevelopment Corporation and other officials associated with the project failed to respond. What is more, black residents raised the critical question of whether officials would establish public housing on a segregated basis. All indicators pointed to the likelihood that it would, despite the recent Supreme Court ruling in *Banks v. Housing Authority of San Francisco* (1953). The Court had upheld the lower court's ruling that found the San Francisco Housing Authority guilty of violating a black couple's Fourteenth Amendment right when it denied their application to the North Beach Place project. NAACP lawyers cited *Shelley v. Kraemer* (1948) as evidence of the court's shift away from the "separate but equal" edict of the *Plessy v. Ferguson* (1896) ruling. While some were skeptical, Kinloch city residents unequivocally celebrated the news that they would receive six hundred thousand dollars in federal money for construction of "a 200-unit public housing project, which will house 2,000 persons, an ultra-modern shopping center, new civic buildings, including a City Hall, and churches, parks and playgrounds." The city hosted celebratory activities for three days, culminating with a parade "through the all-Negro community." An all-black city subject to its own municipal governance, Kinloch had residents who had far greater control over public grants than their black counterparts in St. Louis city.[13]

"The Modern Miracle of Public Housing"

While public policy by no means fully addressed the housing and job crisis plaguing low-income black women and their families, it brought improvements. The 1937, 1949, and 1954 Federal Housing Acts, issued under the Eisenhower administration, included a nondiscrimination clause stipulating that a certain percentage of units should be reserved for black dwellers. Of the new construction authorized by the 1949 Federal Housing Act, officials theoretically set aside just over half for black residents. "Not only has the low-rent housing program provided decent, safe and sanitary homes for Negro families economically unable to rent or buy housing in the private market, but it has also provided employment for both skilled and unskilled Negro workers," read one report, viewing the program from a national perspective. A Public Housing Authority study estimated that three-fourths of black public-housing residents moved out of their apartments on a monthly basis at a rate of less than 2 percent for every one hundred units, and only 2 percent moved out at a rate higher than 5 percent. Approximately 17 percent of black families across the country secured jobs in new public-housing construction during the first half of 1954. The question of integrated public housing was a more complicated one. Housing authorities in Wilmington, Washington, DC, and Baltimore, among others, agreed to operate on an open-occupancy basis, but the reality belied such commitments. Of the rental units across the country reaching full occupancy by June 30, 1954, only 14 percent were "operating on a completed integrated basis."[14]

Carr Square, the first public-housing project opened for black residents in St. Louis city, was originally intended to house families with relative means. The thinking was that low-income residents with families could make affordable rent payments and over time save enough money to afford a down payment on a home of their own. Because the massive housing shortage, coupled with chronic black unemployment and urban renewal projects, had unleashed a wave of black displacement, dispersal, and dislocation, low-income black women and their families, some from Mill Creek Valley and others from similar poorer black districts in the central corridor, flocked to Carr Square, hoping to secure a better place to live. When the Carr Square Village Public Housing Project first opened in 1942, more than four thousand black families, who hoped to escape ramshackle, overcrowded tenements with no electricity and with privies just outside the buildings, were on the waiting list. Moving into the village was a definite improvement. Unable to afford rent payments in middle-income black neighborhoods like the Ville, low-income families who moved to Carr Square had private bathrooms, running water, multiple bedrooms, and two and three stories. Located just northwest of downtown, Carr Square's nineteenth-century inhabitants had included German Protestants, Italians, and Orthodox Jews, who shaped the neighborhood into a diverse, ethnic-immigrant enclave. African Americans began moving into the area during the Great Depression and the World War II period as white ethnic communities moved to inner- and outer-ring suburbs. The public-housing project came to define the Carr Square neighborhood, with its 658 buildings spread across approximately twenty-four acres.[15]

Initially, black working-class women and their families took pride in their new homes; public housing was an unqualified improvement over the tenements or "cold water flats" that they had once occupied. Carr Square resident Imani Mtendaji (formerly Rhonda V. Johnson) lived in the public-housing project for most of her life. Born in 1956, Mtendaji lived there with her four siblings and her parents, Katie Johnson, a seamstress, and Smith Johnson Jr., a mechanic. Katie and Smith's first home in the city was a small, two-room unit, where they lived with their three older children; they moved to a larger unit in the "long rectangular type buildings" of Carr Square in the 1950s. Evelyn Jones's family moved to Carr Square for similar reasons. The house that her family had rented previously was overcrowded and unsanitary, and the ash pits used for trash disposal, located behind the house, attracted vermin. Jones's mother, Dorothy Johnson Ridley, had a best friend, Hazel Davis, who urged her to consider public housing. The two had become friends in the early 1930s, when both frequented a health care clinic on Laclede Avenue. Davis moved to the village in the early 1940s and talked Ridley into applying. Unable to secure a place, however, around the mid-1940s Ridley wrote a letter to President Harry Truman for assistance. The record does not indicate whether it was because of the letter, but Ridley and her family soon moved into an apartment. The family occupied a three-bedroom, one-bath townhouse with the living room and kitchen located on the first floor and bedrooms on the second. The family's new home was "just enough to really live decent [sic]," Jones recalled. In the new setting, she had "space to . . . do something, to have a little privacy." Her old house, by contrast, had two large rooms, where "everybody sees what everybody else [is] doing" but in the village, she said, "We did have rooms with doors to them and we could close them." Carr Square residents believed that their new living situations were a substantial improvement. When friends and relatives visited the village, they tended to remark that residents had it good, citing, for example, the ample space, privacy, and the indoor facility. "They would think that you had something 'cause you stayed in Carr Square Village," Jones recalled. Carol Strickland Ray recalled that her family and friends felt "pride just living in Carr Square." Their new homes had "running water, the inside toilet . . . I mean there was no shame in this," Ray remembered. Water fountains, parks, and playground equipment were scattered around the areas between and directly outside of buildings. Imani Mtendaji's family welcomed the amenities of the new apartment. They owned an automatic washing machine, and, like all other tenants, Mtendaji and her sister took the family's freshly laundered clothing to one of the "drying yards," located between buildings, for drying. "In those days," Mtendaji recalled, "the management was very regimented." There were strict policies regarding maintenance, upkeep, and occupancy, but despite restrictions on the numbers of dwellers in households, which limited occupancy to members of an immediate family, tenants routinely hosted friends and family in need of temporary housing. After a brief stint as a resident at the Phillis Wheatley YWCA, Mtendaji secured a Carr Square apartment of her own in the mid-1970s.[16]

Publicly funded social welfare programs facilitated social bonding, creating the conditions for community development. The Tenant Management Association, partnering with Plymouth House community center, managed by the United Church of Christ, sponsored community activities for children, and recreational facilities provided an outlet. Sixteen years older than Imani Mtendaji, Evelyn Jones also lived in Carr Square Village for most of her life. She recalled having access to an abundance of recreational opportunities both inside and outside the village community. She regularly attended dances held at recreational centers including Poro College; the Neighborhood House; the Phillis Wheatley YWCA; the Carr Square Community Center; Footlong (a restaurant on Franklin Street with a jukebox), where patrons "danced, did the bop"; and Cook's on Eighteenth Street (a small facility managed by a married couple). Jones and her Carr Square friends skated at the Palace Garden Rink at Vandeventer and Finney. Carol Strickland Ray, another resident of Carr Square, likewise recalled multiple opportunities for rich leisure. She swam at the Fifteenth Street Park swimming pool, participated in volleyball tournaments, and participated in the Phillis Wheatley YWCA's programs. Jones went to a baseball game at Sportman's Park on Grand, once home to two major league baseball teams, the St. Louis Cardinals and the St. Louis Browns. Ordinarily, however, Jones stood in long lines to secure baseball tickets for her parents, who, like many black locals, were eager to see their home team play the Los Angeles Dodgers and their black star player Jackie Robinson. Local residents baked goods and sold them to neighbors. A pair of older sisters sold homemade ice cream, and one tenant managed a small confectionary. The same two sisters also organized a drum and bugle corps for children, "and all the kids would want to go there ["on Biddle Street"] and learn how to" play instruments. After worshiping at Washington Tabernacle Baptist Church, where they arrived usually by streetcar, Evelyn Jones and her siblings and friends often went to the Marquette, Comet, or Carver Theater to watch a film. Carr Square Village residents Carol Strickland Ray and Betty Thompson, who later became a state senator, recalled riding the streetcar on Sunday afternoons as a special highlight. Their families would load onto a streetcar, ride the line all the way to Wellston, get off to purchase popcorn, and ride the car back home. Even camping out in the back yard or on a porch to keep cool during sweltering summer months became an important way to build community.[17]

Carr Square Village was not a utopia, however. The area had the highest population density in the city, at twenty-six families per acre, and concerned citizens urged municipal administrators to carefully consider density when planning future projects. It was an area of concentrated black poverty. From 1940 to 1980, more than 90 percent of its inhabitants were tenants, not owners. The median income was $11,523 (1997 dollars) in 1960 and dropped to $9,929 (1997 dollars) twenty years later. Low-income black women outnumbered black males, reaching one thousand more in 1940 and nearly two thousand more in 1960. From 1940 to 1960, black working-class women never exceeded the labor force participation rates of black working-class men, but they came close to matching them, and by 1980 they exceeded them. Such conditions, coupled with a Housing Authority that consistently earned the lowest performance ratings year after year and a gradual withering of public concern for the poor meant that Carr Square Village would soon follow the fate of public-housing structures across the country.[18]

The most potent symbol of detrimental urban planning in St. Louis was the Pruitt-Igoe public-housing project, which opened in 1954. Consisting of thirty-three high-rise buildings that held 11,500 residents, it was made possible by the Federal Housing Act of 1949, which provided direct funds to cities for urban improvements, slum clearance, and public housing. Although at first Pruitt-Igoe did provide an upgrade in housing stock for many of the city's black residents, the project also served to remove and warehouse poor and working-class African Americans from communities clustered around valuable downtown areas that were being primed for redevelopment. For families living in abject poverty, however, living in Pruitt-Igoe was an improvement. Opened in October 1954, the Wendell Oliver Pruitt housing project opened to its first group of residents, Frankie Raglin, aunt and guardian of four children whose parents had recently died. Raglin, "the head of the first family," moved "into a brand new three bedroom unit including a living room bath and kitchen." Evelyn Jones, a Carr Square Village resident who witnessed Pruitt-Igoe's construction as a teenager, said, "I don't think it was a good idea when they stacked everybody up on top of each other. . . . But it was pretty. . . . It was nice. You could, you could walk straight through there at night. They had bands, people playing . . . [an] outdoor band . . . and they had a community center where you could dance. . . . We used to walk up there. Nobody bothered us." The Neighborhood Association–Pruitt Nursery held an open house in April 1956. Children in the public-housing project participated in educational, cultural, and social activities led by a staff of women teachers. Funded by the United Fund, the nursery had just over thirty students with more than twenty on the waiting list. A photo essay of the nursery in the *St. Louis Argus* featured women leading students in art classes, Jimmie Jenkins preparing a meal, Darlene Peterson overseeing naptime, Lucille Thomas "eating the nutritious lunch provided daily," and staff worker and civil rights activist Pearl S. Maddox leading a tour of the facility. Betty Thompson lived in Pruitt-Igoe in the years immediately after its construction. As a teenager, Thompson observed her father's work as a leader of the community-organized White Caps, a voluntary security team of black men who patrolled the community.[19]

Over time, however, the housing development dramatically deteriorated. The subject of considerable national attention, Pruitt-Igoe soon marked the height of municipal negligence, and it quickly deteriorated in the face of inadequate funding. While much public discourse blamed residents for the project's misfortunes, a more accurate and honest assessment of Pruitt-Igoe's failure points to systemic problems, including declining municipal revenues, a poorly managed and poorly financed local housing authority, the mass exodus of factories to the suburbs and cheaper labor markets of the Deep South, strict racial segregation, depopulation, and a shortage of good jobs located close to where residents lived. The project's demise, including the nationally televised implosion of one of its buildings in 1972, marked a spectacular end to the use of high-rises to house low-income residents, and it found many African Americans in St. Louis searching for effective and appropriate responses to problems that the city seemed unwilling or unable to solve. Gateway City residents, as historian Joseph Heathcott notes, witnessed nothing short of "the formation . . . of a new urban vision" that "set about redefining the terms of the debate over the future of the city itself."[20]

Chronic unemployment was intimately linked to the housing crisis. A lack of adequate income made it nearly impossible to improve one's living conditions. "Apart from a few needle trade jobs," writer David A. Hepburn accurately noted about black working-class women's employment prospects, "the kitchen is the only thing open to most women." Two-headed households gripped by poverty demanded that able-bodied adults and children generate income, but this was no simple task. In August 1949 black unemployment was 33 percent, much higher than the rate for white residents, and by the end of September 1948, fewer blacks, approximately thirty-five thousand, were employed than the year before. For black working-class women, the postwar era was not one in which women benefited from postwar economic gains, with unemployment rates for blacks on the rise. A major St. Louis Urban League study, "The Negro in the St. Louis Economy, 1954," completed with research conducted by staff members, Washington University professors, and other volunteers, found that even though black workers had access to greater educational and training opportunities, the group still lagged far behind white workers, "whose economic status is rapidly improving." Put another way, the economic status of black workers at the end of 1953 had not yet matched that of white workers in 1950. Black unemployment was 2.5 times the rate for whites, according to the report. "An indication of this [problem]," journalist Otis N. Thompson summarized, was "the large number of non-white married females taking part in the labor force, obviously to supplement the insufficient earnings of the male worker of the family."[21]

Writer Hattye Thomas penned a poignant story based on her young life, titled "Help Wanted." Published in the *St. Louis Argus* in March 1950, the story ruminated on "where we [black working-class women] stand in the white man's world." Exploding the myth of postwar prosperity, she pointed out that while a small number of black women graduated and secured positions in teaching, nursing, and other professions, "We can't all be nurses or teachers." Thomas argued that the fight to desegregate theaters and other public and private facilities was subordinate to the fight for fair employment. "Can't they all understand that those things are small and unimportant?" "All the papers are screaming of the right to go here or there and some of the papers have gone so far as to discuss interracial marriages. But they don't mention jobs at all." There were thousands, and more, young black women graduates from college, universities, and vocational training schools who were barred from economic opportunity. "We were just two of the thousands of Negro girls all over the world," Thomas wrote, referring to herself and a friend, "who had worked, studied, and tried so hard to prepare for this hard outside world." But in every city and town, there were far too many instances of employers passing over young black women for less qualified white women, she lamented. Depicting a daylong, unsuccessful search for employment, Thomas revealed that she and her friend had met economic rejection three times. Thomas arrived home only to be asked "the dreaded question" of whether or not she had landed a job. Native son Harry S. Truman's civil rights platform missed the point, Thomas maintained:

I do not beg for entrance into your household fair
Nor do I envy you, your treasured heirlooms there.

"I only pray for a chance to prove that there are tools in my brain shop to build for the human race."[22]

For public-housing tenants, public grants provided not only an outlet but also a much-needed employment opportunity. Roughly between the ages of twelve and fifteen, Imani Mtendaji worked as a camp counselor for the United Church of Christ Tenant Management Association, and she later worked for the Carr Central Gateway Center, a community organization that provided services to children, young adults, and senior citizens. Betty Thompson lived in three public-housing projects, Carr Square, Darst-Webbe, and Pruitt-Igoe, from the early 1940s through the mid-1960s, and over the course of those years she worked for the Human

Development Corporation (the headquarters of the city's welfare offices) for twenty-six years, from the mid-1960s to 1980, after a brief stint in the early to mid-1960s of working for the health center of Teamster's Local 688. As an employee of the HDC, Thompson began as a "neighborhood worker" or "housing specialist" and later became a branch manager at the Pruitt-Igoe Center. Darby Robinson described her work history as "hustling," by which she meant that she had held numerous jobs, sometimes more than one at a time, to make ends meet. A widow who cared for her biological children and others in need of a home, Robinson worked as a barmaid for Gully's Lounge, was later one of ten of the first black women to secure jobs as operators at the Southwestern Bell Telephone Company, performed day work as a domestic while attending Hadley Technical High School to "take a trade," labored as a nurse's aide at Jewish Hospital, and worked as a short-order cook and waitress at Geno's Restaurant at Union and Maple. Like her mother, who worked for the HDC in the child care department for twenty years, Robinson took a job as a secretary for the McCormack Realty Company, which managed the Bluemeyer Village Housing Project. In this position, Robinson "handled rent suits, executions of rent, and typed up suits, and you know [performed] the whole nine yards that had something to do with the legal part."[23]

"A Life of Struggle": Ora Lee Malone's Trade Union Activism

As public-housing tenants began fomenting collective struggles to address the jobs and housing crisis, other black working-class women were using the apparatus of the trade union to advance the similar cause for economic dignity. Convinced of the merits of worker organization, Ora Lee Malone developed a critical unionism that pushed organized labor to adopt an expansive social justice platform. One of postwar St. Louis's most important black freedom and economic justice activists, she capitalized on and advanced black working-class women's activism during the 1930s, 1940s, and 1950s. Born in 1918 in Brooksville, Mississippi, and raised in Mobile, Alabama, as the eldest of nine children, her organization of and involvement in antiapartheid and transnational movements, women's counterpublics, and civil rights organizing were as much a part of her trade union organizing as was labor activism itself. An activist who was "mixed up in all these causes," Malone fashioned a cutting-edge activist ethos that merged the struggle for economic justice with that for civil rights and gender equity and the aspirations of poor and working-class persons, people of color, and women.[24] The organizer from the Deep South situated her various calls for reform against the backdrop of the social and political upheavals that gave shape to the post–World War II era. Her critical unionism challenged working-class activists. Black women labor activists like Malone tended to eschew the narrow issue of wage consciousness; their more expansive perspective included workers' broad concerns about living conditions.[25] Malone represented a multifaceted social justice vision that forcefully critiqued certain civil rights, feminist, and labor movement discourses and practices even as it drew from some of these.

When she moved to St. Louis in 1951 at age thirty-three, Malone related that she was not personally pulled by any utopian dreams about a "promised land." On the contrary, she moved to be with her family, who had migrated a year earlier. Disenchanted with the lackluster reality of economic opportunity in the celebrated postwar era, Malone believed that in any new setting, "you had to make your opportunities wherever you go," because "nobody gives you anything." She was conscious of white public discourse that created myths of lazy, desperate, hands-outstretched mobs of blacks begging for federal and state aid, but Malone denounced the notion that she moved because of the promise of help: "Black immigrants had nothing, we just wandered on in and people set up, everyone did the best they could. They had to go to work; they had to find a job on their own. We didn't get any help, no aid or anything." There was little in Malone's historical memory or gathered knowledge from family or friends to suggest that life would become radically different. Wherever she moved, "it was a constant battle." The phrase "a constant battle" crept into most of Malone's recollections. This was a central filter through which she viewed most of her professional interactions.[26]

Moving away from her husband, Sturdivan Malone, a merchant marine and National Maritime Union member, who remained in Alabama, Malone boarded a train at the Gulf Mobile and Ohio railroad where her uncle worked, and she traveled overnight in the *front* car, where blacks were forced to sit because, should the train derail, white lives would likely be saved. When she arrived, Malone moved into a four-family flat where her mother and younger siblings resided on St. Louis Avenue, a street that at the time housed mostly white families. Receiving word from a female cousin who knew the St. Louis job market fairly well, Malone applied to two open positions, one at a paper company on the south side of the city, and the other at the California Manufacturing Company, a predominantly black shop that manufactured men's jackets. She was offered both jobs but chose the California Company because it was closer to home.[27]

Malone's early work experiences matched those of other recent black southern migrants in the mid-twentieth century. She and her coworkers labored under the constant dual threat of economic reprisal and job termination. Though she had the ability to do the more skilled jobs, such as sewing contents tags on jackets, her boss, Joe Berra, often relegated her to the "lowest and dirtiest jobs," perhaps because of her outspokenness. Even so, he periodically elevated other black women workers to positions in which they could oversee clothing orders and record the shop's business with local and state companies. Berra also hired a black woman supervisor to distribute work duties; this position was paid significantly more. But these cases were exceptions. Most employees worked on the shop floor. Because of her dexterity with sewing machines, Malone earned her wage by the piece and took home greater pay than time workers locked into menial wage rates. Paid one penny per jacket, she earned between ten and twelve dollars per day and often made overtime, skirting around the Missouri law that prohibited women from working more than nine hours per day by "clocking out" and then returning immediately. The employees at the manufacturing company received three regular breaks per day, two ten-minute breaks and one lunch break. The employees were mostly black females, but there were also small numbers of black men, Latino women and men, and white men and women.[28]

Because no union had been organized, Joe Berra had complete control over the shop and could cut benefits and fire employees at will. Most of these workers were reluctant to publicly challenge authority, and the area's garment unions were slow to organize shops predominantly populated by persons of color. Yet Malone's ability to do most of the jobs at the shop, coupled with her involvement in the Alabama civil rights movement, placed her in a unique position to lobby on behalf of her coworkers. In Alabama she had campaigned against the Boswell Amendment, passed by the state legislature in 1945 and ratified the following year, which allowed registrars to disqualify aspiring African American voters who "failed" to interpret the US Constitution satisfactorily. It was swift and effective in disenfranchising black voters. In response, the Birmingham and Mobile chapters of the NAACP, as well as the Voters and Veterans League, a black Mobile-based group working to protect the right of African Americans to vote, filed a lawsuit in 1948. A year later the federal district court deemed the amendment unconstitutional on the grounds that it violated the Fifteenth Amendment. The success of this post–World War II campaign bolstered Malone's belief in the efficacy of collective effort.[29]

After witnessing Malone's willingness to challenge daily indignities, one female worker, upset that Berra had just fired her for no apparent reasons and with no advanced notice, asked if it was possible to unionize the shop. Malone remembered it this way: "A woman came to me one day and said she'd been fired. It was an all-black shop; no union was interested in organizing black workers in the men's clothing industry." Not yet well acquainted with the labor movement scene in St. Louis but knowledgeable about national labor leader A. Philip Randolph and the National Maritime Union in Alabama—her husband was a member—Malone was somewhat prepared for the task at hand. She suggested that her coworkers travel to the downtown union office on Washington Street to ask about membership. Malone and others had heard of previous failed attempts to organize black workers in St. Louis. But her opening moves fortunately occurred just as the Amalgamated Clothing and Textile Workers Union was undergoing a jurisdictional dispute with the Garment Workers Union, which meant that both organizations now vied for the workers. An organizer for the ACWU, a white woman, leafleted the company despite calls from management to desist. After months of preparation, union officers permitted the workers to join but were unwilling to pay the cost of bussing all the company's employees to the union hall downtown. Malone and others funded the trip, and the workers were organized in 1956.[30] The new unionists elected Malone shop steward of Local 463, which meant that she served as an advocate for employees by informing managers about workers' grievances and then took the issues to a business representative if matters could not be settled on the floor. As shop steward, Malone interceded for single and married workers whose pay was docked because of unannounced bus schedule changes and sick children, workers who felt the brunt of discriminatory practices based on seniority, and time workers who received significantly smaller wages than pieceworkers. Her efforts as a shop steward, after nineteen years, mushroomed into an international business representative position with the ACWU, where she represented nearly forty shops and stores in St. Louis and southern Missouri, a region with a strong tradition of interracial worker coalitions but considered by many urban African Americans a racial backwater. Malone was among the first generation of black women who came to the fore when women and blacks struggled to secure "decision-making roles in unions." She later became a founding member of local chapters of the A. Philip Randolph Institute and the Coalition of Black Trade Unionists, two organizations at the forefront of black workers' organizing for racial and economic justice.[31]

Ora Lee Malone was also heavily involved in local politics. She campaigned for DeVerne L. Calloway in 1962 when he ran for the state legislature. She recalled, "In any campaign that was going on that I agreed with that particular person's philosophy, I worked on his campaign." While Malone likely agreed with Calloway on the need for legislative solutions to the problem of urban inequality, she sharply diverged with the state senator when it came to the culture of office-holding. About politicians, Malone remarked, "They get up and make a glorious speech . . . many of them leave. They are so far removed from the people." Her criticism of the local NAACP, also Calloway's domain, fell along similar lines: "I'm just kind of tired of the sorority and fraternity crowd being in charge, setting [sic] at their table . . . going to banquets and lining the stage with their things. . . . I just hate their tables." Locating the NAACP and state and local politicians in the same elitist camp, Malone instead wanted leaders to "be at the table with the people who they represent, trying to find out what their problems are." She supported the NAACP's legal work but rejected the organization's classism. Her political focus was on identifying with people who held no titles. She conducted sessions on voter education, discussing local issues with residents and instilling the importance of grassroots civic participation, which she felt was a more valuable use of her time than board meetings or awards dinners.[32]

Housing for low-income women was an issue of special importance for Ora Malone. With colleagues, she generated a list of "suggested action for solutions" to the housing crisis. Included were education and public awareness, advocacy, and leadership development. Groups suggested that they form a working relationship with the Human Development Corporation's staff person, understand and prepare to explain the details of the Fair Housing Act, investigate the "female rent strike" of 1969 to find ways to assist tenants, and "stimulate building of new low- and middle-income housing in the metropolitan area."[33] It was this kind of advocacy that led to various recognitions and promotions. For example, the board of directors of the Greater Saint Louis Committee for Freedom of Residence, an organization founded in 1961 to support integrated housing, nominated Malone to serve on its board, along with other higher-profile leaders in St. Louis's labor and housing scene, including welfare-rights activists Sylvia Miller and Eddie Mae Binion, Ted Gatlin of Clinton-Peabody Tenant Management, and Richard Baron of McCormack & Associates.[34] Members of Black Women's Community Development Foundation, based in Washington, DC, nominated Ora Lee Malone for its Sojourner Truth Award, which the organization "designed to honor the unpraised Black woman who has struggled 'in the Spirit of Sojourner Truth.'"[35]

Community-oriented unionism that merged civil rights, feminist, and labor agendas and prioritized empowering women's voices was a guiding principle that often put Malone "on the cutting edge of the struggle for economic justice for workers and the struggle for civil rights," said two contemporaries. The trade unionist was known for expansive unionism, which centered on "social causes." For this, she "ruffled some feathers" within the labor movement, which Malone did not hesitate to criticize. Unions were crucial, "but their focus is often too narrow[;] they don't reach out enough," she explained. "They concentrate too much on wages, hours and working conditions, which is a part of the job, but they should also be concerned about transportation, and health care, which to most workers are really more important. Most workers are fired over transportation and child care issues." Malone focused on including the voices of women workers. "Women need to learn to fight the unions and make their demands heard," Malone admonished her constituents. For the southern transplant, unionism offered an unprecedented opportunity to speak against injustice with impunity. "I didn't like not being able to have a say when you were treated wrong," she explained. "They would tell you, 'If you don't like it, go home.' It makes you feel better inside when you can say you've been treated wrong, even if you don't get anything else." Bill Hall, leader of the southwest region of Amalgamated Clothing Workers of America (ACWA), headquartered in St. Louis, said of Malone, "She wants to run sometimes when you have to walk. A lot of people called her a rebel, but what she was saying was right. You don't have to be radical just because you're ahead of somebody—you're leading." Joyce Miller, vice president of the ACWA in New York and member of the AFL-CIO executive council, said Malone was "one of the labor movement's early pioneers in terms of civil rights and women's rights—long before it was fashionable and before we had all the formal organizations we have now." These comments came after Malone retired. One would have been hard pressed to locate such positive comments during her heyday.[36]

Black Professional Women's Working-Class Activism

The growing ferment of black women's working-class discontent over jobs and housing in the 1950s and 1960s cannot be fully understood without a discussion of social justice activism among black professional women in housing, law, and politics. As key architects of freedom agendas, black middle-class activist women used their posts to focus on the structural causes of racialized poverty as they exposed the deleterious and compounding effects of "white flight," deindustrialization, decimated tax revenues, public-housing fiascos, and rigid lines of racial segregation affecting black working-class women living in a city hard hit by urban decline. During the 1950s and 1960s, Marian Oldham, Frankie Muse Freeman, and DeVerne Calloway fought locally, challenging urban inequality and traditional civil rights leadership. Their contributions to black working-class women's struggles were a reflection of the larger work of a critical mass of African American women who led the St. Louis struggle for racial and economic equality. They devised strategies to confront the Gateway City's two most trenchant challenges: the fight for fair employment and greater economic opportunity, and the fight for decent, open, and affordable housing.[37]

The tradition of black women's economic activism with respect to employment access and the right to consume extended into the immediate postwar period with the political work of Marian Oldham. Early models of black leaders participating in direct-action protests and education proved key to awakening Oldham's activism. Her first memory of witnessing a picket line was in the late 1930s, one organized by the Colored Clerks' Circle. Outside a black neighborhood store located near Oldham's home was a small group of picketers demanding that the store owner integrate his workforce. By the time she reached young adulthood, Oldham had already witnessed and helped bring about a successful civil rights campaign with the Supreme Court ruling in the 1948 *Shelley v. Kraemer* case. As a Sumner High School student, Oldham worked with scholar Herman Dreer, who, as chair of the Citizens Committee–Shelley Restrictive Covenant Case, had been conducting research for the suit. After school and in the evening, Oldham typed legal briefs for Dreer, and the long hours taught her ways to assist the black freedom struggle. With this experience came the realization that black communities needed basic resources— namely, education and employment, to wage effective campaigns for equal opportunity. Reflecting on her long career, she recalled that "job security" often determined who participated in civil rights efforts. She identified "many, many blacks who wanted to change the situation" but were not "fortunate" enough to have "the ability to speak out."[38]

While Oldham attended Stowe Teachers College, which Dreer helped establish, her political consciousness was raised further by her practicum assignments at schools in some of St. Louis's most poverty-stricken sections. She observed directly the ways economic deprivation affected educational opportunities and school attendance, as she encountered children whose families lived in squalor. They had no plumbing and no heat and scraped by on family budgets of a few dollars per month; the women sometimes had to engage in prostitution merely to make ends meet. For many of the children in these neighborhoods, school was out of the question. Seeing these people struggle to maintain their dignity amid the most abject of conditions and observing the effects of poverty on their children had a profound effect on Oldham. They didn't lack character. They weren't psychologically unequipped to succeed. They hadn't any less interest in formal education or intellectual engagement than anyone else. Poverty prevented the children of these families from engaging with their schooling seriously. These memories Oldham recalled when she later joined collective struggles for fair employment.[39]

Following a stint with Maddox's CCRC and with NAACP activists who conducted boycotts outside the American Theater, which restricted black concertgoers to the "pigeon roost" (balcony seats), Oldham helped establish the St. Louis chapter of CORE. August Meier and Elliott Rudwick described it as one of the most visible and active chapters in the country, known as "an unusually energetic and stable group with a labor union orientation instead of a pacifist one." The St. Louis CORE framed direct-action campaigns against segregation in public accommodation as a part of the battle for basic economic rights that generally inflected the city's black freedom struggle. Oldham had once said that employment in the Gateway City was the sector that made racial segregation most powerfully evident. A key activist who helped mold the chapter along such lines, Oldham distinguished herself through negotiating skill and an adeptness at facilitating discussions. The late 1940s through the early 1960s marked the high point of Oldham's CORE activism, when she involved herself in several important direct-action campaigns. These included negotiations with city drugstores to serve black customers and hire black workers, resulting in African Americans being employed in sales positions and as lunch-counter servers. She also took part in one of the most important and widely covered civil rights protests in St. Louis history: the Jefferson Bank and Trust Company demonstrations of 1963. Oldham and her colleagues demanded that the bank, which was located in a black neighborhood, hire African American tellers. After seven months of protest, during which Oldham was arrested, managers relented and hired five black workers. The quest for economic dignity functioned as the hub of her social activism; she fought for years so that working-class people could improve their situations through living-wage jobs and access to a fuller experience of downtown leisure culture. Echoing the sentiments of Carrie Smith, Cora Lewis, and others, Oldham argued that the core of the injustice for black women was the "feeling of being less than human."[40]

Frankie Muse Freeman's story, like Oldham's, is a microcosm of historical narrative of the modern civil rights movement in the United States; hers is a narrative that especially weaves together the essential threads of legal activism, black institution-building, and the role of state and federal government. Born in the early twentieth century in the last Confederate city—Danville, Virginia—Freeman, along with her family, resisted the segregation laws that required black citizens to sit in the balcony of theaters, ride in the back of streetcars, and stay away from businesses owned and operated by whites where service—in restaurants, at lunch counters, in hotels, and the like—was the main commodity. Educated at two of the premier black educational institutions in the country, Hampton Institute and Howard Law School, Frankie Freeman collected tools to combat Jim Crow. As one of only a few black women to graduate from Howard University Law School, Freeman had worked with Thurgood Marshall, some of whose cases eventually wound their way all the way to the US Supreme Court, resulting in the landmark 1954 ruling in *Brown v. Board of Education*. After she moved to St. Louis in the 1940s, Freeman fine-tuned the method of civil rights activism to fit the border South city of St. Louis, a battleground for struggles over jobs, housing, education, and equal opportunity.[41]

Freeman opened her own law practice in St. Louis, a rarity for women in that period, and black public-housing tenants found their advocate in her. Because the St. Louis Housing Administration failed to practice open occupancy, black activist women like Freeman, who pursued civil rights work on a full-time basis and were leaders of the St. Louis civil rights movement, waged war. Lead attorney Freeman and attorney Constance Baker Motley argued on behalf of a group of black tenants and veterans. Freeman argued that the SLHA had violated black tenants' Fourteenth Amendment right to equal protection, their right to purchase property stipulated by US Code Title 8, section 42, and their rights established by the Federal Housing Act of 1939. Freeman claimed that black tenants had been denied rental units at the Cochran Gardens projects because of racial discrimination. Black journalist Howard B. Woods called the case "the most important and significant . . . to be heard from this area since the 1948 decision in *Shelley v. Kraemer* or the 1857 decision in the historic Dred Scott case." Filing the suit *Ted Davis et al. v. The St. Louis*

Housing Authority in June 1952, NAACP lawyers Freeman and Motley argued their plaintiffs' case in the US District Court in October 1954. In response to the case filed by the NAACP, the SLHA issued a brief in which it admitted to barring black tenants, defending its actions by arguing that it held a special power and responsibility to ensure safety and peace, and enforcing an open-housing policy could jeopardize "the obligation and duty to avoid any conflict which might arise from racial antipathies." Counsel for the authority called for dismissal of the case, claiming that the seminal 1954 *Brown v. Board of Education* US Supreme Court decision did not overturn its "separate but equal" 1896 *Plessy v. Ferguson* ruling. The Housing Authority claimed that no law existed to force the body to integrate and that "no discrimination exists when the Authority follows existing neighborhood patterns in selecting tenants as between white and Negro applicants." Freeman, this time with assistance from Robert L. Witherspoon, filed a new brief in response. They argued that a recent court decision based in San Francisco found the housing authority there making the same "community pattern" argument. One week after the Supreme Court issued the *Brown* decision, it refused to hear the San Francisco case, Freeman pointed out. In late 1955 US District Judge George H. Moore ruled in favor of the plaintiffs in the St. Louis case, agreeing with Freeman's contention that the SLHA, by practicing segregation, was in effect violating black tenants' constitutional rights. In a postscript to the story that hardly anyone could have predicted, shortly after defeating the SLHA in court, Attorney Freeman received an invitation to serve as its general counsel, a post she held for fourteen years. She later became the first woman to serve on the US Commission on Civil Rights, a post she held for sixteen years. In this position, Freeman took the lessons she learned as an advocate for black working-class women in St. Louis and applied them on a national scale.[42]

As Marion Oldham broke down barriers in the consumer and labor sector and Frankie Freeman did the same in law and civil rights, DeVerne Lee Calloway worked in St. Louis city and Missouri state politics. Before moving to St. Louis, Calloway had been active in her native Memphis and in Atlanta and Chicago, organizing the Southern Tenant Farmers Union and CORE, campaigning to equalize teacher salaries, and working at a settlement house. Married to labor leader and St. Louis NAACP head

Ernest Calloway, she moved to St. Louis in 1950, emerged as a political candidate, and in 1962 became the first black woman elected to the Missouri state legislature. It was in St. Louis that she "really began to participate in things." She played an instrumental role, as Pearl S. Maddox had, in drawing people to the St. Louis NAACP and in gathering information about black life in the city. She edited the *New Citizen* (later renamed the *Citizen Crusader*), a left-liberal, community-based periodical that directly captured the turning tide of local black politics. The short-lived *New Citizen* had its finger on the pulse of a rapidly changing 1960s political scene in black St. Louis, as primaries heated up, grassroots factions formed, gerrymandering and redistricting efforts were introduced, new African American leaders emerged within the Democratic Party, and campaign rhetoric for black freedom and liberation escalated. In the middle of all this was Calloway.[43]

Calloway's victory in 1962 to become the state senator from the Fourth Ward's 13th District was nothing less than a political coup in the eyes of African American Democratic Party insiders, who viewed her with deep suspicion. Black opponents criticized her refusal to work within the city's Democratic Party machine, that she "has no Church Affiliation" and "brags about her negative attitude towards God," and her reluctance to affiliate with any particular church; they urged voters to find someone who "would have been more acceptable to the body politic," as a regular political commentator in Calloway's *New Citizen* newspaper put it. But Calloway had tapped into the shifting historical moment, and she helped remap the terrain of St. Louis's black politics, generating a firestorm by bringing a militancy to the local scene that challenged the humdrum patronage of politics as usual. Her impact illustrated the significance of having veteran social justice activists sworn into office, as she took the progressive stances she had honed in the rough-and-tumble world of outsider organizing to the halls of the state legislature.[44]

Calloway built her platform around the idea of social welfare for marginalized people—the poor, the working class, single mothers, and racial minorities. She focused particularly on building the industrial strength of the state, especially in Kansas City and St. Louis, ending racial discrimination in the workforce, and reforming the state's educational system. Eventually she expanded her campaign platform beyond these issues to include rights for the disabled, the young, and the elderly by supporting a variety of Missouri Old Age Assistance and Aid to Dependent Children programs. She lobbied for the passage of fair housing and fair employment bills, supported the Equal Rights Amendment and stronger protective legislation for women workers and their children, and campaigned for increased rights for unemployed pregnant women, a more comprehensive Labor Relations Act, and the passage of a state minimum-wage law.[45]

Calloway's most progressive stances, where she emerged as a leading voice, were in support of reproductive rights and prisoners' rights. Her unsuccessful battle to repeal Missouri's ban on abortion required a formidable organizational effort, including petitions, gathering of signatures, and an extensive letter-writing campaign that urged state residents "to recognize woman as a whole and total person—legally deserving and guaranteed the right to assert and defend her womanhood at every level." In an address to the legislature supporting a family planning bill, Calloway cited repeatedly the needs of African American women, stressing that black women formed a sizable percentage of welfare recipients because almost one-third of them were heads of their households. She also noted that "St. Louis currently has the highest Black infant mortality rate in the nation" and that a disproportionate number of black women died during childbirth. Her advocacy for services and compassion for working-class and poor women emerged at a time when Family Planning Service House Bill 1399 had made it lawful for state-based family planning services "to offer, suggest, or require sterilization," a provision Calloway had battled against. Calloway also served as chair of the State Institutions and Properties Committee. She commissioned the 1974 "Report on the Human Conditions at Missouri State Penitentiary," which documented shocking conditions: high prisoner death rates, physical abuse, inadequate medical care, violations of due process, and racial discrimination. Portions of the study were later used in an American Civil Liberties Union lawsuit, and the study set the stage for penal reform in Missouri. Dubbing herself "an advocate for the urban area," Calloway used poor and working-class African American women's experiences to imagine a political vision wide and deep enough to encompass economically vulnerable persons across Missouri. Calloway's 1962 campaign and reform-minded political work thereafter operated as a nexus at which liberal, feminist, civil rights, labor, and antipoverty agendas met.[46]

It may be unsurprising that Marian Oldham, DeVerne Calloway, and Frankie Freeman were not only colleagues but also friends. Bonds of friendship and care undergirded their shared political interests and a commitment to solidarity. It was against the backdrop of support from women with greater power and institutional backing that black working-class women collectively mobilized for greater economic support.

Black women's working-class struggles against urban inequality in St. Louis took multiple forms in St. Louis. Some challenged negative images by producing counternarratives of urban poverty that blamed structural forces instead of individual behavior. The women who challenged power holders' managing of state funds, as well as the apparatus of state funding itself, drew links between housing and jobs to show they were the interlocking bedrocks of women's economic experiences. Public-housing tenants built communities and drew connections between their living conditions and their precarious position as marginalized and excluded urban workers. Other black working-class women, such as Ora Lee Malone, having been steeped in the principles of black trade union activism as a young woman in the Deep South, battled to unionize workers of color. Supported by black professional women with greater access to resources and influence, black women workers in St. Louis gained momentum in their struggles, benefited as they were by a growing ferment of black freedom struggle that centered on working-class experiences.

Through the prism of black women's economic experience in postwar St. Louis, we can reimagine the history of urban decline in St. Louis. To be sure, postwar St. Louis was a poster child for the fall of the American city. Because of white flight, rapid deindustrialization, population loss, decimating revenues, municipal neglect, and rigid racial segregation, St. Louis experienced a precipitous fall. The postwar period witnessed many urban losses, which St. Louis bore in dramatic fashion. But the lived experiences of women such as Imani Mtendaji, Hattye Thomas, and Evelyn Jones, along with the activism of Ora Lee Malone, Marian Oldham, Frankie Muse Freeman, and DeVerne L. Calloway, suggest that the particular ways in which black women encountered and responded to urban decline became fertile ground for an emerging politics. Black women's activism centered on their experiences as urban residents; their politics underscored connections between employment, housing, and opportunities for a better economic existence for the working classes. Urban inequality made building connections through political work and family and community life a matter of survival. Learning to develop an economic analysis and politics that anticipated and marked the constitutive elements of urban decline, and to also devise ways to negotiate them, black activist women of the 1950s and 1960s laid the groundwork for subsequent struggle. Out of the crucible of intense battles waged over the future of their city, they forged alliances, communities, and networks to help make possible one of the most important working-class struggles of twentieth-century St. Louis, the rent strike of 1969.[47]

Conclusion

The Legacies of Black Working-Class Women's Political Leadership

Jean King, a St. Louis transplant from Osceola, Arkansas, and Memphis, Tennessee, in the fall of 1968 spotted a young Andre Smallwood eating a piece of bread he found on the snow-covered ground outside of their Darst public-housing development located just south of downtown. King soon learned that Smallwood's mother had a monthly welfare check that amounted to less than the newly stipulated rent increase. The contrast between King and Smallwood's mother could not have been more striking, although both resided in the same housing project. King and her husband, employed and married with one child, had the means to avoid routine visits from caseworkers, fluctuating welfare payments, and rent schedules that continually increased. But negotiating these realities was typical for most other black women, many of whom functioned as their family's breadwinners. Public-housing tenants had already been meeting regularly to discuss the possibility of conducting a rent strike when King attended a tenants' meeting at the nearby Blumeyer Housing Project in midtown St. Louis. After King shared the story of her encounter with Smallwood's mother, tenants elected her president of the Citywide Rent Strike Committee. Like many "organic intellectuals" who emerged as leaders of grassroots social movements, King came out of a local movement that was already organized when the time to strike arrived. King, along with other black women community organizers, went on to spearhead one of the nation's largest and earliest rent strikes in the postwar era. Women's militant mass action garnered national attention and later influenced public policy reform. Because of the long and distinguished activism of black working-class women, a groundswell of grassroots organizing on a national scale, and federal action in support of antipoverty measures, the rent strike came to be understood by sympathetic supports as a working-class struggle led by black women for economic dignity.[1]

The rent strike occurred in early 1969, staged by more than one thousand tenants, about a quarter of the city's public-housing residents. It was sparked by the SLHA's decision to raise rents sixfold, which threatened to price many poor people on fixed incomes out of their residences and leave them homeless. Facing these desperate circumstances, women from a number of developments—including Darst-Webbe and Clinton-Peabody on the south side of town, Carr Square Village, Vaughn, and Cochran near the north side of town, and the massive Pruitt-Igoe project—took radical action to protect themselves and their families. Women activists had been pushing for housing reform for years through appeals and demonstrations, so the seven-month period during which nearly one-quarter of Gateway City public-housing tenants withheld their rent payments was the culmination of numerous smaller-scale demonstrations that had begun earlier. The success of the rent strike illustrated St. Louis as an incubator for women's leadership that pushed forward the national progressive agenda. The rent strike in St. Louis helped usher in a national development, a series of demonstrations waged by increasingly vocal and influential public-housing and welfare rights movements during the late 1960s that were led primarily by working-class African American women.[2]

In an immediate sense, the origins of the rent strike date back to two years before, when black working-class women launched campaigns for jobs and economic opportunity. Nine black women staged a sit-in at the HDC, led protests against the SLHA, and picketed City Hall to demand living-wage jobs and improved living conditions. The nine-woman August 1967 occupation of the HDC offices to demand living-wage jobs received significant media attention and led to an injunction against the protestors. They committed acts of civil disobedience by jamming the locks on doors and filing cabinets and preventing the use of vending machines by applying a "foreign substance." When the city sheriff ordered protestors to disperse, the black women defied him. Public-housing resident Lillie Marshall let the injunction document fall to the floor as he attempted to hand it to her. Picketer Delores Smith told him, "I don't plan to walk out of here unless I have a job. They'll have to carry me out." Birdie Lou Saine responded, "I guess we'll be arrested but that's okay. Next time you come back with the contempt citation bring some food with you." Some of the demonstrators received job offers, they explained, but rejected them because the pay, between $1.65 and $2.44 per hour, was meager. Delores Smith told the press that the women had tried to secure jobs at more than fifteen private companies in the city and county but were met with racial discrimination. Taking their grievances to the HDC, which managed the city's welfare rolls, the women placed responsibility on the corporation because it was the main body charged with assisting black women in finding jobs. Smith told reporters that the group would continue the protest "until the jobs walk in the door." The nine freedom fighters camped out with their children, politicizing motherhood, their status as workers, and the particular breadwinning roles that black working-class women disproportionately played.[3]

In November 1967, public-housing tenants demonstrated outside the SLHA. They called for rent reductions, increased representation on the Housing Authority Board of Commissioners, improved maintenance of rental units, better pest control and police protection, improved utilities services, and financial transparency in the operation of city housing projects. Community resident Mattie Trice served as spokesperson, telling the press that she represented hundreds of residents from the Pruitt-Igoe, Carr Square, Vaughn, and Cochran developments, "When you get a [monthly] check for $75 how can you possibly eat if you are going to pay $50 to $55 [monthly] rent? These buildings were built for us, for poor people." Picketers registered new voters, sang "We Shall Overcome" and other protest songs, and waved "homemade signs" that read "Rent Hike Unfair," "Make the Roaches Pay Rent, Too," "Don't Move—Fight," "Sure Fire Riot Control—Lower Rent," and "March Now—Eat Later." The group threatened to use the ultimate weapon, the rent strike, if their demands were not met.[4]

The multipronged, citywide movement gathered momentum, and by the spring of 1968 there were two hundred black protestors, many of them women, conducting pickets outside City Hall to demand jobs and increased welfare payments. Barbara Bates, chair of the St. Louis chapter of the League for Adequate Welfare, led the demonstration with support from the Black United Front, a consortium of local Black Power groups. The Zulu 1200s and the Action Committee to Improve Opportunities for Negroes (ACTION), two of St. Louis's most active black social justice groups in the late 1960s, served as march marshals. Strikers wound their way through the city from one major housing development to another, Pruitt-Igoe, Vaughn, Carr Square, and to City Hall. "We're not looking for handouts," Bates said. "There are many people on welfare [that want] jobs." Fear, she noted, was the main reason only a small number of residents had joined the demonstration. "It saddened me to go through the Pruitt-Igoe housing project and come out with only the handful of people we did. Some say they're afraid to come out because they may be cut off welfare. But if we as black people unite and work together there's nothing the authorities can do." The group's demands were concrete: two thousand minimum-wage jobs at $2 per hour, a 50 percent rent reduction, a 60 percent decrease in the cost of food stamps, advance notice if welfare checks were to be terminated or reduced, the requirement that city caseworkers inform tenants of their right to a hearing if their benefits were to be reduced or terminated, a formal investigation of more than seventy-five caseworkers "for alleged improper acts," and the firing of Proctor N. Carter, Missouri's director of welfare. Bates shared that Missouri was one of seven states that dispersed the most meager welfare checks in the country. Hoping to gain new supporters to turn their engagement into political change, demonstrators also registered new voters. Other groups joined in the fight. The National Welfare Rights Organization affiliate Parents for Progress conducted a Mother's Day protest, where demonstrators marched from Fountain Park to the St. Louis office of the State Division of Welfare and placed a black drape over its door. "Motherhood is dead," they declared, pointing out the difficulties working-class women encountered in fulfilling their roles as mothers when they lacked steady and sufficient incomes. The flurry of protests for economic dignity that black working-class women organized in the late 1960s put St. Louis on the map of antipoverty struggles. The rent strike would make it a national leader.[5]

Rent strikers issued a set of comprehensive demands when they began their protest in early 1969. Before a gathering of approximately one hundred residents at St. Stephen's Episcopal Church, strikers sketched out the group's agenda. Tenants called upon SLHA director Irvin Dagen, the former St. Louis Congress on Racial Equality leader, who was a colleague of Marian Oldham, to determine rents based on income rather than apartment size, capping the total amount at 25 percent of occupants' monthly earnings. Most tenants were on fixed incomes, they pointed out, so they called for policies that would permit partial rent payments, stipulate that no suits would be filed against tenants who could not make payments without first securing approval from the Tenants Affairs Board, prevent adding repair costs to rent payments, and require sharing Housing Authority job openings with tenants before announcing them to the general public. Tenants also wanted cooperative economic models like community-run businesses and co-ops, while others aimed to protect themselves by guaranteeing "due process" in property damage cases. They demanded better police protection, improved maintenance, and leases with a three-year rent freeze. Strikers' most important demands clustered around tenant control over and representation in the decision-making process, including a tenant affairs board, representation on the Board of Commissioners of the SLHA, budget oversight to ensure "fiscal responsibility," and the authority to create rent schedules and hold veto power over executive hiring decisions. The group demanded social services, housing for senior citizens, recreational facilities, updated units, and new tenants to occupy vacant units. To protect themselves, strikers demanded that no legal action be taken against anyone who participated in the strike.[6]

The women's action became useful to emerging Black Power groups that lent their support and framed the case of black working-class women as powerful symbols of the public-private profiteering that had funded the suburbs and impoverished the city as a matter of government policy. St. Louis CORE, which had by then expelled its white members and engaged in militant acts of physical confrontation, teamed with local organizations such as Plymouth House, represented by the Reverend Buck Jones, local community housing activist Ivory Perry's Metropolitan Tenants Organization, Zulu 1200, Black Liberators, Black Nationals, and ACTION. Leaders issued a statement of formal support, promising to become "fully involved at such time as we consider it helpful to the people." ACTION proposed the building of a "tent city" in Shaw Park, located in nearby Clayton, Missouri, where Irvin Dagen lived. St. Stephen's Episcopal Church Reverend William L. Matheus informed the

Clayton Board of Alderman, "ACTION plans to bring any evicted public-housing tenant that volunteers to dramatize the human suffering and poverty of the urban public-housing concentration camps to the City of Clayton." Members juxtaposed the "green slopes," "clean streets," and "attractive shops" of a posh St. Louis suburb with the "human misery and poverty and degradation of the urban concentration-like camps" in the city. ACTION leaders publicly identified black women such as Lizzie J. Lee, a southside public-housing resident facing eviction and the first willing to join the tent city, as tragic examples. After all, ACTION spokespersons declared, a portion of public-housing tenants' meager welfare checks funded Dagen's salary, which in turn subsidized the director's tax payments to the city of Clayton. "The plight of homeless black women and children evicted and set out on city sidewalks amidst their belongings" best represented the economic dimensions and profit motive of the urban crisis, Matheus explained in his statement to the Clayton Board of Alderman. These links proved powerful for gaining traction in heated debates about race and poverty.[7]

In addition to connecting with movements for Black Power, the women who participated in the collective action drew upon elements of worker organization through use of the strike method. Seven months into the rent strike, not one participant had been evicted, and it became clear that the Housing Authority would be forced to declare bankruptcy if it did not give in to the tenants' demands. The underfunded Housing Authority relied almost exclusively on rents to generate revenue, and with nearly six hundred thousand dollars withheld, it had no choice but to capitulate. The strike ended on October 29, 1969, with tenants winning nearly all of their demands, including representation and an unprecedented measure of decision-making power. St. Louis Teamsters leader Harold Gibbons played an indispensable role in helping to bring the strike to an end by helping to organize the Civic Alliance, but it was the group of striking tenants that inspired him to do so. Gibbons rightly saw in the rent strike the "total person unionism" that he had worked hard to implement. For Gibbons, the quest for dignity was the ultimate fight for any serious labor movement, and this was the quest at the core of the rent strike and housing struggles in general. The fight was principally "enabling the poor who live in the low-cost housing areas to find dignity, security and human values in their homes and neighborhoods," he observed. Such was "the fundamental principle that trade unionism is all about." Gibbons drew an important parallel between workers' rights movement of the 1930s and 1940s, when "workers began to take matters into their own hands, and discovered they could never build a better life unless they organized and built the kind of strength necessary to demand and win what was coming to them in America," and the "new movement" generated by black working-class women. In drawing this historical trajectory, Gibbons outlined the basic contours of black women's working-class activism in St. Louis from the New Deal to the Great Society.[8]

A tradition of working-class struggle generated by black women helped to frame the rent strike as an instance of self-organization by black women workers who toiled in low-wage sectors and performed essential unpaid labor as mothers and community leaders. Nut shellers and domestic workers in the 1930s, black young women who aspired to work as clerks in the shops located in their own neighborhoods, and defense and garment workers in the 1940s and 1950s made public the varied dimensions of their economic lives and labors, transforming them into a platform from which to make claims to economic dignity. Women's demands in the late 1960s echoed those of the generation that preceded them. In a powerful way, the rent strike closed the chapter in which black women's working-class struggles took center stage in the St. Louis black freedom and economic justice movement, just as the Funsten Nut Strike of 1933 had opened it.

Black women's working-class struggles continued in the 1970s, but the terrain upon which women mobilized altered in form. The changing social, political, and economic order increasingly began to reflect a turn against black women's activism for economic justice. Reagan-era tax cuts and the evisceration of public funding for antipoverty programs found traction in the antistatist position of political conservatives. The specter of the "welfare queen" became a most effective tool. Low-income black women became one of Ronald Reagan's primary targets as his administration attempted to dismantle "big government" and the logic of American liberalism that conceptualized the state as protector of the economically vulnerable. Why attack black working-class women in particular? It was the *success* of black women's movements against poverty and economic indignity—movements that reached their apex in the 1960s but had roots in struggles of the thirties, forties, and fifties—that motivated War on Poverty detractors. To attack the state was to, in effect, attack black *working-class* women and their status as political actors.[9]

The case study of black women's economic activism in St. Louis illuminates why black working-class women had become a political threat. As the Gateway City underwent major economic, political, and social transformations, black women's activism indelibly marked the urban political agendas that shaped the local struggle. Black women forged an effective, community-based culture of resistance and organizing that emphasized economic dignity, or the right to jobs; a living wage; welfare; suitable working conditions; affordable, quality public housing and child care; and access to public accommodations. Operating at the intersection of struggles for economic, racial, and gender justice, working-class black women made economic dignity foundational, incorporated a wide array of living concerns into their political platforms, and challenged masculinized images of the American worker. Domestics, food processors, garment workers, defense employees, clerks, public-housing tenants, and the underemployed and unemployed struggled with their sympathizers to find their economic footing by staging a long and entrenched battle for economic power through community institutions, unions, family networks, coalitions, migration, and labor testimony. Their economic politics became key components of major campaigns in twentieth-century social movements. Black working-class women's laboring bodies and their unpaid and paid labors constituted the social and political order that animated justice-making in St. Louis. Within the liminal and contested boundaries marking struggles for racial and economic justice, black working-class women located opportunities for political experimentation.

Acknowledgments

I am filled with deep gratitude for those who made this book possible. Writing a book is, by far, a collective undertaking. I would like to thank my mentor, Andrea Friedman, for graciously reading *many* drafts of this work. Andrea offered such wonderful suggestions for making this book stronger and coached me through the writing process from start to finish. I am forever in her debt. I would also like to extend special thanks to Iver Bernstein, Mary Ann Dzuback, Maggie Garb, and David Roediger for reading and commenting on earlier drafts of the book. Their insights pushed me to think harder and draw connections that I had not imagined. This project would not be half of what it is without the steadfast encouragement of Sheri Notaro, Gerald Early, Mary Laurita, Amy Gassel, and the fellows of Washington University's Chancellor's Graduate Fellowship Program, who convinced me that becoming a professor was possible. Many thanks to Dr. Caryl McFarlane, Ina Noble, and the staff of the Andrew W. Mellon Foundation and the Woodrow Wilson National Fellowship Foundation for offering crucial support to see this project to completion. Thanks to Dr. Calvin Howell and Debbie Wahl, whose leadership of the Mellon Mays Undergraduate Fellowship Program at Duke University made all the difference. So many of us benefited from your commitment to changing the professoriate for the better. Sadly, Raymond Gavins and Leslie Brown, two brilliant historians and generous members who have had a major influence upon my career as a historian, did not live to see this book. But their impact on my thinking and approach is on every page.

I could not have hoped for a better editorial team than Anne Dean Dotson, Patrick O'Dowd, Jackie Wilson, and David Cobb of the University Press of Kentucky. Their enthusiasm for this project sustained me in tough moments and their professionalism guided me through the many stages required to bring the book to completion.

My former Bowdoin College colleagues—Judith Casselberry, Tess

Chakkalakal, Matt Klingle, Patrick Rael, Jen Scanlon, Anne Clifford, Rosemary Effiom, and Femi Vaughn—along with members of the Southern Maine American History Research Group made my time in Brunswick, Maine, special. Through dinners, writing groups, colloquia, and many conversations, I learned so much about the craft of historical research and writing. Thank you for helping me discover new ways to think about my research. My former colleagues at Luther College were no less wonderful. Novian Whitsitt, Martin Klammer, Guy Nave, and Richard Mtisi became fast friends, and Shelia Radford-Hill and Wintlett Taylor-Browne made the work worthwhile. Brian Caton, Ed Tebbenhoff, Marvin Slind, Jackie Wilkie, Victoria Christman, Robert Christman, Gregg Narber, and the late Lawrence Williams of Luther's History Department were strong supporters of my work. I have had the good fortune to land in a department that has supported my research in innumerable ways. My History Department colleagues at the University of Missouri have generously supported me through the final stages of this book. I would especially like to thank Wilma King, Catherine Rymph, John Wigger, Robert Smale, Linda Reeder, Kerby Miller, Michelle Morris, Jerry Frank, Ilyana Karthas, Mark Carroll, Daniel Domingues, and Ted Koditschek. Catherine, Robert, Emma Lipton, and Elizabeth Chang made sure that I stayed on task at our weekly writing sessions.

This project could not have been completed without the wonderful assistance of the archivists and librarians who answered my many queries and pointed me in such fruitful directions. I would especially like to extend thanks to the staff of the State Historical Society of Missouri, the Missouri History Museum's Library and Research Center, and Special Collections at Washington University in St. Louis, Southern Illinois University–Carbondale's Special Collections Research Center, and Southern Illinois University–Edwardsville's Special Collections Library. I would like to offer my sincere thanks to Frances Levine, Melanie Adams, Elizabeth Pickard, and Sarah Sims of the Missouri History Museum for their assistance and encouragement.

I extend my most sincere thanks to the many historians whose intellectual labors laid the groundwork for my own. I would especially like to thank Priscilla Dowden-White and Clarence Lang, two of my most treasured colleagues and friends. Priscilla and Clarence supported this project in innumerable ways and provided me with multiple opportunities to share my work. Their important work on the history of black St. Louis made this book possible. David Lucander, Kenneth Stuart Jolly, and Gary Kremer shared insights based on their extensive knowledge of St. Louis and Missouri history. Premilla Nadasen, Eileen Boris, Dayo Gore, Sarah Haley, Prudence Cumberbatch, Michael Ezra, Annelise Orleck, and Jenny Carson read portions of the manuscript and made important contributions to the book through their insightful commentary. Rosemary Feurer, Jefferson Cowie, Anne Volk, Jean Allman, Nancy MacLean, Ileen DeVault, and members of the Urban Studies Faculty Seminar of the Hall Center for the Humanities at the University of Kansas also read portions of the work. I would also like to thank the anonymous readers of the manuscript for their thorough and insightful comments, which greatly improved the book. It was truly a pleasure to work with my personal editor, Cynthia Gwynne Yaudes, and my cartographer, George Stoll. I wish to extend special thanks to Wiley Price, an extraordinary photographer for the St. Louis American who graciously shared his photo of Ora Lee Malone.

My family and friends kept me grounded through the writing and revising process. My parents, Dorothy K. Ervin and the late E. J. Ervin Jr., encouraged me at every turn. This book belongs to them in every imaginable way. Michelle Purdy stood by me and this book when we needed her the most. And finally, I wish to extend heartfelt thanks to Rachel Darrylyn Dickson, who makes all of this research and writing worth it all. Rachel lived with this project for far too long; she endured all of my stress and anxiety over the status of this work and constantly reminded me of why I chose to write the book. Her unwavering support, wonderful sense of humor, and fierce love sustained me. This project would not exist without her.

As Leslie says in her acknowledgments: all of the good things in this manuscript are because of the people I listed here and the many more whom I failed to mention. All mistakes are mine alone.

Notes

Abbreviations

CaP	DeVerne L. Calloway Papers, State Historical Society of Missouri, Columbia
EG	Edna Gellhorn Papers, University Archives, West Campus Library, Washington University in St. Louis, St. Louis, MO
FC	Fannie Cook Papers, Missouri History Museum Library and Research Center, St. Louis, MO
ILGWU-SIUC	ILGWU Papers, Lovejoy Library, Southern Illinois University–Carbondale
NS	Negro Scrapbook, Missouri History Museum Library and Research Center, St. Louis, MO
SHSM	Urban League of St. Louis, State Historical Society of Missouri, St. Louis
SLUL	St. Louis Urban League Records, University Archives, Washington University in St. Louis, St. Louis, MO
TDM	D. McNeal Scrapbook, s0321, Manuscript Collection, State Historical Society of Missouri

Introduction

1. "Rent Strikers' Liaison Group to Meet Here," *St. Louis Post-Dispatch,* May 11, 1969; Wesley, Price, and Morris, *Lift Every Voice and Sing,* 181; Harper Barnes, "What Started as a Rent Strike," *St. Louis Beacon,* November 13, 2012; Karp, "St. Louis Rent Strike of 1969"; Lang, *Grassroots at the Gateway,* 212–16; Lipsitz, *Life in the Struggle,* 9–14.

2. Lipsitz, *American Studies,* xiv.

3. Carrie Smith and Cora Lewis, "We Strike and Win," *Working Woman* (1933): 8–9; "Mayor Hears Wage Protest of Nut Strikers," *St. Louis Star Times,* May 23, 1933; "Mayor's Group Takes Up Strike of Nut Pickers," *St. Louis Post-Dispatch,* May 23, 1933; Feurer, "Nutpickers' Union," 36–40; Lang, *Grassroots at the Gateway,* 29–34.

4. Friedman, "Strange Career of Annie Lee Moss."

5. Nadasen, *Household Workers Unite;* and Jones, *Labor of Love,* for example, focus on the politics of black women's activism in the paid labor market and

in the context of women's community and family work. Others examine black women's economic activism primarily through the prism of antipoverty organizing. See, for example, Williams, *Politics of Public Housing;* Orleck, *Storming Caesar's Palace;* Levenstein, *Movement without Marches;* Nadasen, *Welfare Warriors;* Countryman, *Up South;* and Greene, *Our Separate Ways.* On the making of black left feminism and black women activists as political strategists, organizers, and rank-and-file participants in diasporic radicalism, see Gore, *Radicalism at the Crossroads;* McDuffie, *Sojourning for Freedom;* Washington, "Childress, Hansberry, and Jones"; and Washington, *Other Blacklist.* For a history of black economic activism, see Ezra, *Economic Civil Rights Movement.*

6. Roediger, "What If Labor?, 73, 74; Rank of the General Occupational Divisions by Nativity and Color of the Employed Woman, St. Louis, MO, 1930, Women Workers of St. Louis, Missouri, 1930, s0348, Manuscript Collections, State Historical Society of Missouri, St. Louis; US Bureau of the Census, *U.S. Census of Population: 1950,* vol. 2, *Characteristics of the Population,* part 25, Missouri (Washington, DC: Government Printing Office, 1952), 276.

7. This book is grounded in historical interpretations that expand older models or understandings of labor history. While there are too many to list here, see, for example, Kelley, "'Not What We Seem.'"

8. Leflouria, *Chained in Silence;* Haley, *No Mercy Here;* Nadasen, *Household Workers Unite;* Boris and Nadasen, "Historicizing Domestic Workers' Resistance and Organizing"; Harris, *Sex Workers, Psychics;* Blair, *I've Got to Make My Livin'.* On feminist studies, women's labor, and black women's labor in particular, and on the erasure of black working-class women and women of color from earlier studies in women's labor history, see Brewer, "Theorizing Race, Class and Gender"; Davis, *Women, Race and Class;* Janiewski, *Sisterhood Denied;* Boris and Kleinberg, "Mothers and Other Workers"; Kessler-Harris, *Gendering Labor History.*

9. Xiomara Santamarina, *Belabored Professions: Narratives of African American Working Womanhood* (Chapel Hill: University of North Carolina Press, 2005).

10. "Women in Organized Labor: Profiles in Labor: Ora Malone," *St. Louis American,* August 28–September 3, 1986; Philip Dine, "Trade Group Honors Area Union Activist," *St. Louis Post-Dispatch,* November 27, 1988, Ora Lee Malone Papers, series 383, folder 1, Manuscript Collections, SHSM; Ora Lee Malone, interview by Keona Ervin, November 4, 2003, American Lives Project, Washington University in St. Louis, St. Louis, MO.

11. Korstad, *Civil Rights Unionism;* Skotnes, *New Deal for All?;* Korstad and Lichtenstein, "Opportunities Found and Lost"; Gill, *Beauty Shop Politics,* 19–21, 42–43; Reese, "Domestic Drudges to Dazzling Divas," 176–77; Wright, *Discovering African American St. Louis,* 69.

12. Friedman, "Strange Career of Annie Lee Moss."

13. Primm, *Lion of the Valley,* 463–68; Douglass, *St. Louis Church Survey,* 45–46; Dorothy W. Burke, *Economic Status of Saint Louis* (St. Louis, 1935), 11; Lang, "Community and Resistance," 534; Ernest Calloway, "The Negro Social and Economic Thrust: Containment Apparatus Changes as Negro Awoke to Political Potential," *Missouri Teamster,* December 20, 1963.

14. Report of the Industrial Bureau of the St. Louis Chamber of Commerce quoted in Burke, *Economic Status,* 13; Feurer, *Radical Unionism in the Midwest,* 7; Corbett and Seematter, *In Her Place,* 218–19 ("light").

15. Crossland, *Industrial Conditions,* 101, 22, 94; Occupational Distribution of St. Louis Female Workers by Color and by Nativity: 1930, Facts and Figures for Speakers on Race Relations, Department of Race Relations, St. Louis Community Council, September 1934, p. 4, series 1, box 4, folder 12, FC; Reid, *Industrial Status of Negroes,* 20; Rank of the General Occupational Divisions by Nativity and Color of the Employed Woman, St. Louis, MO, 1930, Women Workers of St. Louis, Missouri, 1930, s0348, Manuscript Collections, State Historical Society of Missouri, St. Louis.

16. Brown, *Upbuilding Black Durham;* Crossland, *Industrial Conditions,* 12; "Black Population by Sex and Age for Census Tracts: 1930," in *1930 Federal Census for Metropolitan St. Louis Tabulated by Enumeration Districts and Census Tracts* (St. Louis: Research Committee of the St. Louis Community Council, 1932); "Black Population in St. Louis from U.S. Census, 1940," in *Population and Housing Statistics for Census Tracts, St. Louis, Mo. and Adjacent Area* (Washington, DC: Government Printing Office, 1942), 6, Missouri State Employment Service, New Deal and Black Agencies, Missouri File, Special Collections, University of Missouri–Columbia; Osofsky, *Harlem,* 4; Black Population in St. Louis, from U.S. Census, 1910–1933, in *Population and Housing Statistics,* p. 6, Missouri State Employment Service, New Deal and Black Agencies, Missouri File, Special Collections, University of Missouri–Columbia.

17. Skotnes, *New Deal for All?*

18. Korstad and Lichtenstein, "Opportunities Found and Lost," 786 ("increasingly urban"), 788 ("workplace-oriented"); Korstad, *Civil Rights Unionism;* Skotnes, *New Deal for All?;* Hall, "Long Civil Rights Movement"; Harris, "Running with the Reds"; Kelley, *Hammer and Hoe;* Lucander, *Winning the War for Democracy.*

19. Lang, *Grassroots at the Gateway,* 4–5; Biondi, *To Stand and Fight,* 2.

20. Calloway, "Negro Social and Economic Thrust; Lang, *Grassroots at the Gateway,* 12; Richard Dudman, "St. Louis' Silent Racial Revolution," *St. Louis Post-Dispatch,* June 11, 1990; Joseph, *Waiting 'Til the Midnight Hour,* 50–53; Robnett, *How Long?,* 19–23; Edwards, *Charisma and the Fictions.*

21. Lang, *Grassroots at the Gateway,* 4–5, 7–13; Gordon, *Mapping Decline;* Dowden-White, *Groping toward Democracy;* Lipsitz, *Life in the Struggle;* Jolly, *Black Liberation in the Midwest;* Heathcott, "Black Archipelago"; Lucander,

Winning the War for Democracy; Lang, "Locating the Civil Rights Movement";
Campbell, *Gateway Arch.*

22. Ora Lee Malone, interview by Keona Ervin, November 11, 2003.

1. "We Strike and Win"

1. Smith and Lewis, "We Strike and Win."

2. Lang, *Grassroots at the Gateway,* 29–34; Feurer, "Nutpickers' Union";
Brunn, "Black Workers and Social Movements," 341–96.

3. "Looking Back on a Strike," *St. Louis Post-Dispatch,* May 25, 1933.

4. 1930 Annual Report, series 4, box 6, folder 79, SLUL; Jennie C. Buckner quoted in Fichtenbaum, *Funsten Nut Strike,* 19; see also 15–20.

5. Voris, "Women in Missouri Industries," 39, 40; Bill Gebert, "The St.
Louis Nut Strike an Example of Correct Strike Tactics," *Daily Worker,* June 1,
1933; Bill Gebert, "The St. Louis Strike and the Chicago Needle Trades Strike,"
Communist: A Magazine of the Theory and Practice of Marxism-Leninism 12, no.
8 (August 1933): 802; Fichtenbaum, *Funsten Nut Strike,* 20.

6. Charley Jordan and "Hi" Henry Brown, "Nut Factory Blues" (Vocalion
Records, 1932); Scott, *Blues Empress in Black Chattanooga;* Kelley, "Not What
We Seem"; Hunter, *To 'Joy My Freedom;* Davis, *Blues Legacies and Black Femi-
nism;* Carby, "It Jus Be's Dat Way"; Baraka, *Blues People,* 6.

7. Jordan and Brown, "Nut Factory Blues"; Baraka, *Blues People,* 121;
Clark to Kirk Latta, November 18, 1941, series 4, box 1, folder General Correspondence 1941, SLUL.

8. Jordan and Brown, "Nut Factory Blues"; Reid, *Industrial Status of
Negroes,* 7–8; Brown, *Upbuilding Black Durham.*

9. Davis, *Blues Legacies and Black Feminism;* Gross, *Colored Amazons;*
McGuire, *Dark End of the Street;* Hine, "Rape and Black Women."

10. Mumford, *Interzones.*

11. Jordan and Brown, "Nut Factory Blues."

12. Gebert, "St. Louis Strike and Needle Trades Strike; "Woman Reported
Hurt in City Hall Riot Dies," *St. Louis Argus,* August 19, 1932; "Workers Halt
Eviction in St. Louis, MO," *Daily Worker,* March 24, 1932 ("among them quite
a few Negro workers"); "'Reds' Storm City Hall and Four Are Shot, 20 Injured,"
St. Louis Globe-Democrat, July 12, 1932 "City Hall Riot Charges Faced by 5
Negroes," *St. Louis Argus,* July 15, 1932; Rosemary Feurer, "City Hall and the
Unemployed Protests," in Feurer, *St. Louis Labor History Tour,* 21–23; Feurer,
Radical Unionism in the Midwest, 36–43; Brunn, "Black Workers and Social
Movements," 147, 197, 218, 221, 229, 232, 254–56.

13. Ralph Shaw, "St. Louis' Biggest Strike," *Labor Unity,* August 1933,
8–11 ("brought in the Scottsboro case"); "Girls Both White and Negro," in
Fichtenbaum, *Funsten Nut Strike,* Appendix I ("organize ourselves"); Smith and

Lewis, "We Strike and Win" ("the white girls stayed inside"; "floorlady"); "Nut Pickers Ask Mayor to Act as Arbiter in Strike," *St. Louis Post-Dispatch*, May 18, 1933; "Mayor's Group Takes Up Strike" ("Animals in the Zoo"; "Fight for the Freedom of Labor"); "Women in Organized Labor: Through the Past, Partly: Women Record Triumph and Turmoil in Struggle for Equality," *St. Louis American*, August 28–September 3, 1986, p. 3C.

14. Gebert, "St. Louis Strike and Needle Trades Strike," 801 (strikers' quotes), 801–6; Shaw, "St. Louis' Biggest Strike," 8, 9, 10; "Mayor's Group Takes Up Strike"; Smith and Lewis, "We Strike and Win," 8, 9; Brunn, "Black Workers and Social Movements," 147, 254–56.

15. Gebert, "St. Louis Strike and Needle Trades Strike," 804 ("What a change"; "Negro woman"), 801 ("It is important to note"), 804.

16. "To the Workers of St. Louis," in Fichtenbaum, *Funsten Nut Strike*, Appendix II.

17. Carrie Smith quoted in Gebert, "St. Louis Nut Strike an Example"; Gebert, "St. Louis Strike and Needle Trades Strike"; Shaw, "St. Louis' Biggest Strike," 9; Feurer, "Nutpickers' Union."

18. Smith and Lewis, "We Strike and Win"; "Mayor Hears Wage Protest."

19. "Mayor Hears Wage Protest."

20. "Mayor's Arbiters Settle Strike of 1200 Nut Pickers," *St. Louis Post-Dispatch*, May 24, 1933; Shaw, "St. Louis' Biggest Strike."

21. Shaw, "St. Louis's Biggest Strike," 10, 11; Gebert, "St. Louis Strike and Needle Trades Strike"; "Smashing Victory, Pay Increases Are Won by St. Louis Nut Pickers," *Daily Worker*, May 25, 1933; Smith and Lewis, "We Strike and Win," 8–9 ("We have no more terror").

22. Gebert, "St. Louis Strike and Needle Trades Strike," 805–6 ("Under no circumstances"); Gebert, "St. Louis Nut Strike an Example"; Shaw, "St. Louis' Biggest Strike."

23. Gebert, "St. Louis Nut Strike an Example" ("the strike"; "shows what potentialities"; "these comrades"); rank-and-file AFL workers quoted in Shaw, "St. Louis' Biggest Strike," 11; Gebert, "St. Louis Strike and Needle Trades Strike," 804; "A.F. of L. Leaders Betray Strike on St. Louis Levee," *Daily Worker*, April 17, 1934; Smith and Lewis, "We Strike and Win," 8–9 ("The working women"; "can and should be followed"); "Women Nut-Pickers' Strike Continues," *St. Louis Post-Dispatch*, May 17, 1933.

24. Floyd J. Collins, "Today and Yesterday: The Nut Pickers' Strike," *St. Louis Argus*, May 26, 1933; Reid, *Industrial Status of Negroes*, 38–40, 48, 49; Gebert, "St. Louis Strike and Needle Trades Strike," 800 ("a historical role"), 805 ("do as the nut pickers did"); "Strike of Nut Pickers Strong in St. Louis; 2,000 Out for Pay Raise," *Daily Worker*, May 23, 1933 ("The majority of the strikers"); "Another St. Louis Food Factory Goes Out on Strike," *Daily Worker*, May 22, 1933; "Nut Pickers Win Strike," *St. Louis Argus*, July 21, 1933; "John-

son Tries to Sell NRA Codes to Working Women," *Daily Worker,* August 16, 1933; "Nut Pickers Vote to 'Down Tools' May Day," *Daily Worker,* April 24, 1934; "New St. Louis Laundry Union Calls Meeting," *St. Louis Post-Dispatch,* August 9, 1933; Shaw, "St. Louis' Biggest Strike," 11 ("given leadership"; "the outstanding feature").

25. Gebert, "St. Louis Strike and Needle Trades Strike," 803; Smith and Lewis, "We Strike and Win," 8–9.

26. "William Scarlett—An Appreciation," May 7, 1950, p. 4, Ferdinand J. Isserman Papers, Jacob Rader Marcus Center of the American Jewish Archives, Hebrew Union College, Cincinnati, OH; Ferdinand J. Isserman, "The Friendship between Christ Church Cathedral and Temple Israel," November 30, 1962, pp. 1–2, ibid.; Ferdinand J. Isserman, "The Five Outstanding Events of 1933," December 29, 1933, ibid.; Ferdinand J. Isserman, "Judaism and Race Relations," December 14, 1945, ibid.; "Mayor Orders Inquiry in Nut Pickers' Strike," *St. Louis Post-Dispatch,* May 19, 1933; Smith and Lewis, "We Strike and Win."

27. Ferdinand J. Isserman, "The Moral of the Nut-Pickers' Strike," May 25, 1933, reprinted in Fichtenbaum, *Funsten Nut Strike,* 69–70.

28. Clark to Rev. J. F. Moreland, November 3, 1933, series 1, box 9, SLUL; Clark to Ruth Ford, May 8, 1933, ibid.; St. Louis Urban League 1933 Annual Report, p. 3, series 4, box 6, folder 82, ibid.; J. Buckner quoted in Fichtenbaum, *Funsten Nut Strike,* 45.

29. Tuck, *We Ain't What We Ought;* "Looking Back on a Strike"; "Nut Pickers on Strike," *St. Louis Post-Dispatch,* May 20, 1933 ("instance right at home"; "of wage-slashing and sweat shop conditions"); Denning, *Cultural Front;* "Women in Organized Labor: Through the Past."

30. "Offers More Pay to End Strike of 500 Nut Pickers," *St. Louis Post-Dispatch,* May 16, 1933 ("There has been some improvement); "500 Negro Women Offered Pay Rise, Continue Strike," *St. Louis Star-Times,* May 16, 1933; "Mayor Arbiters Settle Strike of 1200 Nut Pickers, *St. Louis Post-Dispatch,* May 24, 1933.

31. "Public Trial Will Expose Layoffs in Nut Pickers' Fight," *Daily Worker,* October 5, 1933; "Firing of Union Nut Pickers in St. Louis Plotted," *Daily Worker,* September 8, 1933 ("Food Workers of St. Louis"); *St. Louis Star Times,* May 15, 16; October 19, 1933; Shaw, "St. Louis' Biggest Strike," 9; *St. Louis Globe-Democrat,* May 18, 1933; *St. Louis Post-Dispatch,* May 18, 1933; *St. Louis Argus,* October 13, 1933; "Win Relief; Call United Meet in East St. Louis," *Daily Worker,* May 26, 1934; January 1937 Report, series 4, box 4, folder Monthly Report, Assistant Industrial Secretary, 1937, January–June, S. R. Williams, SLUL.

32. Quotes in "Nut Factory Closes," *St. Louis Argus,* October 6, 1933; Floyd J. Collins, "The Nut Pickers' Strike," *St. Louis Argus,* May 26, 1933.

33. Shaw, "St. Louis' Biggest Strike," 11; *St. Louis Post-Dispatch,* May 24, 26, 1933; "Two Strikes Here Settled through Mediation Board," *Daily Worker,*

October 19, 1933; "Conditions Worse under N.R.A., Says Food Union," *Daily Worker,* November 6, 1933.

34. Shaw, "St. Louis' Biggest Strike," 10; "Mayor Orders Inquiry"; *Daily Worker,* May 22, 1933; *St. Louis Globe-Democrat,* May 19, 1933; *St. Louis Post-Dispatch,* January 22, 1930; "Thugs Kidnap, Beat Packers' Strike Leader," *Daily Worker,* May 17, 1934; "Women Picket Nut Factories in Strike," *St. Louis Argus,* May 19, 1983; ""Communist Strikes Judge over Negroes," *St. Louis Argus,* March 30, 1934.

35. González, "Carolina Munguía and Emma Tenayuca," 213; *Pecan Shellers of San Antonio,* xv–xvi, xvii, 111; Vargas, "Tejana Radical," 565.

36. Vargas, "Tejana Radical," 565; González, "Carolina Munguía and Emma Tenayuca," 213; *Pecan Shellers of San Antonio,* xv, xvii, xviii.

37. González, "Carolina Munguía and Emma Tenayuca," 213, 214 ("temporary charter"), 215, 216, 222 ("operated at the crossroads"); *Pecan Shellers of San Antonio,* xvi; Vargas, "Tejana Radical," 554, 555, 556 ("largest labor strike"); Ruiz, *Cannery Women, Cannery Lives,* 41–84.

38. Lang, *Grassroots at the Gateway,* 38.

39. "Looking Back on a Strike."

2. "Their Side of the Case"

1. Nadasen, *Household Workers Unite.*

2. Annual Report of the Urban League of St. Louis for the Year 1933, p. 5, s0093, SHSM.

3. Ibid.; Nadasen, "'Sista' Friends and Other Allies"; Nadasen, "'Tell Dem Slavery Done'"; Boris and Nadasen, "Domestic Workers Organize!"; Kessler-Harris, *Pursuit of Equity;* Jones, *Labor of Love, Labor of Sorrow,* 171–74.

4. Lang, *Grassroots at the Gateway,* 13; Dowden-White, *Groping toward Democracy,* 2, 12–16, 116–23; Dowden, "Urban League of St. Louis"; Storrs, *Civilizing Capitalism,* 33, 91–123, 196–98.

5. Rank of the General Occupational Divisions by Nativity and Color of the Employed Woman, St. Louis, MO, 1930, Women Workers of St. Louis, Missouri, 1930, s0348, SHSM; Burke, *Economic Status,* 13.

6. September and November 1930 Reports, series 4, box 4, folder 36, SLUL; July 1931 Monthly Report, series 4, box 4, folder 39, ibid.; January 1932 Monthly Report, series 4, box 4, folder 42, ibid. ("$5.00 per week"); February 1934 Report, series 4, box 4, folder 46, ibid.; Lucy Randolph, "The Perfect Treasure," *American Junior League Magazine,* February 1934, 36, 37 ("a basement room").

7. August 1931 Monthly Report, series 4, box 4, folder 39, SLUL; January 1932 Monthly Report, series 4, box 4, folder 42, ibid.; July 1931 Monthly Report, series 4, box 4, folder 39, ibid.

8. Mary Young to Clark, May 17, 1937, series 1, box 9, folder 21, May 1937, SLUL; Ellen Hockett to Clark, November 19, 1930, St. Louis Urban League Papers, ibid.; Luella Webster to Jennie C. Buckner, n.d., series 4, box 1, folder 13, ibid.; Young to Clark, May 12, 1937, series 1, box 9, folder 21, ibid.; Young to Clark, May 17, 1937, series 1, box 9, folder 19, ibid.; Annual Report of Executive Secretary of Urban League of St. Louis, 1930, SHSM; Henryetta Makins to Clark, November 28, 1928, series 1, box 9, folder 4, SLUL; Jane Story to Clark, April 19, 1929, series 1, box 9, folder 5, ibid.; Clark to Henry V. Ghem, May 10, 1933, series 1, box 9, folder 11, ibid.; Makins to Clark, November 28, 1928, series 1, box 9, folder 4, ibid.; Story to Clark, April 19, 1929, series 1, box 9, folder 5: General Correspondence, 1929, ibid.; Clark to Ghem, May 10, 1933, series 1, box 9, folder 11, May 1933, ibid.; Webster to Buckner, n.d., series 1, box 1, folder 13, ibid.; Young to Clark, May 12, 1937, series 1, box 9, folder 21, May 1937, ibid.; Clark-Lewis, *Living In, Living Out*.

9. Annual Report of the Urban League of St. Louis for the Year 1933, p. 1 ("because the question"), SHSM; Reid, *Industrial Status of Negroes,* 1; Facts and Figures for Speakers on Race Relations, St. Louis Community Council, Department of Race Relations, September 1934, p. 4, box 4, folder 2, FC; "J. T. Clark Called to N.Y. by Urban League," *St. Louis Argus,* March 30, 1934; Dowden, "We Are Determined to Fight," 79–80. The literature on the National Urban League is voluminous. Some representative works include Reed, *Not Alms but Opportunity;* Weiss, *National Urban League;* Strickland, *Chicago Urban League;* Parris and Brooks, *Blacks in the City;* Moore, *Search for Equality.*

10. Annual Report of the Urban League of St. Louis for the Year 1933, p. 1, SHSM; A Digest of Fields Explored and Services Given by the Urban League of St. Louis, n.d., p. 3, box 15, folder 5, Mary T. Hall Papers, Missouri History Museum, St. Louis ("During the depression"); January 1938–June 1938 Monthly Reports, series 4, box 5, folder 1, SLUL; July 1938 Report of Industrial Secretary, series 4, box 5, folder 1, ibid.; January 1944 Comparative Table of Employment Statistics, series 4, box 5, folder 7, ibid.; 1929 Monthly Report, series 4, box 4, folder 32, ibid.; 1930 Monthly Report, series 4, box 4, folder 36, ibid.; 1932 Monthly Report, series 4, box 4, folder 42, ibid.; 1933 Monthly Report, series 4, box 4, folder 44, ibid.; Clark to John W. George, n.d., series 1, box 9, folder 24, ibid.; Clark to Arthur, October 24, 1933, series 1, box 9, folder 10 ("white girls could be had"), ibid.; Charles A. Collier Jr. to Freeman L. Martin, June 24, 1933, series 4, box 1, folder 9, ibid.; Myrtle McKinney to Industrial Committee of Urban League, 8 June 1933, series 4, box 1, folder 9, ibid.; Martin to Industrial Committee of the Urban League, June 16, 1933, series 4, box 1, folder 9, ibid.

11. March 1929 Report, Urban League of St. Louis, Industrial Department (Women and Girls), SLUL; Report for March 1929, series 4, box 4, folder 32, ibid.; Twentieth Anniversary, 1919 to 1938, Urban League of St. Louis, St.

Louis Urban League Papers, s0093, box 1, folder Urban League of St. Louis, Annual Reports, 1938–1942, 1944–1945, 1957, 1960, 1964–1970, 1972, 1974, SHSM; V. D. Abbington, February 1945 Report, p. 1, St. Louis Urban League Records, series 4, box 5, folder 13, SLUL.

12. Jennie C. Buckner and Marie C. Wilburn, "Orders from Bachelors," series 4, box 4, folder 36, Report of Industrial Secretary, 1936 all, series 4, box 4, folder 50, SLUL; McGuire, *Dark End of the Street,* xviii–xix, xx, 201–3.

13. Annual Report of the Urban League of St. Louis for the Year 1933, p. 5 ("Evidences"), SHSM; Meeting of General Household Workers, September 21, 1933, box 4, folder 1, FC; "Domestic Workers Problems Are Discussed in a Meeting," *St. Louis Argus,* October 6, 1933; Clark to Mrs. George Gellhorn, September 20, 1933, series 3, box 10, folder 20 ("apparently our meeting"), EG.

14. Clark to Mrs. George Gellhorn, September 20, 1933, series 3, box 10, folder 20, EG ("We are trying"); Meeting of General Household Workers, September 21, 1933, box 4, folder 1, FC ("to arrive at some code"); "Domestic Workers Problems Are Discussed"; Annual Report of the Urban League of St. Louis for the Year 1933, p. 4 ("understand the complicated"), SHSM; September 1933 Report, p. 2, series 4, box 4, folder 43, SLUL.

15. August 1930 Monthly Report, series 4, box 4, folder 36, SLUL; Meeting of General Household Workers, September 21, 1933, box 4, folder 1, FC ("live comfortably"; "Using her own"); Annual Report of the Urban League of St. Louis for the Year 1933, p. 5 ("authority"; "well trained women"), SHSM.

16. T. Arnold Hill, "Domestic Service to the Front," *Opportunity* 4 (April 1930): 120.

17. Quotes in ibid.; Women's Conference on Household Employment Relations, March 18, 1930, series 3, box 10, folder 20, EG; Standard Certificate of Death, Florence Eldridge, Division of Health of Missouri, Filed November 2, 1949, Date of Death, November 2, 1949; Hunter, *To 'Joy My Freedom,* 57–65; Kelley, "'Not What We Seem.'"

18. Women's Bureau, US Department of Labor, "Suggested Minimum Standards for the Full-Time General Houseworker," Proposed in 1931 by the National Committee on Employer-Employee Relationships in the Home, 1931, box 4, folder 1, FC; Hazel Kyrk, "A Fine Art—an Undesired Job," *Life and Labor Bulletin* 9, no. 10 (December 1931): 1, serial no. 97, *National Women's Trade Union League of America, Life and Labor Bulletin* (10 vols., 1922–1932), http://books.google.com/books?id=5urmAAAAMAAJ&ots=adX8Qofm5k&dq=life%20and%201abor%20national%20women's%20trade%20union%20UL&pg=PA1#v=onepage&q&f=false ("Recent re-discovery of household workers"); Smith, "Regulating Paid Household Work," 851; "Unionizing the 'Hired Girl,'" *Literary Digest,* May 9, 1931, 23, www.unz.org/Pub/Literary Digest-1931may09–00023 ("Magna Carta").

19. "Unionizing the 'Hired Girl,'" 23.

20. Ella Baker and Marvel Cooke, "The Bronx Slave Market," *Crisis* 42, no. 11 (1930): 330–32; Wilson, *Segregated Scholars,* 173–214; Palmer, *Domesticity and Dirt,* 111–35; Gore, *Radicalism at the Crossroads,* 15–45, 106–12; McDuffie, *Sojourning for Freedom,* 3–6, 10–16.

21. Quotes in "Domestic Workers Problems Are Discussed"; Minutes of Meeting of Committee on Household Service Problems, October 17, 1933, box 4, folder 1, FC.

22. Minutes of Meeting of Committee on Household Service Problems, October 17, 1933, p. 2, box 4, folder 1, FC; Clark to Edna Gellhorn, October 20, 1933, series 3, box 10, folder 20, EG ("to adopt"); Edna Gellhorn to Father William N. Markoe, October 24, 1933, series 4, box 1, folder 9, SLUL; 1933 Annual Report, p. 2, series 4, box 6, folder 82, ibid.; March 1932 Monthly Report, series 4, box 4, folder 42, ibid.; Twentieth Anniversary, 1919 to 1938, UL of St. Louis, St. Louis Urban League Papers, s0093, box 1, folder UL of St. Louis, Annual Reports, 1938–1942, 1944–1945, 1957, 1960, 1964–1970, 1972, 1974, SHSM ("the first minimum standard").

23. January 1934 Report, p. 2, series 4, box 4, folder 46, 1934, SLUL; Annual Report of Industrial Secretary, 1934, p. 2, folder 83 ("naturally"; "willing to work for less"; "We emphasized"); UL Placement Service and the Transfer of This Responsibility to the State Employment Service, n.d., series 4, box 1, folder 16, ibid. ("This agreement was ignored"); 1939 Annual Report, series 4, box 6, folder 89, ibid. ("the [standard] rates"); Collier to Buckner, March 13, 1934, series 4, box 1, folder 10, ibid.; and Collier to Clark, March 13, 1934, series 4, box 1, folder 18, SLUL; Clark to Collier, October 30, 1933, series 3, box 10, folder 20, EG; Lang, *Grassroots at the Gateway,* 36.

24. 1933 Annual Report, p. 2, series 4, box 6, folder 82, SLUL ("The action"); Labor Program, by Charles A. Collier, Industrial Secretary, p. 8, series 4, box 6, folder 83, ibid.; December 1933 Report, p. 2, series 4, box 4, folder 43, ibid. ("further action").: Charles Collier, Report of Industrial Secretary, February 1936, series 4, box 4, folder 50, ibid; Lang, *Grassroots at the Gateway,* 36; Ransby, *Baker and the Black Freedom Movement.*

25. Some Observations of Women's Employment, 1943, series 4, box 6, folder 93, SLUL ("petty faults"); Charles Collier, Report of Industrial Secretary, February 1936, series 4, box 4, folder 50, ibid; Ava Simmons to Clark, October 4, 1937, series 1, box 9, folder 19, ibid.; Report of the Industrial Secretary, May 1936, series 4, box 4, folder 50, ibid. ("The girls were not justified"; "sometimes Negro employees"); Report of the Industrial Secretary, April 1936, series 4, box 4, folder 50, p. 2, ibid. ("a program"); Collier, Report of Industrial Secretary, 1936 all, p. 2, ibid.; and June 1935 Report of the Industrial Secretary, p. 2, series 4, box 4, folder 48 ("some real strength"; "a nucleus of the formation"), ibid.; Clark-Lewis, *Living In, Living Out,* 37.

26. Annual Report of the Urban League of St. Louis for the Year 1933, p.

5, SHSM; Suggestions for Elimination of Domestic Employment Load, series 4, box 1, General Correspondence 1949, SLUL; Plan for Setting into Our Industrial Department a Very Minimum Cost Charge, series 4, box 1, folder 16, ibid.; Clark to Mrs. William Scarlett, June 15, 1942, series 4, box 1, folder 16, ibid.; Leah V. R. Scarlett to Clark, June 6, 1942, ibid.; Clark to Jewish Employment & Vocational Service, June 6, 1942, ibid.; UL Placement Service and the Transfer of This Responsibility to the State Employment Service, n.d., ibid.; Industrial Committee Minutes, June 9, 1949, series 4, box 1, folder 23, SLUL; A Review of the Program of the St. Louis Urban League, Health and Welfare Council Social Conditions, 1948, SHSM; Cohen, *Making a New Deal,* 2–9; Fine and Gordon, "Strengthening Labor Standards Enforcement."

27. 1937 Report, p. 3, Urban League Papers, series 4, box 6, folder Annual Report, Industrial Secretary, 1937, SLUL ("household employment"); Arnold B. Walker, "Household Employment Conference (Urban League)," p. 3, Annual Report of Industrial Secretary, January 8, 1942, series 4, box 6, Annual Reports, Industrial Secretary, Field Industrial Secretary, Women's Division, 1941, ibid.; "A Digest of Fields Explored and Services Given by the Urban League of St. Louis: During Twenty-Five Years—1918–1943," 1–4, n.d., box 15, folder 5, Mary T. Hall Papers, Missouri History Museum, St. Louis ("not one"); "What Happened to the Domestic Servant?" *Bulletin of the Urban League of St. Louis,* 24, No. 2 (1943), p. 4, box 14, folder 1, ibid. ("irate"; "go begging for days"); 1941 Annual Report, page 3, series 4, box 6, folder Annual Reports, Industrial Secretary, Field Industrial Secretary, Women's Division, 1941, SLUL ("mad scramble").

28. "What Happened to the Domestic Servant?"; "Some Observations of Women's Employment, 1943," p. 1, series 4, box 6, Annual Reports, Industrial Secretary, Field Secretary, 1943, SLUL; Anderson, "Last Hired, First Fired," 82; Santamarina, *Belabored Professions;* Brown-Nagin, *Courage to Dissent.*

29. 1941 Annual Report, p. 3, series 4, box 6, folder Annual Reports, Industrial Secretary, Field Industrial Secretary, Women's Division, 1941, SLUL; Voluntary Agreement—Household Employment, n.d., FC.

30. "Tentative Draft of Household Standards in St. Louis," St. Louis, Missouri, n.d., box 4, folder 1, FC.

31. 1941 Annual Report, p. 4, series 4, box 6, folder Annual Reports, Industrial Secretary, Field Industrial Secretary, Women's Division, 1941, SLUL.

32. "Suggestions for Elimination of Domestic Employment Load," series 4, box 1, General Correspondence 1949, SLUL; "Plan for Setting into Our Industrial Department a Very Minimum Cost Charge," series 4, box 1, General Correspondence, 1942, ibid.; Clark to Mrs. William Scarlett, June 15, 1942, ibid.; Leah V. R. Scarlett to Clark, June 6, 1942, ibid.; Clark to Jewish Employment & Vocational Service, June 6, 1942, ibid.; "Urban League Placement Service and the Transfer of This Responsibility to the State Employment Service," n.d.,

ibid.; Industrial Committee Minutes, June 9, 1949, series 4, box 1, folder Industrial Committee Minutes, Agenda, Members, 1941–1949, SLUL;; "Local U. League Made 411 Job Placement," *St. Louis American,* September 17, 1954; for a notion of "incrementalism" useful in understanding black women domestics' approach to labor activism, particularly how steady changes over a long period led to key shifts in black women's employment by the period of World War II, see Kessler-Harris, *Out to Work;* and Alice Kessler-Harris, "'Not a Man's Union': Women Teamsters in the United States during the 1940s and 1950s," *Journal of Women's History* 24 (Autumn 2001): 169–92.

33. "Need for Domestic Help Grows," *St. Louis Argus,* March 3, 1950.

3. "The Fight against Economic Slavery"

1. "Need for Domestic Help Grows"; "Housewives League History," History of the St. Louis Housewives League, St. Louis Housewives League (s0155), Manuscript Collection, State Historical Society of Missouri, SHSM; "Brief History of the National Housewives' League of America, Inc.," 43rd Annual Meeting Program of the National Housewives' League in St. Louis, Missouri, 1980, St. Louis Housewives League Scrapbook (s0155), Manuscript Collection, ibid.; quote in "A Housewive's Organization," *St. Louis Argus,* September 22, 1933; Greenberg, *Or Does It Explode,* 116–17; Hine, "Housewives' League of Detroit."

2. Arnold B. Walker, Woolworth 5 & 10 Store Memo, June 20, 1940, series 4, box 11, folder 1, SLUL; Chatelain, *South Side Girls,* 171 ("used girls' employment"), 128–29, 116–18; Mitchell, *Righteous Propagation.*

3. Anne Valk, "Housewives' League," in Corbett and Seematter, *In Her Place,* 258–60.

4. Hine, "Housewives' League of Detroit"; Dowden-White, *Groping toward Democracy,* 248–52; Greenberg, *Or Does It Explode,* 7–8, 114, 116, 117, 119, 138, 139; Lang, *Grassroots at the Gateway,* 38–39; quotes in John A. Davis, "We Win the Right to Fight for Jobs," *Opportunity* 5 (August 1938): 230–31.

5. "Housewives League History," s0155, SHSM ("to do all"; "the first to adopt"; "the need of building"); Young, *Your St. Louis and Mine,* 54, 79; Valk, "Housewives' League," 259.

6. "House-wives League Rally Song," series 1, subseries 22, box 7, folder 27, SLUL; "A Housewive's Organization," *Argus,* September 22, 1933; Roediger, "Making Solidarity Uneasy," 225, 226 ("brought together").

7. Valk, "Housewives' League," 259.

8. Samuel P. Bills, "Fleshpots of St. Louis," *St. Louis Argus,* June 7, 1940, series 4, box 11, folder 1, SLUL ("without saying a word"); "Chicago Whip Editor Speaks to Big Crowd," *St. Louis Argus,* May 1, 1931 ("The uniting"; "large and enthusiastic crowd"; "Now is the time"), series 1: subseries 22, box 7, folder 27, ibid.; "St. Louis Housewives League," *St. Louis Argus,* May 1, 1931, series 1:

subseries 22, box 7, folder 27, ibid.; "Housewives League to Hold Meeting May 6," *St. Louis Argus,* May 1, 1931, series 1: subseries 22, box 7, folder 27, ibid.; "Housewives League," *St. Louis Argus,* March 4, 1932, series 1: subseries 22, box 7, folder 27, ibid.; "Housewives League," *St. Louis Argus,* May 15, 1931," series 1, subseries 22, box 7, folder 27, ibid.; "Housewives League History," s0155, SHSM.

9. "Housewives League History," History of the St. Louis Housewives League, St. Louis Housewives League (s0155), Manuscript Collection, State Historical Society of Missouri, SHSM; "Brief History of the National Housewives' League of America, Inc.," 43rd Annual Meeting Program of the National Housewives' League in St. Louis, Missouri, 1980, St. Louis Housewives League Scrapbook (s0155), ibid.

10. "History of the Colored Clerks' Circle," n.d., p. 1, series 2, box 4, folder 10, SLUL ("Economic pressure"; "the unwillingness"; "a city wide demand"); Amended Articles of Agreement of Colored Clerks Circle Association, p. 1, October 1941, series 4, box 11, folder 1, ibid.; Colored Clerks' Circle Letter to Black Churches, n.d., ibid. ("the fight"; "the Negro").

11. The Constitution of the Colored Clerks' Circle, n.d., pp. 1, 5, 6, series 4, box 11, folder 1, SLUL.

12. Ibid.; "History of the Colored Clerks' Circle," pp. 1 ("grew almost overnight"), 2, 5 ("the membership"), 6, 7, series 2, box 4, folder 10, SLUL; Colored Clerks' Circle Membership Roll, n.d., series 4, box 11, folder 1, ibid.; Colored Clerks' Circle Letter to Black Churches, n.d., ibid.

13. Young, *Your St. Louis and Mine,* 54, 79; History of the Colored Clerks' Circle, pp. 1, 2, 3, series 2, box 4, folder 10, SLUL ("no partiality"; "the person best qualified"); Stanley High, "Black Omens," *Saturday Evening Post,* June 4, 1938, p. 37; Colored Clerks' Circle Letter to Black Churches, n.d., series 4, box 11, folder 1, SLUL ("thirty days").

14. History of the Colored Clerks' Circle, p. 1, series 2, box 4, folder 10, SLUL; Arnold B. Walker, Woolworth 5 & 10 Cent Store Memo, June 17, 1940, series 4, box 11, folder 1, ibid. ("a small room"); Colored Clerks' Circle to Friend, n.d., ibid. ("It is our policy"; "Negro dressed"; "Do not be misled").

15. Colored Clerks' Circle to Friend, n.d., series 4, box 11, folder 1, SLUL ("We are not union"; "the dangerous union obstacle"); Sidney R. Williams and Arnold B. Walker, "Pressure Tactics," *Opportunity* 7 (December 1939): 368 ("through workers' organizations"); Colored Clerks' Circle Letter to Black Churches, n.d., series 4, box 11, folder 1, SLUL ("Don't walk"); History of the Colored Clerks' Circle, p. 1, series 2, box 4, folder 10, ibid.; Lang, *Grassroots at the Gateway,* 36, 37 ("broad swath").

16. High, "Black Omens," 37 ("white-owned"); History of the Colored Clerks' Circle, p. 5, series 2, box 4, folder 10, SLUL ("This protest"); Sidney R. Williams to B. T. McGraw, October 20, 1940, ibid. ("have lead numerous strug-

gles"); Colored Clerks' Circle Letter to Black Churches, n.d., series 4, box 11, folder 1, ibid. ("In 1939"); History of the Colored Clerks' Circle, pp. 1, 2, series 2, box 4, folder 10, ibid.

17. For a history of black protest politics, see, for example, Bates, *Pullman Porters and Protest Politics;* Williams and Walker, "Pressure Tactics," 368 ("new technique"; "Today there is rapidly developing"; "outmoded racial 'line'"; "shocked them"; "Mass pressure"); Williams to McGraw, October 30, 1940, series 4, box 11, folder 1, SLUL ("who fail to agree"); High, "Black Omens," 37.

18. Williams to McGraw, October 30, 1940, series 4, box 11, folder 1, SLUL. On the intersection of black activism and the New Deal, see, for example, Sullivan, *Days of Hope;* and Sitkoff, *New Deal for Blacks.*

19. Colored Clerks' Circle Letter to Black Churches, n.d., series 4, box 11, folder 1, SLUL.

20. Ibid.

21. Williams and Walker, "Pressure Tactics," 368; Arnold B. Walker to Frank M. Jones, December 4, 1937, series 4, box 11, folder 1, SLUL; Walker to Colored Clerks' Circle Executive Council, December 8, 1939, ibid.; Walker to Herman Webb, April 10, 1939, ibid.; Dowden-White, *Groping toward Democracy,* 248–52.

22. History of the Colored Clerks' Circle, p. 1, series 2, box 4, folder 10, SLUL.

23. T. D. McNeal interview by Richard Resh and Franklin Rother, Black Community Leaders Project (T-024), July 22, 1970, Manuscript Collection, SHSM; Colored Clerks' Circle Membership Roll, n.d., series 4, box 11, folder 1, SLUL; Lucander, *Winning the War for Democracy,* 137.

4. "Riveting the Sinews of Democracy"

1. Loretta Owens, "FEPC to Rule on Injustices," *St. Louis Argus,* August 3, 1944.

2. Ibid.; TDM; Lang, *Grassroots at the Gateway,* 65–66; Lucander, *Winning the War for Democracy,* 85, 137; Kersten, *Race, Jobs, and the War.*

3. "Negroes Decry Discrimination," *St. Louis Globe-Democrat,* August 15, 1942, TDM ("equal rights now"; "promised equal rights"); "12,000 Hear Randolph at St. Louis Meet," *Chicago Defender,* August 1942, ibid.; Sally Parham quoted in Dona Blakeley, "Woman's Role in March on Washington Movement," *Chicago Defender,* August 22, 1942, ibid. Unidentified Woman to the March on Washington Committee, March 16, 1944, ibid.

4. "Ordinance Plant Strike Spreads," *St. Louis Globe Democrat,* May 11, 1943, TDM; Howard B. Woods, "6,000 in St. Louis to Lose War Jobs," *Chicago Defender,* July 7, 1945, ibid.; quotes in 1943 Annual Report of the Indus-

trial Secretary, p. 1, series 4, box 6, folder Annual Reports, Industrial Secretary, Women's Division, 1943, SLUL; "1000 Face Layoffs at St. Louis Arms Plant," *Chicago Defender,* November 27, 1943, TDM.

5. Howard B. Woods, "17,000 St. Louis Women Jobless as Racial Barriers Prevent Hiring," *Chicago Defender,* May 6, 1944 ("With the country"; "acute"); "1000 Face Layoffs at St. Louis Arms Plant," *Chicago Defender,* November 27, 1943, TDM; 1943 Annual Report of the Industrial Secretary, p. 2, series 4, box 6, Annual Reports, Industrial Secretary, Women's Division, 1943, SLUL ("dropped everything"); 1943 in Review, August and September, p. 5, Annual Report of the Industrial Secretary, 1943, series 4, box 6, Annual Reports, Industrial Secretary, Women's Division, Women's Field Secretary, ibid.; Honey, *Bitter Fruit;* Shockley, *"We, Too, Are Americans";* "NAACP Letter States Bias Exists at St. Louis Plant," *Pittsburgh Courier,* March 6, 1943, TDM ("It is common knowledge").

6. "March Committee Asks Women to Fight for Jobs," n.p., n.d., TDM ("Pointing out"); "Young Women with Factory Experiences," n.p., n.d., ibid. ("young women with factory experience"); March on Washington Committee to Black Churches, July 11, 1944, ibid. ("Women workers wanted"; "new rules of War Manpower Commission"); "Job Situation for Women Here Serious," n.p., n.d., pp. 1–2, ibid. ("use mass picketing"; "face the necessity"; "There is no other city"; "all race-minded individuals"); Roy A. Hoglund to Wagner Electric Corporation, June 28, 1944, FEPC Records, RG 228, Closed Cases, 1943–1945, box 5, folder Wagner Electric Corporation, 9-BR-157, St. Louis, MO, Ollie Haynes, National Archives, Kansas City, MO ("because of the considerable number"); Wagner Electric Corporation, Case 9-BR-157 and 171, June 23, 1944, p. 4, ibid.; "NAACP Letter States Bias Exists at St. Louis Plant," *Pittsburgh Courier,* March 6, 1943, TDM.

7. Fair Employment Practices Commission, House of Representatives, Committee on Labor, Statement of David M. Grant, June 6, 1944, Washington, DC, g3, g23, g7, 76, 95–96, TDM.

8. "Racial Complaint against 4 More Firms Taken Up," *St. Louis Post-Dispatch,* August 2, 1944, TDM.

9. Loretta Owens, "FEPC to Rule on Injustices," *St. Louis American,* August 3, 1944, TDM; "Inquiry Opens Today in Negro Charges of Discrimination," *St. Louis Globe-Democrat,* August 1, 1944, ibid; "Negroes Tell of Job Seeking at Amertorp," n.p., n.d., ibid.

10. United States of America Executive Office of the President's Committee on Fair Employment Practice, Notice of Hearing, Case no. 61, FEPC Records, RG 228, Closed Cases, 1943–1945, box 1, folder Amtertorp Corporation, 9-BR-164, St. Louis, MO, Thelma Shuford, et. al., National Archives, Kansas City, MO; Bussman's Manufacturing Company, Case no. 9-BR-172, FEPC Records, RG 228, Closed Cases, 1943–1945, box 1, folder Bussman's Manufacturing

Company, 9-BR-172, St. Louis, MO, ibid.; Albertine Burrill Affidavit, June 20, 1944, FEPC Records, RG 228, Closed Cases, 1943–1945, box 5, folder Wagner Electric Corporation, 9-BR-157, St. Louis, MO, Ollie Haynes, ibid.; S. R. Redmond to Fair Employment Practice Committee, February 9, 1944, FEPC Records, RG 228, Closed Cases, 1943–1945, box 1, folder Carter Carburetor Co., 9-BR-141, St. Louis, MO, March on Washington Movement, ibid.; Vora L. Thompson FEPC Complaint, February 16, 1944, ibid.; Vora L. Thompson Affidavit, St. Louis, Missouri, 1944, ibid.; Pearl S. Maddox Affidavit, ibid.

11. Loretta Owens, "FEPC to Rule on Injustices," *St. Louis American,* August 3, 1944, TDM ("I had never worked"; "equally proportioned"); "Racial Complaint against 4 More Firms Taken Up," *St. Louis Post-Dispatch,* August 2, 1944, TDM; Owens, "FEPC to Rule on Injustices"; Lucander, *Winning the War for Democracy,* 85; Lang, *Grassroots at the Gateway,* 50.

12. "That St. Louis Woman with Machine Is New Wartime Thing," n.p., n.d., TDM; "The Sinews of Democracy at Curtiss-Wright," n.p., n.d. ("slacks and overalls"); "Curtiss-Wright Employing Negro Women in Skilled Jobs," *St. Louis Star-Times,* February 5, 1943, ibid.; "St. Louis Negro Women Building Warplanes," *St. Louis Post-Dispatch,* February 5, 1943, ibid.; "Employees of Curtiss-Wright Plant Receive Praise," *St. Louis American,* February 4, 1943, ibid.; Arnold B. Walker, January 6, 1943, 1942 Annual Report of Industrial Secretary, p. 3, series 4, box 6, folder Annual Report, Industrial Secretary, Women's Division, 1942, SLUL.

13. Ollie Haynes, FEPC Complaint, Filed February 16, 1944, Case Number 9-BR-154, FEPC Records, RG 228, Active Cases, 1943–1946, box 1, folder Bell Telephone Company, 9-BR-1154, St. Louis, MO, Mrs. Ollie Haynes, National Archives, Kansas City, MO; Annie Dove Bizzle, FEPC Complaint of Discrimination, Filed April 13, 1945, FEPC Records, RG 228, Active Cases, 1943–1946, box 1, folder U.S. Employment Service, 9-GR-1490, St. Louis, MO, Complaint Visit, Annie Bizzle, et. al., ibid.

14. Candace Little, FEPC Complaint, January 29, 1945, Case Number 9-BR-1459, FEPC Records, RG 228, Closed Cases, 1943–1945, box 3, folder McQuay-Norris Manufacturing Company, 9-BR-1459, St. Louis, MO, Complaint Visit, Mary Little, et. al., National Archives, Kansas City, MO; Mary Little, ibid.; Thelma Shuford FEPC Complaint, Filed March 6, 1964, Case Number 9-BR-172, FEPC Records, RG 228, Closed Cases, 1943–1945, box 1, folder Bussman's Manufacturing Company, 9-BR-1172, St. Louis, MO, Thelma Shuford, ibid.; Modestine Thorton Affidavit, St. Louis, Missouri, June 15, 1944, ibid.; Geneva Coleman, FEPC Complaint, October 17, 1944, Case Number, 9-BR-417, FEPC Records, RG 228, Active Cases, 1943–1946, box 1, folder Wagner Electric Corporation, 9-BR-1499, St. Louis, MO, Geneva Coleman, National Archives, Kansas City; Wagner Electric, Case Number 9-BR-171, March 29, 1944, FEPC Records, RG 228, Closed Cases, 1943–1945, box 5,

folder Wagner Electric Corporation, 9-BR-157, St. Louis, MO, Ollie Haynes, ibid.

15. Mary Johnson to Franklin D. Roosevelt, April 4, 1945, FEPC Records, RG 228, Active Cases, 1943–1946, box 1, folder U.S. Employment Service, 9-BR-1490, St. Louis, MO, Complaint Visit, Annie Bizzle et al; Hattie Mann to Franklin D. Roosevelt, December 11, 1944, FEPC Records, RG 228, Closed Cases, 1943–1945, box 4, folder U.S. Cartridge Company, 9-BR-1449, St. Louis, MO, Complaint, Multiple Complainants, National Archives, Kansas City, MO.

16. Ethel Mattingly to Franklin D. Roosevelt, October 24, 1944, FEPC Records, RG 228, Closed Cases, 1943–1945, box 4, folder U.S. Cartridge Company, 9-BR-1449, St. Louis, MO, Complaint, Multiple Complainants, National Archives, Kansas City, MO; Annie Dove Bizzle and Arlean Ward to Franklin D. Roosevelt, February 26, 1945, ibid.; Enola Sampa to Franklin D. Roosevelt, April 4, 1945, ibid.; Hattie Mann (January 3, 1945), Annie Dove Bizzle (March 21, 1945), Arlean Ward (March 21, 1945), Enola Sampa (April 26, 1945) Complaints to FEPC, ibid.

17. Martha MacGregor, "George Washington Carver Prize Novel," *New York Post,* February 19, 1946, series 5, vol. 9, *Mrs. Palmer's Honey,* May 1945–April 1946, FC.

18. "Briefly Notes," n.p., n.d., series 5, vol. 9, *Mrs. Palmer's Honey,* May 1945–April 1946, FC; D. S., "The Metamorphosis of Honey Hoop," *Christian Science Monitor,* February 26, 1946, ibid. ("when the urgency").

19. Book review of *Mrs. Palmer's Honey, Saturday Review of Literature,* February 9, 1946, series 5, vol. 9, *Mrs. Palmer's Honey,* May 1945–April 1946, FC; *New York Times* Best Sellers List, March 3, 10, 17, 24, 31, 1946, ibid.; "What America Is Reading," *New York Herald Tribune,* April 7, 1946, ibid.; "Fannie Cook Receives George Washington Carver Award," *Publishers Weekly,* February 23, 1948, ibid.

20. D. S., "The Metamorphosis of Honey Hoop," *Christian Science Monitor,* February 26, 1946, series 5, vol. 9, *Mrs. Palmer's Honey,* May 1945–April 1946, FC ("union organizers"); "From Where I Sit," *Saturday Review of Literature* (Doubleday, n.d.), 27, ibid. ("an outstanding work"); Martha MacGregor, "George Washington Carver Prize Novel," *New York Post,* February 19, 1946, ibid. ("more tract than novel"); "Briefly Notes" n.p., n.d., ibid. ("her almost neurotic loyalties").

21. Betty Burnett, *St. Louis at War,* 8, 20, 21; 1941 Annual Report of the Industrial Secretary, pp. 2, 3, series 4, box 6, Annual Reports, Industrial Secretary, Field Industrial Secretary, Women's Division, 1941, SLUL; Annual Report, Employment for Women, pp. 1, 2, series 4, box 4, ibid.; 1942 Annual Report of Industrial Secretary, series 4, box 6, Annual Report, Industrial Secretary, Industrial Field Secretary, Women's Division, Women's Field Secretary, 1942, ibid.;

1942 Industrial Report, Field Work (Women's Department), 1942, St. Louis Urban League Records, series 4, box 6, ibid.; Wilkerson, *Warmth of Other Suns.*

22. Burnett, *St. Louis at War,* 8, 20, 21; 1941 Annual Report of the Industrial Secretary, pp. 2, 3, series 4, box 6, p. 1, Annual Reports, Industrial Secretary, Field Industrial Secretary, Women's Division, 1941, SLUL ("hoped that the defense boom"; "the picture remains"); Annual Report, Employment for Women, pp. 1, 2, series 4, box 4, ibid.; 1942 Annual Report of Industrial Secretary, series 4, box 6, p. 1, Annual Report, Industrial Secretary, Industrial Field Secretary, Women's Division, Women's Field Secretary, 1942, ibid. ("Since the outbreak"); 1942 Industrial Report, Field Work (Women's Department), 1942, St. Louis Urban League Records, series 4, box 6, ibid.; Wilkerson, *Warmth of Other Suns.*

23. "War Plant Firings Stir Negro Protest," *St. Louis Post-Dispatch,* June 16, 1942, TDM; "Negro Protest March Set at Ordinance Plant," *St. Louis Star-Times,* June, 18, 1942, ibid.; "200 Reported Out at Small Arms Plant," *St. Louis Argus,* June 12, 1942, ibid.; "Protest Parade in St. Louis," *Pittsburgh Courier,* June 25, 1942, ibid.; "Protest Gets Negro Unit at Arms Plant," *Chicago Defender,* June 27, 1942, ibid.; "Training to Begin for All-Negro Ammunition Unit," *St. Louis Post-Dispatch,* June 21, 1942, ibid.; "War Plant Here to Hire Negro Unit," *St. Louis Globe Democrat,* June 21, 1942, ibid.; "Small Arms Plant Demonstration Gets Results," *St. Louis American,* June 25, 1942, ibid.; Statement of David Grant, Fair Employment Practices Committee on Labor, House of Representatives, June 6, 1944, Washington, DC, pp. 79–80, ibid.; Rosemary Feurer, "WWII and the Remaking of the St. Louis Economy and the St. Louis Working Class," in Feurer, *St. Louis Labor History Tour,* 33; Burnett, *St. Louis at War,* 22–23.

24. T. D. McNeal, March on Washington Committee, to Roy A. Englund, January 15, 1944, FEPC Records, RG 228, General Records, 1943–1946, box 3, folder St. Louis Unit, March on Washington Movement, 1943–1944, National Archives, Kansas City, MO; Irene Barnett Mason Affidavit, St. Louis, Missouri, 1944, FEPC Records, RG 228, Closed Cases, 1943–1945, box 1, folder Carter Carburetor Co, 9-BR-141, St. Louis, MO, March on Washington Movement, ibid.; Helen Patterson Affidavit, ibid.

25. Owens, "FEPC to Rule on Injustices," *St. Louis American,* August 3, 1944, TDM; "Negroes Say They Sought Jobs but Were Not Hired," *St. Louis Post-Dispatch,* August 2, 1944, ibid.; "Negroes Tell of Job Seeking at Amertorp," n.p., n.d., ibid.; quotes in "Negro Hiring Practice 'Set by Community,'" *St. Louis Star-Times,* August 2, 1944, ibid.; "Fair Practices Session Here Reveal Firms Willing to Cooperate in 'All-American' Plan," *St. Louis American,* August 3, 1944, ibid.

26. 1944 Annual Report of the Industrial Secretary, pp. 1, 2 ("slightest intention"), series 4, box 6, folder 94, SLUL; January 1945 Report, p. 2 ("share[d]

equally"), February 1945, and March 1945, St. Louis Urban League Records, series 4, box 5, folder 13, ibid.

27. July 1945 Report, p. 2, series 4, box 5, folder Monthly Report, Women's Division, Field Contacts, 1945 Jan.–Mar, June, July, Dec., SLUL; June 1945 Report, p. 1 ("industrial jobs are practically closed"; "forced to return"), ibid.; December 1945 Report, p. 2 ("The average peace time"), ibid.; 1944 Annual Report of the Industrial Secretary, p. 1, series 4, box 6, Annual Reports, Industrial Secretary, Women's Division, 1944, Highlights of Annual Reports, 1926–43, ibid.; Bertha Brown, FEPC Affidavit, July 10, 1944, FEPC Records, RG 228, Closed Cases, 1943–1945, box 4, folder United States Cartridge Company, 9-BR-69, St. Louis, Missouri, National Archives, Kansas City, MO; Emilee T. Lee Complaint, July 13, 1941, ibid.; Ollie M. Haynes Complaint, July 13, 1944, ibid.; Emilee T. Lee Affidavit against Wagner Electric Company, June 15, 1944, FEPC Records, RG 228, Closed Cases, 1943–1945, box 5, folder Wagner Electric Corporation, 9-BR-157, St. Louis, MO, Ollie Haynes, National Archives, Kansas City, MO.

28. Tyson, *Radio Free Dixie*, 29; Ransby, *Baker and the Black Freedom Movement*; Cobble, *Other Women's Movement*; McGuire, *Dark End of the Street*.

29. "Group Visits Department Store Here," *St. Louis Argus*, May 19, 1944; "Silent Protests Staged by Loyal American Citizens in Downtown Department Stores," *St. Louis Argus*, July 14, 1944; Lucander, *Winning the War for Democracy*; Lang, *Grassroots at the Gateway*.

30. "Mrs. Pearl Maddox Answers T. D. McNeal," *St. Louis Argus*, November 17, 1944; Lang, *Grassroots at the Gateway*, 65–68; Lucander, *Winning the War for Democracy*, 141.

31. Greenberg, *Or Does It Explode*, 116–17; Hine, "Housewives League of Detroit"; High, "Black Omens"; Young, *Your St. Louis and Mine*, 54; History of the Colored Clerks' Circle, n.d., series 2, box 4, folder 10, SLUL; Dowden-White, *Groping toward Democracy*, 248–49.

5. "Beneath Our Dignity"

1. John T. Clark to "My Dear," March 17, 1943, St. Louis Urban League Records, series 4, box 1, folder 17, SLUL; Clark to "Factory Worker," March 30, 1943, ibid.

2. Boris, "'You Wouldn't Want One of 'Em'"; Lipsitz, *Rainbow at Midnight*; Cobble, *Other Women's Movement*, 3; Zieger, *Jobs and Freedom*; Shockley, "*We, Too, Are Americans*"; Honey, *Bitter Fruit*.

3. Denning, *Cultural Front*; Biondi, *Stand and Fight*; Griffin, *Harlem Nocturne*; Mullen, *Popular Fronts*; Santamarina, *Belabored Professions*; Lipsitz, *Rainbow at Midnight*; Kelley, *Race Rebels*; Fones-Wolf, "Industrial Unionism and Labor Movement Culture," 25; Gore, *Radicalism at the Crossroads*; McDuffie,

Sojourning for Freedom; Washington, *Other Blacklist;* McCallum, "Gospel of Black Unionism," 3; Redmond, *Anthem,* 141–78.

4. 1940 Annual Report, St. Louis Urban League Papers, series 4, box, 4, folder Annual Report, SLUL; "Garment Industry," 10/23/37, series 4, box 4, folder Monthly Report, Industrial Secretary, 1937, ibid.; October 1938 Report of the Industrial Secretary, p. 2, series 4, box 5, folder 1, ibid.; "Labor Relations," p. 3, February 1945 Report, series 4, box 5, Monthly Report, Women's Division, Field Contacts, 1945, ibid.; Reginald A. Johnson to Mr. Kessler, October 15, 1930, series 4, box 6, folder 20, ibid.; "New St. Louis Laundry Union Calls Meeting," August 9, 1933, *St. Louis Post-Dispatch;* "The Strike of Needle Crafts," *St. Louis Globe-Democrat,* September 5, 1933, sl 39, folder ILGWU: Programs of Theatricals, 1933–1975, Photographs, Newspapers, ILGWU Papers, SHSM; Clark to Edna Gellhorn, September 8, 1933, series 1, box 9, folder 1933, SLUL.

5. "Textile and Garment Industries," p. 4, series 4, box 6, folder 1941, SLUL ("Necessity as a result of the war"); "1941 in Review," p. 1, Textile and Garment Industries, series 4, box 6, folder Annual Reports, Women's Division, 1941, ibid.; "Garment Industry," *Urban League of St. Louis Industrial News,* vol. 25, November 1943, no. 8, series 1, box 9, folder 35, ibid.; Richard H. Jefferson to Clarence E. Mitchell, September 21, 1943, series 4, box 1, folder 73, ibid.; 1943 Annual Report of the Industrial Secretary, p. 3 ("rushed in"), series 4, box 6, folder Annual Reports, 1943, ibid.; 1944 Annual Report, pp. 1–2, series 4, box 6, folder Annual Reports, Women's Division, Highlights of Annual Reports, 1926–43, ibid.; "Labor Relations," p. 3, St. Louis Urban League Records, February 1945 Report, series 4, box 5, folder Monthly Report, Women's Division, Field Contacts, 1945, ibid.

6. Portnoy Garment Company Log, January 20, 1944 ("is a most promising"; "practically no exits"), series 4, box 6, folder Portnoy Garment Company, 1943–50, SLUL; Belle-McKay Dress Company Log, April 13, 1944 ("negative philosophy"), August 14, 1944 ("failed and have failed"), and November 27, 1944 ("rises and subsides"), series 4, box 6, folder Belle McKay Company, 1943–48, ibid.; "ILGWU, AFL, Installation of Local 516 Report," February 28, 1949, series 4, box 5, folder Monthly Report, Women's Field Secretary, 1949, ibid. ("practically all refused"); Ace Uniform Company Log, March 23, 1945 ("at the rate"), series 4, box 6, folder Ace Uniform Company, 1945–47, ibid.; Kearnes Brothers Dress Company, Incorporated, Log, January 4, 1947 ("An entirely integrated setup"), and July 9, 1947 ("the shop has become"), series 4, box 6, folder Kearns Brothers Dress Company, Inc. 1947, ibid.; "Labor Relations," p. 3 ("As far as it can be ascertained"), February 1945 Report, series 4, box 5, folder Monthly Report, Women's Division, Field Contacts, 1945, ibid.

7. March 1946 Report, p. 2, series 4, box 4, folder Executive Secretary of the Urban League of St. Louis, Monthly Reports, 1946, SLUL; United Cap, Hatters, and Millinery Workers Union Log, October 7, 20, 24; November 22,

December 8, 11, 1944 (all quotes from this report); December 15, 1944; January 5, 27; March 7, 29; June 15, 1945, series 4, box 6, folder United Cap, Hatters, and Millinery Workers Union, AFL, 1944–49, ibid.; Percy Ginsburg, Special Notice, n.d.; Percy Ginsburg to "Gentlemen," August 13, 1945; Julius A. Thomas to Valla Abbington, January 4, 1949, series 4, box 6, folder United Cap, Hatters, and Millinery Workers Union, AFL, 1944–49, ibid.

    8. Leather and Luggage Workers' Union, Local 60 (CIO) Log, series 4, box 6, folder Leather and Luggage Workers Union, Local 60, CIO, 1945, SLUL; Boot and Shoe Workers Union (AFL) Log, March 26, 1946, series 4, box 6, folder Boot and Shoe Workers Union (AFL), 1946–48, ibid.; Abbington to Ben Berk, November 14, 1947; Berk to Abbington, November 19, 1947; Abbington to Berk, January 23 1948, and Berk to Abbington, January 27, 1948, ibid.

    9. Bernard Handbag Manufacturing Company Report, March 20, 1946, series 4, box 6, 1946, folder Bernard Handbag Manufacturing Company, 1946, SLUL; V. Abbington, "International Ladies' Garment Workers Union, A.F. of L., Installation of Local 516," series 4, box 5, Monthly Report, Women's Field Secretary, 1949 January–May, September, ibid.

    10. Day Placements—Women's Division, p. 3 ("called [the] employer," "stole clothes"; "broke employer's perfume bottles"; "refused to follow"), Women's Division, Report of Industrial Secretary, February 1944, series 4, box 5, folder Monthly Report, Industrial Secretary, 1944, all, Jefferson, SLUL; Permanent Placements—Women's Division, p. 3 ("[wanted to give] orders"; "too slow"), Women's Division, Report of Industrial Secretary, February 1944, series 4, box 5, folder Monthly Report, Industrial Secretary, 1944, all, Jefferson, ibid.; March 1944 Report, p. 2 ("laid the employer out"; "fussed with her"), ibid.; Garment Industry, p. 3 ("because the only ones"; "Absenteeism, lateness"), April 1944 and March 1944 Reports, ibid; Hunter, *To 'Joy My Freedom;* Kelley, *Hammer and Hoe;* Kelley, "'Not What We Seem.'"

    11. Portnoy Garment Company Log, January 3, 1944 ("out in front"), March 16, 1945, May 19, 1945 ("the pressure"; "methods used"), series 4, box 6, folder Portnoy Garment Company, 1943–50, SLUL; Belle McKay Company Log, October 22, 1943 ("they feel they are being exploited"), December 2, 1943, January 12, 1944, April 13, 1944, August 1, 14, 22 ("decided [she] didn't like"), 24, 1944, November 3, 27, 1944, January 16, 19, 1945, series 4, box 6, folder Belle McKay Company, 1943–48, ibid.; Abbington to David Portnoy, September 17, 1945, series 4, box 6, folder Portnoy Garment Company, 1943–50, ibid.

    12. Dollies and Birdies Hat Shop Incorporated, May 10, 1944, series 4, box 6, folder Dollie's Birdies Hat Shop Inc., 1944, SLUL; Regal Manufacturing Company Log, January 18, 1945, and June 5, 1945, folder Regal Manufacturing Company, 1945, ibid.; Regal Manufacturing Company Log, June 5, 1945, 1945, ibid.; J. H. Mittaman Hat Company Report, November 17, 1942 ("got

into a heated argument"), April 10, 1943, series 4, box 6, ibid.; "Investigation—
J. H. Mittaman Hat Company, 1407 Washington Avenue, April 1, 1942, series
4, box 6, ibid.

13. J. H. Mittaman Hat Company Log, November 17, 1942, series 4, box 6,
folder Mittaman Millinery Company, 1942–43, SLUL; Lewin and Mathes Company Log, p. 2, July 1944 Report, series 4, box 5, folder Monthly Report, Industrial Secretary, 1944, all, Jefferson, ibid.

14. "Negro Factory Girls Slow to Join Unions," *Urban League of St. Louis
Bulletin* 24, no. 5 (1943): 1, 4, box 14, folder 1, Mary T. Hall Papers, Missouri
History Museum, St. Louis; Ruth Adler Dress Company Log, June 2; August
4, 20; September 2, 7, 1943, series 4, box 6, folder Novelty Frocks, Ruth Adler
Dress Company, 1943–44, SLUL; United Cap, Hatters, and Millinery Workers
Log, March 29, 1945, series 4, box 6, folder United Hatters, Cap, and Millinery
Workers, AFL, 1944–49, ibid.; Bernard Handbag Manufacturing Company Log,
March 20, 1946, series 4, box 6, folder Bernard Handbag Manufacturing Com-
pany, 1946, ibid. ("there are certain privileges").

15. March 1944 Report, series 4, box 5, Monthly Report, Industrial Secretary, 1944, SLUL; 1944 Report of the Industrial Secretary, p. 5, series 4, box 6,
Annual Reports, Women's Division, 1944, ibid.; "Even Results Can Be Obtained
with 'Bottom of the Barrel Labor,'" *St. Louis Urban League Bulletin,* n.d., p. 3;
"Sixteen Points on How to 'Make Good,'" issued by the Industrial Department
of the Urban League, n.d., box 15, folder 5, Mary T. Hall Papers, Missouri History Museum, St. Louis; Clark to Grace Bullard, April 19, 1944, series 4, box 6,
Portnoy Garment Company, 1943–1950, SLUL; Portnoy Garment Company
Report, March 2, 10, 1944, ibid.

16. March 1944 Report, series 4, box 5, Monthly Report, Industrial Secretary, 1944, SLUL; 1944 Report of the Industrial Secretary, p. 5, series 4, box 6,
Annual Reports, Women's Division, 1944, ibid.; February 1945 Report, Factory
Highlights, series 4, box 5, Monthly Report, Women's Division, 1945 Jan.–Mar.,
June, July, Dec., ibid.; "Even Results Can Be Obtained with 'Bottom of the Barrel Labor,'" *St. Louis Urban League Bulletin,* n.d., p. 3 ("the morale"; "they were
unwilling"); Clark to Factory Worker, March 30, 1943, series 4, box 1, folder 17,
ibid. ("so suspicious").; V. D. Abbington, September 17, 1945, series 4, box 6,
Portnoy Garment Company, 1943–1950, ibid.

17. Doris Preisler, KSD, *St. Louis Post-Dispatch* Interview, February 14, 1940,
p. 3 ("self-confidence"), box 1, folder 6, ILGWU-SIUC; "Report of Educational
Dep't, St. Louis, Mo. by Doris Preisler for Five Year Jubilee—Kansas City, Oct.
1939," box 1, folder 5, ibid.; Doris Preisler, "St. Louis an Alma Mater," March,
1, 1939, ibid.; Meyer Perlstein, "Native Intelligence at Work," *St. Louis Garment
Worker* 1, no. ?, Oct. 16, 1939, ibid. ("acquire the knowledge"); Denning, *Cultural Front;* Glen, *Highlander;* Horton and Friere, *We Make the Road by Walking.*

18. Marguerite Martyn, "The New Era for Garment Workers," *St. Louis*

Post Dispatch, December 11, 1935, box 1, folder 5, ILGWU-SIUC ("It would be fine"); "Remembering the 1911 Triangle Factory Fire," Cornell University, Industrial and Labor Relations School, Kheel Center for Labor-Management Documentation and Archives, https://trianglefire.ilr.cornell.edu/primary/songsPlays/StoryOfILGWUEpisodeV.html; Elizabeth Fones-Wolf, *Waves of Opposition: Labor and the Struggle for Democratic Radio* (Urbana: University of Illinois Press, 2006), 2, 21–22, 45–47, 56; "International Ladies' Garment Workers Union," n.p, n.d., Pageant Clippings, box 1, folder 5, ILGWU-SIUC; "Pageant of Unionism Coming to Kansas City Saturday Night, Ang. 29" ("how trade union organization"), ibid.; "This and That from St. Louis" ("The unfortunates"), ibid.; "Justice and Greed in Leading Roles at Union Pageant" ("mark[ed] the first time"), ibid.; "'Surging Forward': A Pageant," ibid.; "Surging Forward to Be Presented Saturday Night," August 28, 1936, ibid.; Dorothy Coleman, "Workers' Theater Movement in St. Louis," *St. Louis Post-Dispatch,* June 8, 1936 ("fundamentally a group project"; "solo dances"), ibid.; "Report of Educational Dep't, St. Louis, Mo. by Doris Preisler for Five Year Jubilee—Kansas City, Oct. 1939," box 1, folder 5, ibid.; "Pageant Begins to Take Form," ILGWU Records, ibid.

19. Clark to "My Dear," March 17, 1943, series 4, box 1, General Correspondence 1943, SLUL; Clark to "Factory Worker," March 30, 1943, ibid.

20. *Tomorrow Must be Ours,* act 1, act 2, April 9–12, 1943, pp. 8, 9, box 8, folder 6, ILGWU-SIUC.

21. Clark to "My Dear," March 17, 1943, St. Louis Urban League Records, series 4, box 1, folder 17, SLUL (all Clark quotes); Clark to "Factory Worker," March 30, 1943, ibid; Sandage, "Marble House Divided"; Arsenault, *Sound of Freedom;* Redmond, *Anthem,* 144.

22. "Let Freedom Swing Again," May 17–18, 1943, including publicity and review, box 8, folder 8, ILGWU-SIUC ("Al Jolson"; "effective song"); "Let Freedom Swing" Playbill, March 8, 9, 15, 16, 1946, ibid.; "The Sharecropper's Song," words and music by Mark Silverstone, n.d., ibid.; "Let Freedom Swing," Script, Lyrics, and Notes, ILGWU Records, ibid.; Redmond, *Anthem,* 99–139.

23. ILGWU Southwest Regional Conference Program, St. Louis, June 1942, box 1, folder 6, ILGWU-SIUC; Micki McElya, *Clinging to Mammy,* p. 13 ("became a way"); "Missouri History: What Is Missouri's State Song?," Records and Archives Division, Missouri Secretary of State, www.sos.mo.gov/archives/history/song.asp; Hunter, *To 'Joy My Freedom;* Kelley, "'Not What We Seem.'"

24. Mississippi Revels Information Sheet/Promotional Material, February 15, 16, 17, 1949, box 1, folder 11, ILGWU-SIUC ("wronged woman"); Doris Preisler to St. Louis Race Relations Commission, ca. February 1949, ibid.; Dudley Murphy and W. C. Handy, *St. Louis Blues,* digital, produced by R.C.A. Gramercy Studios, distributed by Radio Pictures (later RK Productions Distributing Corporation, 1929) ("I hate to see"); "Congratulations Were Extended,"

St. Louis Globe-Democrat, n.d., box 9, folder 4, ILGWU-SIUC; "Valentine Show in the Making," February 14, 1949, *St. Louis Globe-Democrat*, ibid.

25. "To Give 'Mississippi Revels' on Oldtime Showboat," *St. Louis Argus*, February 11, 1949, box 9, folder 4, ILGWU-SIUC; Union Art Students, *St. Louis Post-Dispatch*, December 4, 1949, ibid.

26. Preisler to St. Louis Race Relations Commission, ca. February 1949, box 1, folder 11, ILGWU-SIUC; Doris Preisler, "One Friend's Loving Memories of Rita Oberbeck," box 9, folder 6, ibid.; *St. Louis Garment Worker*, October 16, 1939, box 1, folder 5, ibid.; "To Give 'Mississippi Revels' On Oldtime Showboat," *St. Louis Argus*, February 11, 1949, box 9, folder 4, ibid.; "'St. Louis Blues' on the Riverfront Again," n.d., box 9, folder 2, ibid.

6. "Jobs and Homes . . . Freedom"

1. Odell W. Morris, "Modern Housing to Rise in 'Worst Slum' Area," *St. Louis Argus*, January 6, 1950.

2. Williams, *Politics of Public Housing*; Orleck, *Storming Caesar's Palace*; Hinton, *From the War on Poverty*; Heathcott, "City Quietly Remade," 223; Williams, *Politics of Public Housing*; Orleck, *Storming Caesar's Palace*; Levenstein, *Movement without Marches*; Kelley, *Yo Mama's Disfunktional!*; Nadasen, *Welfare Warriors*.

3. Bussel, *Fighting for Total Person Unionism*.

4. Richard G. Baumhoff, "Progress or Decay? St. Louis Must Choose," *St. Louis Post-Dispatch*, March 5, 1950; U.S. Bureau of the Census, "Table 18: Population of the 100 Largest Urban Places: 1950," https://www.census .gov/population/www/documentation/twps0027/tab18.txt; U.S. Bureau of the Census, "Table 19: Population of the 100 Largest Urban Places: 1960," https://www.census.gov/population/www/documentation/twps0027/tab19 .txt; U.S. Bureau of the Census, Table 20: Population of the 100 Largest Urban Places: 1970," https://www.census.gov/population/www/documentation/ twps0027/tab20.txt; U.S. Bureau of the Census, "Table 21: Population of the 100 Largest Urban Places: 1980," https://www.census.gov/population/www/ documentation/twps0027/tab21.txt; Gordon, *Mapping Decline*, 8–10.

5. David Hepburn, "Shocking St. Louis," *Our World* 5, no. 2 (February 1950): 10–20; "St. Louis Full of Vice, Jim Crow—Our World," *Carolina Times*, January 7, 1950; "Deplore National Mag's Piece on St. Louis, Declare It 'Untrue,'" *St. Louis Argus*, January 13, 1950.

6. Hepburn, "Shocking St. Louis"; "St. Louis Full of Vice"; "Deplore National Mag's Piece."

7. Henry Winfield Wheeler, "Shocking St. Louis: Libelous and Ludicrous," *St. Louis American*, January 19, 1950 ("We challenge them"); "St. Louis Full of Vice"; "Deplore National Mag's Piece" ("If they had said"; "who probably"; "unfortunately much"); "'Our World' Hastily Maligns St. Louis," *St. Louis*

American, January 12, 1950 ("a malicious job"); Howard B. Woods, "2 Women Lawyers Make Impressive Scene in Housing Suit Argument," *St. Louis Argus,* October 8, 1954 ("this city's 'Mr. Civil Rights'").

8. Morris, "Modern Housing to Rise."

9. "Mother, Five Children Face Street Eviction: Woman in Wheelchair, Youngers All under 12," *St. Louis Argus,* February 17, 1950; Morris, "Modern Housing to Rise."

10. "The Second Great Migration," *Overview, in Motion: The African-American Migration Experience,* www.inmotionaame.org/migrations/topic .cfm?migration=9&topic=1 (accessed April 2, 2014); Hepburn, "Shocking St. Louis"; Self, *American Babylon;* Anne Valk, "Women and Postwar St. Louis," in Corbett, *In Her Place,* 283.

11. "Mill Creek Valley," University of Missouri–St. Louis, www.umsl.edu/ virtualstl/phase2/1950/mapandguide/millcreeknode.html (accessed April 7, 2014); "Mill Creek Slum Demolition Work Gets under Way," *St. Louis Post-Dispatch,* February 16, 1959; Harry Wilensky, "Market Street Area Next Site for Slum Clearance, Industrial Redevelopment Is Major Purpose: Section Bounded by Grand, Olive, 20th Street and Railroad Yards," *St. Louis Post-Dispatch,* August 8, 1954; Lang, *Grassroots at the Gateway,* 139–43.

12. "Where Four Died in Explosion and Fire" and "12 Living in House Built for Four Families," *St. Louis American,* January 12, 1950; Otis N. Thompson, "Advisory Committee Awaits Date for First Meeting," *St. Louis Argus,* August 13, 1954.

13. Thompson, "Advisory Committee Awaits Date" ("The visions"); Steve Duncan, "Area Residents Ask Fair Share," *St. Louis Argus,* August 13, 1954 ("We need new buildings"; "so long as 'poor'"); "We Will Wait, and See," *St. Louis Argus,* August 13, 1954 ("Recently"; "there were speeches"); "2 Women Lawyers"; "Suit on Housing Segregation Heard in Federal District Court," *St. Louis Argus,* October 8, 1954; Freeman, *Song of Faith and Hope,* 57–63. "Kinloch Jubilant over Redevelopment Plans," *St. Louis Argus,* June 22, 1956.

14. "38 Percent Occupancy in Low Cost Housing," *St. Louis Argus,* November 5, 1954.

15. "Carr Square" and "Neighborhood Research," in *Through the Eyes of a Child.*

16. Imani Mtendaji, Tape 1: 4, 5–6, 8–9, 10–11, 18–19, 20–21, 21–22; Tape 2: 3–4, 11–12; Tape 3: 4, 10–11, Part 4: 7, 11; Evelyn Jones, Tape 2: 14–15, 18–19, 20; Carol Strickland Ray, Tape 3: 2, 17, all in *Through the Eyes of a Child.*

17. Evelyn Jones, Tape 1: 12–19; Tape 2: 9–10; Tape 3: 1–3, 10–11; Tape 4: 17; Betty Thompson, Tape 1: 15, Tape 2: 9; Carol Strickland Ray, Tape 1: 17; Tape 2: 17, 19; Tape 3: 10, 13–14, all in *Through the Eyes of a Child.*

18. "League Warns of Increasing Area Density," *St. Louis Argus,* January 27, 1950; "Carr Square" and "Neighborhood Research."

19. "Pruitt Nursery Announces Open House for Sunday, April 8 (photo essay)," *St. Louis Argus,* March 16, 1956; Bristol, "The Pruitt-Igoe Myth"; Evelyn Jones, Part 3: 17–18; Betty Thompson, Part 1: 5–6, in *Through the Eyes of a Child;* "First Families Move into Pruitt," *St. Louis Argus,* October 15, 1954 ("the head of the first family"); Valk, "Women and Postwar St. Louis," 285.

20. Heathcott, "City Quietly Remade"; Freidrichs, Freidrichs, Fehler, and Woodman, *Pruitt-Igoe Myth.*

21. Hepburn, "Shocking St. Louis"; Otis N. Thompson, "Survey Shows Negroes Extensively Underemployed: Race Bars Up Despite Ability," *St. Louis Argus,* November 12, 1954.

22. Hattye Thomas, "Help Wanted," *St. Louis Argus,* March 24, 1950.

23. Imani Mtendaji, Tape 2: 3, 4, 5, 8–12; Evelyn Jones, Tape 1: 2, 23–26; Tape 3: 9–10; Betty Thompson, Tape 1: 3, 4–5, 19, 20, 21, 22; Darby Robinson, Part 1: 3, 4, 5, 6, 9, 10–11, 13, 25–26, all in *Through the Eyes of a Child.*

24. Dine, "Trade Group Honors Union Activist" ("mixed up").

25. Ibid.; "Not Bad for a Factory Worker," *Southwest Progress* (Winter 1989); "Women in Organized Labor: Profiles in Labor," p. 7C; Ora Lee Malone, interview by Keona Ervin, November 11, 2003; Dine, "Trade Group Honors Union Activist."

26. Malone interview, November 4, 2003.

27. Ora Lee Malone, interview by Keona Ervin, November 11, 2003; Dine, "Trade Group Honors Union Activist."

28. Malone interview, November 11, 2003; Dine, "Trade Group Honors Union Activist"; Anderson, "Last Hired, First Fired," 87.

29. Malone interview, November 11, 2003; Tenth Annual Women's Conference Luncheon Program, Coalition of Black Trade Unionists, Los Angeles, California, May 22, 1992, in Ervin's collection.

30. Malone interview, November 11, 2003; Tenth Annual Women's Conference Luncheon Program; Dine, "Trade Group Honors Union Activist."

31. Malone interview, November 11, 2003; Tenth Annual Women's Conference Luncheon Program; Dine, "Trade Group Honors Union Activist" ("decision-making roles"); "Women in Organized Labor: Profiles in Labor," p. 7C; Amalgamated Clothing Workers of America Leadership Training Certificate for Ora Lee Malone, September 23, 1960, sl 670, box 1, folder 1 Awards, 1940–1990, Ora Lee Malone Papers, Western Historical Manuscripts Collection, Thomas Jefferson Library, University of Missouri–St. Louis.

32. "Women in Organized Labor: Profiles in Labor"; Malone quoted in Dine, "Trade Group Honors Union Activist"; Ora Lee Malone, interview by Bill Morrison, May 3, 1973, St. Louis, MO, pp. 10, 11, 16, 20; Gloria S. Ross, "Ora Lee Malone: Labor Leader Who Fought for Voting Rights, Civil Rights and Women's Rights," *St. Louis Beacon,* https://www.stlbeacon.org/#!/content/27904/ora_malone_obit_110612 (accessed March 11, 2015); Kelley, *Freedom Dreams.*

33. "Suggested Action for Solution," n.d., Ora Lee Malone Papers (s670), box 1, folder 2, SHSM, Manuscript Collection.

34. James V. Stepleton to Board member, March 10, 1975, Ora Lee Malone Papers (s670), box 1, folder 2, SHSM, Manuscript Collection.

35. Inez Smith Reid to Ora Malone, July 30, 1974, Ora Lee Malone Papers (s670), box 1, folder 2, SHSM, Manuscript Collection.

36. Dine, "Trade Group Honors Union Activist" ("on the cutting edge"; "social causes"; "ruffled some feathers"; "she wants to run sometimes"; "one of the labor movement's"); "Not Bad for a Factory Worker" ("but their focus"; "I didn't like"); "Women in Organized Labor: Profiles in Labor" ("Women need to learn").

37. Lang, *Grassroots at the Gateway*, 4–5; Gordon, *Mapping Decline*; Dowden-White, *Groping toward Democracy*; Lipsitz, *Life in the Struggle*; Jolly, *Black Liberation in the Midwest*; Heathcott, "Black Archipelago"; Lucander, *Winning the War for Democracy*; Lang, "Locating the Civil Rights Movement"; Skotnes, *New Deal for All?*; Williams, *Politics of Public Housing*; Orleck, *Storming Caesar's Palace*; Levenstein, *Movement without Marches*; Nadasen, *Welfare Warriors*.

38. CORE Report on Marian Oldham, told by Charles Oldham, interview by Margaret and Irvin Dagen, August 19, 1995, Margaret and Irvin Dagen History of St. Louis CORE Collection, s0661, box 2, folder 19, SHSM; Charles Oldham, interview by Maggie and Irv Dagen, August 19, 1995, s0661, box 2, folder 18, p. 10, Margaret and Irvin Dagen History of St. Louis CORE Collection, box 2, folder 19, ibid.; Oldham quoted in interview by Sister Prince, "I, Too, Sing America Oral History Project," July 6, 1987, Missouri Historical Society, St. Louis, MO, 16, 30–31; Lang, *Grassroots at the Gateway*, 81, 114.

39. CORE Report on Marian Oldham, 7–8.

40. "Marian Oldham Dies at 66," *St. Louis Post-Dispatch*, March 13, 1966; Lang, *Grassroots at the Gateway*, 114, 183; Valk, "Women and Postwar St. Louis," 289; Meier and Rudwick, *CORE*, 190 (quote), 49, 74; CORE Report on Marian Oldham, 12–17, 20–21; Oldham quoted in "I, Too, Sing America," 12, 15; "11 from City, County Appointed to Civil Rights Advisory Panel," *St. Louis Post-Dispatch*, February 6, 1977; "Ex-CORE Head Calls Jobs Bias Serious Here," *St. Louis Globe-Democrat*, August 28, 1964; Korstad and Lichtenstein, "Opportunities Found and Lost"; Lang, *Grassroots at the Gateway*, 80–83, 114, 184; Kimbrough and Dagen, *Victory without Violence*.

41. Freeman, *Song of Faith and Hope*, 1–19, 29–38.

42. "2 Women Lawyers"; "Suit on Housing Segregation"; "Housing Body Files Its Answer in Legal Battle: Admits Its Barring of Races," *St. Louis Argus*, November 19, 1954; "Case Now Ready for Decision," *St. Louis Argus*, December 3, 1954; "Housing Authority Plans to Follow Judge Moore's Ruling: Plaintiffs Will Get Priority," *St. Louis Argus*, January 6, 1956.

43. Calloway quote from interview by Irene Cortinovis, September 9, 1971, Black Community Leaders Project, University of Missouri–St. Louis, 18, 19; Robert Bussel, "'A Trade Union Oriented War on the Slums': Harold Gibbons, Ernest Calloway, and the St. Louis Teamsters in the 1960s," *Labor History* 44, no. 3 (2003): 49–76; Lang, *Grassroots at the Gateway,* 123, 125, 127, 145.

44. "Big Shop Talk" in "In Our Town," *New Crusader,* n.d. ("has no Church Affiliation"; "brags about her negative"), and "Big City Shoptalk" in "In Our Town," *New Crusader,* June 5, 1962 ("Would have been more acceptable"), box 1, folder 4, CaP; Calloway interview by Irene Cortinovis, 19–20; Lang, *Grassroots, at the Gateway,* 100–104.

45. DeVerne Calloway Campaign Flyer, n.d., box 1, folder 4, CaP; Marge Cunningham, "Capitol Profile: DeVerne Calloway," *Communicator,* April 18, 1977; "DeVerne Calloway Dead at 76," *St. Louis Post-Dispatch,* January 25, 1993; Charles E. Burgess, "Unusual Husband-Wife Team," *St. Louis Globe-Democrat,* April 23, 1977; "Design-Builders of Democracy: The Calloways of St. Louis," *Labor Today* 12 (Fall 1962): 24–25, Ernest Calloway Addenda Papers, box 1, folder 12, SHSM.

46. George E. Curry, "Inquiry Sought in Charges of Oppression at Prison," *St. Louis Post-Dispatch,* Oct. 17, 1975, box 1, folder 7, CaP; DeVerne Calloway, interview by Kenn Thoms, February 23, 1983, Oral History Program, State Historical Society of Missouri, Columbia, 1–9; Calloway interview by Irene Cortinovis, 27–30; Untitled draft of Calloway address to a legislative committee regarding abortion, box 1, folder 1, CaP; "Family Planning Service House Bill 1399," Calloway address to House Committee on Family Planning Service— House Bill 1399, n.d., ibid. ("to recognize woman"; "St. Louis currently").

47. Sugrue, *Origins of the Urban Crisis;* Gordon, *Mapping Decline.*

Conclusion

1. Jean King, interview by Doris A. Wesley, in Wesley, Price, and Morris, *Lift Every Voice and Sing,* 180; Barnes, "What Started as a Rent Strike Revolutionized Public Housing," *St. Louis Beacon,* November 13, 2012; Karp, "St. Louis Rent Strike of 1969"; "Strikers' Liaison Group to Meet Here"; Lang, *Grassroots at the Gateway,* 212–16; Lipsitz, *Life in the Struggle,* 9–14.

2. "Rent Strikers' Liaison Group to Meet Here," *St. Louis Post-Dispatch,* May 11, 1969; Wesley, Price, and Morris, *Lift Every Voice and Sing,* 181; Barnes, "What Started as a Rent Strike"; Karp, "St. Louis Rent Strike of 1969"; Lang, *Grassroots at the Gateway,* 212–16.

3. "HDC Asks Writ to End 9-Day Sit-in at Office," *St. Louis Globe-Democrat,* August 23, 1967; Delores Smith and Birdie Lou Saine quoted in "Women Face Forcible Removal in HDC Sit-in," *St. Louis Globe-Democrat,* August 25, 1967, NS.

4. "Tenants Picket Public Housing Agency Offices," *St. Louis Post-Dispatch,* November 8, 1967; Mattie Trice quoted in "Public Housing Tenants to Continue Picketing," *St. Louis Globe-Democrat,* November 9, 1967, NS.

5. All quotes in "200 Negroes March on City Hall," *St. Louis Post-Dispatch,* March 13, 1968, NS; Wesley, Price, and Morris, *Lift Every Voice and Sing,* 181; Lang, *Grassroots at the Gateway,* 212–16; Williams, *Politics of Public Housing,* 325–26; Nadasen, *Welfare Warriors;* Orleck, *Storming Caesar's Palace.*

6. "1,000 Tenants Open Rent Strike," February 3, 1969, NS; "Pruitt-Igoe Rent Strike Demands" and "City-Wide Rent Strike Committee Demands," series 2, box 49, folder 3, Alfonso J. Cervantes Records, University Archives, Special Collections, Washington University in St. Louis; "Nine-Month Rent Strike Hopefully Coming to End," *Missouri Teamster,* September 19, 1969.

7. "Joint Action," series 1, box 32, folder 26, Alfonso J. Cervantes Records, University Archives, Special Collections, Washington University in St. Louis; News Release from ACTION, April 23, 1969, series 2, box 51, folder 4, ibid.; Statement by Rev. William L. Matheus, Minister-in-Charge of St. Stephen's Episcopal Church, to Clayton Board of Alderman, April 22, 1969, ibid.; ACTION News Release, April 18, 1969, ibid.; "St. Louis to Host Nationwide Tenants Group Convention," *Missouri Teamster,* September 19, 1969; Williams, *Politics of Public Housing;* Williams, "Tired of Being Treated like Dogs."

8. "Gibbons, Rent Strikers Propose Housing Coalition," *St. Louis Post-Dispatch,* October 10, 1969; "Housing Alliance Brought Needed Aid to Strikers," *Missouri Teamster,* November 21, 1969; "Rent Strike Hopefully Coming to End"; "Stalemate in Public Housing," *St. Louis Globe Democrat,* August 29, 1969; "Civic Alliance for Housing Ends Strike, Begins Needed Changes," *Missouri Teamster,* November 21, 1969; Ernest Calloway, "Reflections: Public Housing in St. Louis," *St. Louis Sentinel,* February 21, 1970; Gibbons quotes all in Harold Gibbons, "The Poor Must Find Dignity, Security in Housing," *Missouri Teamster,* September 19, 1969; Bussel, *Fighting for Total Person Unionism.*

9. Kohler-Hausmann, "Crime of Survival."

Bibliography

Primary Sources

Burke, Dorothy W. *Economic Status of Saint Louis Negroes.* St. Louis: Welfare Plan Committee, February 1935.

Crossland, William A. *Industrial Conditions among Negroes in St. Louis.* St. Louis: Press of Mendle Printing, 1914.

Douglass, H. Paul. *The St. Louis Church Survey: A Religious Investigation with a Social Background.* New York: George H. Doran, 1924.

Henry, Alice. *Women and the Labor Movement.* New York: G. H. Doran, 1923. http://nrs.harvard.edu/urn-3:HBS.BAKER:130629.

I, Too, Sing America Oral History Project. St. Louis: Missouri Historical Society, 1988.

Johnson, Charles S. *The Economic Stats of Negroes: Summary and Analysis of the Material Presented at the Conference on the Economic Status of the Negro.* Nashville: Fisk University Press, 1933.

Negro Women in Industry. Washington, DC: Government Printing Office, 1922. http://nrs.harvard.edu/urn-3:HBS.BAKER:136864.

Nelson, Eleanor Crosby. *Women at Work.* Washington, DC: Government Printing Office, 1933. http://nrs.harvard.edu/urn-3:HBS.BAKER:140326.

The Pecan Shellers of San Antonio: The Problem of Underpaid and Unemployed Mexican Labor. Washington, DC: Government Printing Office, 1940.

Pidgeon, Mary Elizabeth. *Employment Fluctuations and Unemployment of Women.* Washington, DC: Government Printing Office, 1933. http://nrs.harvard.edu/urn-3:HBS.BAKER:140306.

———. *Negro Women in Industry in 15 States.* Washington, DC: Government Printing Office, 1929. http://nrs.harvard.edu/urn-3:HBS.BAKER:455500.

Reid, Ira De A. *Industrial Status of Negroes in St. Louis.* New York: Department of Research, National Urban League, September 1934.

———. *Negro Membership in American Labor Unions by the Department of Research and Investigations of the National Urban League.* New York: Negro Universities Press, 1989. Originally published 1930.

St. Louis City Plan Commission. *A Housing Program for the City of St. Louis, 1970–1980.* April 1971.

A Strong Seed Planted: The Civil Rights Movement in St. Louis, 1954–1968. St. Louis: Missouri Historical Society, 1989.

Through the Eyes of a Child Oral History Project. St. Louis: Missouri Historical Society, 1998–1999.

Voris, Ruth Irene. "Women in Missouri Industries: A Study of Hours and Wages." *Bulletin of the Women's Bureau* 35 (1924): 39–44. http://nrs.harvard.edu/urn-3:HBS.BAKER:292904.

Young, Nathan B. *Your St. Louis and Mine*. St. Louis: N. B. Young, 1937.

Secondary Sources

Adams, Luther. *Way Up North in Louisville: African American Migration in the Urban South, 1930–1970*. Chapel Hill: University of North Carolina Press, 2010.

Adams, Patricia L. "Fighting for Democracy in St. Louis: Civil Rights during World War II." *Missouri Historical Review* 80, no. 1 (1985): 58–75.

Albertan, Chris. *Bessie*. New Haven, CT: Yale University Press, 2003.

Allen, Ernest, Jr. "Waiting for Tojo: The Pro-Japan Vigil of Black Missourians, 1932–1943." *Gateway Heritage* 16 (Fall 1995): 38–55.

Anderson, Karen Tucker. "Last Hired, First Fired: Black Women Workers during World War II." *Journal of American History* 69, no. 1 (1982): 82–97.

———. *Wartime Women: Sex Roles, Family Relations and the Status of Women during World War II*. Westport, CT: Greenwood Press, 1981.

Appleby, Joyce. *The Relentless Revolution: A History of Capitalism*. New York: W. W. Norton, 2010.

Arnesen, Eric. *Brotherhoods of Color: Black Railroad Workers and the Struggle for Equality*. Cambridge, MA: Harvard University Press, 2001.

———. "Up from Exclusion: Black and White Workers, Race, and the State of American Labor History." *Reviews in American History* 26, no. 1 (1998): 146–74.

Arsenault, Raymond. *Sound of Freedom: Marian Anderson, the Lincoln Memorial, and the Concert that Awakened America*. New York: Bloomsbury Press, 2009.

Baldwin, Davarian L. *Chicago's New Negroes: Modernity, the Great Migration, and Black Urban Life*. Chapel Hill: University of North Carolina Press, 2007.

Baraka, Amiri [LeRoi Jones]. *Blues People: Negro Music in White America*. 1963. New York: Harper Perennial, 1999.

Barnett, Bernice McNair. "Invisible Southern Black Women Leaders in the Civil Rights Movement: The Triple Constraints of Gender, Race, and Class." *Gender and Society* 7 (1993): 162–82.

Baron, Ava, ed. *Work Engendered: Toward a New History of American Labor*. Ithaca, NY: Cornell University Press, 1991.

Bates, Beth Tompkins. *The Making of Black Detroit in the Age of Henry Ford*. Chapel Hill: University of North Carolina Press, 2012.

———. "A New Crowd Challenges the Agenda of the Old Guard in the NAACP, 1933–1941." *American Historical Review* 102, no. 2 (1997): 340–77.

————. *Pullman Porters and the Rise of Protest Politics in Black America, 1925–1945*. Chapel Hill: University of North Carolina Press, 2001.

Baybeck, Brady, and E. Terrence Jones, eds. *St. Louis Metromorphosis: Past Trends and Future Directions*. St. Louis: Missouri Historical Society Press, 2004.

Biondi, Martha. "How New York Changes the Story of the Civil Rights Movement." *Afro-Americans in New York Life and History* 31, no. 2 (2007): 15–31.

————. *To Stand and Fight: The Civil Rights Movement in Postwar New York City*. Cambridge, MA: Harvard University Press, 2003.

Blackwelder, Julia Kirk. *Women of the Depression: Caste and Culture in San Antonio, 1929–1939*. College Station: Texas A&M University Press, 1984.

Blair, Cynthia M. *I've Got to Make My Livin': Black Women's Sex Work in Turn-of-the-Century Chicago*. Chicago: University of Chicago Press, 2010.

Boris, Eileen. "Black Women and Paid Labor in the Home: Industrial Homework in Chicago in the 1920s." In *Homework: Historical and Contemporary Perspectives on Paid Labor at Home,* edited by Eileen Boris and Cynthia R. Daniels, 33–53. Urbana: University of Illinois Press, 1989.

————. "Black Workers, Trade Unions, and Labor Standards: The Wartime FEPC." In *Historical Roots of the Urban Crisis: African Americans in the Industrial City, 1900–1950,* edited by Henry Louis Taylor Jr. and Walter Hill, 251–73. New York: Garland, 2000.

————. *Home to Work: Motherhood and the Politics of Industrial Homework in the United States*. New York: Cambridge University Press, 1994.

————. "The Power of Motherhood: Black and White Activist Women Redefine the 'Political.'" In *Mothers of a New World: Maternalist Politics and the Origins of the Welfare State,* edited by Sonya Michel and Set Koven, 213–45. New York: Routledge, 1993.

————. "'The Right to Worlds the Right to Live!': Fair Employment and the Quest for Social Citizenship." In *Two Cultures of Rights: The Quest for Inclusion and Participation in Modern America and Germany,* edited by Manfred Berg and Martin H. Geyer, 121–42. New York: Cambridge University Press, 2002.

————. "'You Wouldn't Want One of 'Em Dancing with Your Wife': Racialized Bodies on the Job in World War II." *American Quarterly* 50, no. 1 (1998): 77–108.

Boris, Eileen, and Jennifer Klein. *Caring for America: Home Health Workers in the Shadow of the Welfare State*. New York: Oxford University Press, 2012.

Boris, Eileen, and S. J. Kleinberg. "Mothers and Other Workers: (Re)Conceiving Labor, Maternalism, and the State." *Journal of Women's History* 15, no. 3 (2003): 90–117.

Boris, Eileen, and Premilla Nadasen. "Domestic Workers Organize!" *Working USA* 11 (December 2008): 413–37.

———. "Historicizing Domestic Workers' Resistance and Organizing." *International Labor and Working-Class History* 88 (Fall 2015): 4–10.

Boris, Eileen, and Annelise Orleck. "Feminism and the Labor Movement: A Century of Collaboration and Conflict." *New Labor Forum* 20 (Winter 2011): 33–41.

Borstelmann, Thomas. *The Cold War and the Color Line: American Race Relations in the Global Arena*. Cambridge, MA: Harvard University Press, 2001.

Boyle, Kevin. "Labour, the Left, and the Long Civil-Rights Movement." *Social History* 30, no. 3 (2005): 366–72.

Bracey, John H., Jr., and August Meier. "Allies or Adversaries? The NAACP, A. Philip Randolph, and the 1941 March on Washington." *Georgia Historical Quarterly* 75, no. 1 (1991): 1–17.

Brewer, Rose M. "Theorizing Race, Class, and Gender: The New Scholarship of Black Feminist Intellectuals and Black Women's Labor." In *Theorizing Black Feminisms: The Visionary Pragmatism of Black Women,* edited by Stanlie M. James and Abena P. A. Busia, 13–30. New York: Routledge, 1993.

Bristol, Katharine G. "The Pruitt-Igoe Myth." *Journal of Architectural Education* 44, no. 3 (1991): 163–71.

Brody, David. "Radical Labor History and Rank-and-File Militancy." *Labor History* 16 (1985): 117–26.

Brown, Leslie. *Upbuilding Black Durham: Gender, Class, and Black Community Development in the Jim Crow South*. Chapel Hill: University of North Carolina Press, 2008.

Brown-Nagin, Tomiko. *Courage to Dissent: Atlanta and the Long History of the Civil Rights Movement*. New York: Oxford University Press, 2012.

Burnett, Betty. *St. Louis at War: The Story of a City, 1941–1945*. Tucson: Patrice Press, 1972.

Bussel, Robert. *Fighting for Total Person Unionism: Harold Gibbons, Ernest Calloway, and Working-Class Citizenship*. Urbana: University of Illinois Press, 2015.

———. "'A Trade Union Oriented War on the Slums': Harold Gibbons, Ernest Calloway, and the St. Louis Teamsters in the 1960s." *Labor History* 44, no. 3 (2003): 49–76.

Bynum, Cornelius L. *A. Philip Randolph and the Struggle for Civil Rights*. Urbana: University of Illinois Press, 2010.

Campbell, Tracy. *The Gateway Arch: A Biography*. New Haven, CT: Yale University Press, 2013.

Cantor, Louis. "A Prologue to the Protest Movement: The Missouri Sharecropper Roadside Demonstration of 1939." *Journal of American History* 55, no. 4 (1969): 804–22.

Capeci, Dominic J., Jr. *The Lynching of Cleo Wright*. Lexington: University Press of Kentucky, 1998.

———. "The Lynching of Cleo Wright: Federal Protection of Constitutional Rights during World War II." *Journal of American History* 72, no. 4 (1986): 859–87.

Carby, Hazel. "It Jus Be's Dat Way Sometime: The Sexual Politics of Women's Blues." *Radical America* 20 (1987): 9–22.

———. "Policing the Black Woman's Body in an Urban Context." *Critical Inquiry* 18 (1992): 738–55.

Cayton, Horace R., and George S. Mitchell. *Black Workers and the New Unions.* 1939. Reprint, College Park, MD: McGrath, 1969.

Cha-Jua, Sundiata Keita, and Clarence Lang. "The Long Movement as Vampire: Temporal and Spatial Fallacies in Recent Black Freedom Studies." *Journal of African American History* 92, no. 2 (2007): 265–88.

Chateauvert, Melinda. *Marching Together: Women of the Brotherhood of Sleeping Car Porters.* Urbana: University of Illinois Press, 1998.

Chatelain, Marcia. *South Side Girls: Growing up in the Great Migration.* Durham, NC: Duke University Press, 2015.

Christensen, Lawrence O., William E. Foley, Gary R. Kremer, and Kenneth H. Winn, eds. *Dictionary of Missouri Biography.* Columbia: University of Missouri Press, 1999.

Clark-Lewis, Elizabeth. *Living In, Living Out: African-American Domestics in Washington, D.C.* Washington, DC: Smithsonian Institution Press, 1994.

Cobble, Dorothy Sue. *The Other Women's Movement: Workplace Justice and Social Rights in Modern America.* Princeton, NJ: Princeton University Press, 2004.

———. *The Sex of Class: Women Transforming American Labor.* Ithaca, NY: Cornell University Press, 2007.

Cohen, Lizabeth. *Making a New Deal: Industrial Workers in Chicago, 1919–1939.* Cambridge: Cambridge University Press, 2008.

Collier-Thomas, Bettye. *Jesus, Jobs, and Justice: African American Women and Religion.* New York: Alfred A. Knopf, 2010.

Connolly, N. D. B. *A World More Concrete: Real Estate and the Remaking of Jim Crow South Florida.* Chicago: University of Chicago Press, 2014.

Corbett, Katherine T. *In Her Place: A Guide to St. Louis Women's History.* St. Louis: Missouri Historical Society Press, 1999.

———. "No Crystal Stair: Black St. Louis, 1920–1940." *Gateway Heritage* 8, no. 2 (1987): 8–15.

Countryman, Matthew J. *Up South: Civil Rights and Black Power in Philadelphia.* Philadelphia: University of Pennsylvania Press, 2005.

Cowie, Jefferson R. *The Great Exception: The New Deal and the Limits of American Politics.* Princeton, NJ: Princeton University Press, 2016.

———. *Staying Alive: The 1970s and the Last Days of the Working Class.* New York: New Press, 2012.

Crosby, Emilye, ed. *Civil Rights History from the Ground Up: Local Struggles, a National Movement.* Athens: University of Georgia Press, 2011.

Cumberbatch, Prudence, Dayo F. Gore, and Sarah Haley. "Guest Editors' Note." In "Black Women's Labor: Economics, Culture, and Politics," special issue, *Souls* 18, no. 1 (2016): 1–10.

Davis, Angela Y. *Blues Legacies and Black Feminism: Gertrude "Ma" Rainey, Bessie Smith, and Billie Holiday.* New York: Vintage, 1998.

———. *Women, Race and Class.* New York: Random House, 1981.

Dawson, Michael C. *Black Visions: The Roots of Contemporary African-American Political Ideologies.* Chicago: University of Chicago Press, 2001.

De Jong, Greta. *Invisible Enemy: The African American Freedom Struggle after 1965.* Malden, MA: Wiley-Blackwell, 2010.

D'Emilio, John. *Lost Prophet: The Life and Times of Bayard Rustin.* New York: Free Press, 2003.

Denning, Michael C. *The Cultural Front: The Laboring of American Culture in the Twentieth Century.* New York: Verso Books, 1997.

Dill, Bonnie Thornton. *Across the Boundaries of Race and Class: An Exploration of Work and Family among Black Female Domestic Servants.* New York: Garland, 1994.

Dittmer, John. *Local People: The Struggle for Civil Rights in Mississippi.* Urbana: University of Illinois Press, 1995.

Dowden, Priscilla. "Over This Point We Are Determined to Fight: The Urban League of St. Louis in Historical Perspective." *Gateway Heritage* 13, no. 4 (1993): 32–47.

———. "The Urban League of St. Louis in Historical Perspective." *Gateway Heritage* (1993): 32–47.

Dowden-White, Priscilla. *Groping toward Democracy: African American Social Welfare Reform in St. Louis, 1910–1949.* Columbia: University of Missouri Press, 2011.

Drake, St. Clair, and Horace Cayton. *Black Metropolis: A Study of Negro Life in a Northern City.* 1945. Reprint, Chicago: University of Chicago Press, 1993.

Dudziak, Mary L. *Cold War Civil Rights: Race and the Image of American Democracy.* Princeton, NJ: Princeton University Press, 2000.

Early, Gerald, ed. *Ain't but a Place: An Anthology of African American Writings about St. Louis.* St. Louis: Missouri Historical Society Press, 1998.

Edwards, Erica R. *Charisma and the Fictions of Black Leadership.* Minneapolis: University of Minnesota Press, 2012.

Egerton, John. *Speak Now against the Day: The Generation before the Civil Rights Movement in the South.* New York: Alfred A. Knopf, 1994.

Endersby, James W., and William T. Horner. *Lloyd Gaines and the Fight to End Segregation.* Columbia: University of Missouri Press, 2016.

Enstad, Nan. *Ladies of Labor, Girls of Adventure: Working Women, Popular Culture, and Labor Politics at the Turn of the Twentieth Century.* New York: Columbia University Press, 1999.

Estes, Steve. *I Am a Man! Race, Manhood, and the Civil Rights Movement.* Chapel Hill: University of North Carolina Press, 2005.

Ezra, Michael, ed. *The Economic Civil Rights Movement: African Americans and the Struggle for Economic Power.* New York: Rutledge, 2013.

Fairclough, Adam. *Better Day Coming: Blacks and Equality, 1890–2000.* New York: Viking, 2001.

Feurer, Rosemary. "The Nutpickers' Union, 1933–1934: Crossing the Boundaries of Community and Workplace." In *"We Are All Leaders": The Alternative Unionism of the Early 1930s,* edited by Staughton Lynd, 27–50. Urbana: University of Illinois Press, 1996.

———. *Radical Unionism in the Midwest, 1900–1950.* Urbana: University of Illinois Press, 2006.

———, ed. *The St. Louis Labor History Tour.* St. Louis: Bread and Roses, 1994.

———. "William Sentner, the UE, and Civic Unionism in St. Louis." In *The CIO's Left-Led Unions,* edited by Steve Rosswurm, 95–117. New Brunswick, NJ: Rutgers University Press, 1992.

Fichtenbaum, Myrna. *The Funsten Nut Strike.* New York: International, 1991.

Fine, Janice, and Jennifer Gordon. "Strengthening Labor Standards Enforcement through Partnerships with Workers' Organizations." *Politics and Society* 38, no. 4 (2010): 552–85.

Fink, Gary M. *Labor's Search for Political Order: The Political Behavior of the Missouri Labor Movement, 1890–1940.* Columbia: University of Missouri Press, 1973.

Fleming, Cynthia Griggs. *Soon We Will Not Cry: The Liberation of Ruby Doris Smith Robinson.* New York: Rowman and Littlefield, 1998.

Foner, Philip S. *Organized Labor and the Black Worker, 1619–1973.* New York: International, 1974.

———. *Women and the American Labor Movement: From World War I to the Present.* New York: Free Press, 1980.

Fones-Wolf, Elizabeth. "Industrial Unionism and Labor Movement Culture in Depression-Era Philadelphia." *Pennsylvania Magazine of History and Biography* 109, no. 1 (1985): 3–26.

Frank, Dana. *Buy American: The Untold Story of Economic Nationalism.* Boston: Beacon Press, 1999.

Franklin, V. P., and Bettye Collier-Thomas. "For the Race in General and Black Women in Particular: The Civil Rights Activities of African American Women's Organizations, 1915–50." In *Sisters in the Struggle: African American Women in the Civil Rights–Black Power Movement,* edited by Bettye Collier-Thomas and V. P. Franklin, 21–41. New York: New York University Press, 2001.

Fraser, Nancy. "Rethinking the Public Sphere: A Contribution to the Critique of an Actually Existing Democracy." In *Habermas and the Public Sphere,* edited by Craig Calhoun, 109–42. Cambridge: MIT Press, 1992.

Fraser, Nancy, and Linda Gordon. "A Genealogy of Dependency: Tracing a Key-word of the U.S. Welfare State." *Signs* 19 (1994): 309–36.

Fraser, Steve, and Gary Gerstle, eds. *The Rise and Fall of the New Deal Order, 1930–1980.* Princeton, NJ: Princeton University Press, 1989.

Freeman, Frankie Muse. *A Song of Faith and Hope: The Life of Frankie Muse Free-man.* St. Louis: Missouri Historical Society Press, 2003.

Freeman, Joshua B. "Delivering the Goods: Industrial Unionism during World War Two." *Labor History* 19, no. 4 (1978): 170–93.

———. *Working-Class New York: Life and Labor since World War II.* New York: New Press, 2000.

Friedman, Andrea. *Citizenship in Cold War America: The National Security State and the Possibilities of Dissent.* Amherst: University of Massachusetts Press, 2015.

———. "The Strange Career of Annie Lee Moss: Rethinking Race, Gender, and McCarthyism." *Journal of American History* 94, no. 2 (2007): 44–68.

Freidrichs, Chad, Jaime Freidrichs, Paul Fehler, and Brian Woodman *The Pruitt-Igoe Myth.* DVD. Directed by Chad Freidrichs. Unicorn Stencil, 2001.

Gabin, Nancy. "'They Have Placed a Penalty on Womanhood': The Protest Action of Women Auto Workers in Detroit-Area UAW Locals, 1945–1947." *Feminist Studies* 8 (1982): 373–98.

———. "Wins and Losses: the UAW Women's Bureau after World War II." In Groneman and Norton, *"To Toil the Livelong Day,"* 233–49.

Gaines, Kevin. *Uplifting the Race: Black Leadership, Politics, and Culture in the Twentieth Century.* Chapel Hill: University of North Carolina Press, 1996.

Gallagher, Julie A. *Black Women and Politics in New York City.* Urbana: University of Illinois Press, 2012.

Garb, Margaret. *City of American Dreams: A History of Home Ownership and Housing Reform in Chicago, 1871–1919.* Chicago: University of Chicago Press, 2005.

———. *Freedom's Ballot: African American Political Struggles in Chicago from Abolition to the Great Migration.* Chicago: University of Chicago Press, 2014.

Garfinkel, Herbert. *When Negroes March: The March on Washington Movement in the Organizational Politics for FEPC.* 1959. Reprint, New York: Atheneum, 1973.

Gellman, Erik S. "Carthage Must Be Destroyed: Race, City Politics, and the Campaign to Integrate Chicago Transportation Work, 1929–1943." *Labor* 2, no. 2 (2008): 81–114.

———. *Death Blow to Jim Crow: The National Negro Congress and the Rise of Militant Civil Rights.* Chapel Hill: University of North Carolina Press, 2012.

Gellman, Erik, and Jared Roll. *Gospel of the Working Class: Labor's Southern Prophets in New Deal America.* Urbana: University of Illinois Press, 2011.

Gerstle, Gary. "The Protean Character of American Liberalism." *American Historical Review* 99, no. 4 (1994): 1043–73.

Giddings, Paula. *In Search of Sisterhood: Delta Sigma Theta and the Challenge of the Black Sorority Movement.* New York: Amistad, 2002.

———. *When and Where I Enter: The Impact of Black Women on Race and Sex in America.* New York: William Morrow, 1984.

Gill, Tiffany M. *Beauty Shop Politics: African American Women's Activism in the Beauty Industry.* Urbana: University of Illinois Press, 2010.

Gilmore, Glenda Elizabeth. "'Am I a Screwball or a Pioneer?': Pauli Murray's Civil Rights Movement." In *Profiles in Leadership: Historians on the Elusive Quality of Greatness,* edited by Walter Isaacson, 261–82. New York: W. W. Norton, 2010.

———. *Defying Dixie: The Radical Roots of Civil Rights, 1919–1950.* New York: W. W. Norton, 2008.

———. *Gender and Jim Crow: Women and the Politics of White Supremacy in North Carolina, 1896–1920.* Chapel Hill: University of North Carolina Press, 1996.

———. "Race and the CIO: The Possibilities for Racial Egalitarianism during the 1930s and 1940s." *International Labor and Working-Class History* 44 (September 1993): 1–32.

Glen, John M. *Highlander: No Ordinary School.* 2nd ed. Knoxville: University of Tennessee Press, 1996.

Glenn, Evelyn Nakano. "Racial Ethnic Women's Labor: The Intersection of Race, Gender and Class Oppression." *Review of Radical Political Economics* 17, no. 3 (1985): 86–108.

———. *Unequal Freedom: How Race and Gender Shaped American Citizenship and Labor.* Cambridge, MA: Harvard University Press, 2002.

Glickman, Lawrence B. *A Living Wage: American Workers and the Making of Consumer Society.* Ithaca, NY: Cornell University Press, 1997.

Glymph, Thavolia. *Out of the House of Bondage: The Transformation of the Plantation Household.* Cambridge: Cambridge University Press, 2003.

Goldberg, David E., and Trevor Griffey. *Black Power at Work: Community Control, Affirmative Action and the Construction Industry.* Ithaca, NY: Cornell University Press, 2010.

Golland, David Hamilton. *Constructing Affirmative Action: The Struggle for Equal Employment Opportunity.* Lexington: University Press of Kentucky, 2011.

Gonda, Jeffrey D. *Unjust Deeds: The Restrictive Covenant Cases and the Making of the Civil Rights Movement.* Chapel Hill: University of North Carolina Press, 2015.

González, Gabriela. "Carolina Munguía and Emma Tenayuca: The Politics of Benevolence and Radical Reform." *Frontiers* 24, nos. 2–3 (2003): 200–229.

Gordon, Colin. *Mapping Decline: St. Louis and the Fate of the American City.* Philadelphia: University of Pennsylvania Press, 2008.

Gordon, Linda. "Black and White Visions of Welfare: Women's Welfare Activism, 1890–1945." *Journal of American History* 78 (1991): 559–90.

———. *Pitied but Not Entitled: Single Mothers and the History of Welfare.* Cambridge, MA: Harvard University Press, 1994.

Gore, Dayo F. "'The Danger of Being an Active Anti-Communist': Expansive Black Left Politics and the Long Civil Rights Movement." *American Communist History* 11, no. 1 (2012): 45–48.

———. *Radicalism at the Crossroads: African American Women Activists in the Cold War.* New York: New York University Press, 2011.

Gore, Dayo F., Jeanne Theoharis, and Komozi Woodard. *Want to Start a Revolution? Radical Women in the Black Freedom Struggle.* New York: New York University Press, 2009.

Gottlieb, Peter. *Making Their Own Way: Southern Blacks' Migration to Pittsburgh, 1916–1930.* Urbana: University of Illinois Press, 1987.

Grant, Gail Milissa. *At the Elbows of My Elders: One Family's Journey toward Civil Rights.* St. Louis: Missouri History Museum, 2008.

Gray, Brenda Clegg. *Black Female Domestics during the Depression in New York City, 1930–1940.* New York: Garland, 1993.

Green, Adam. "Race, Gender, and Labor in 1960s Memphis: 'I Am a Man' and the Meaning of Freedom." *Journal of Urban History* 30 (2004): 465–89.

———. *Selling the Race: Culture, Community, and Black Chicago, 1940–1955.* Chicago: University of Chicago Press, 2007.

Green, Laurie B. *Battling the Plantation Mentality: Memphis and the Black Freedom Struggle.* Chapel Hill: University of North Carolina Press, 2007.

Green, Venus. *Race on the Line: Gender, Labor, and Technology in the Bell System, 1880–1980.* Durham, NC: Duke University Press, 2001.

Greenberg, Cheryl Lynn. *Or Does It Explode: Black Harlem in the Great Depression.* New York: Oxford University Press, 1991.

———. *To Ask for an Equal Chance: African Americans in the Great Depression.* Lanham, MD: Rowman and Littlefield, 2009.

Greene, Christine. *Our Separate Ways: Women and the Black Freedom Movement in Durham, North Carolina.* Chapel Hill: University of North Carolina Press, 2005.

Greene, Debra Foster. "'Just Enough of Everything': The St. Louis Argus: An African American Newspaper and Publishing Company in Its First Decade." *Business and Economic History* 4 (2006): 1–11.

Greene, Lorenzo J., Gary R. Kremer, and Antonio Holland. *Missouri's Black Heritage.* Rev. ed. Columbia: University of Missouri Press, 1993.

Greene. Lorenzo J., and Carter G. Woodson. *The Negro Wage Earner.* New York: Russell and Russell, 1930.

Griffin, Farah Jasmine. *Harlem Nocturne: Women Artists and Progressive Politics during World War II*. New York: Basic Civitas, 2013.

Groneman, Carol, and Mary Beth Norton, eds. *"To Toil the Livelong Day": America's Women at Work, 1790–1980*. Ithaca, NY: Cornell University Press, 1987.

Gross, Kali. *Colored Amazons: Crime, Violence, and Black Women in the city of Brotherly Love, 1880–1910*. Durham, NC: Duke University Press, 2006.

Grossman, James R. *Land of Hope: Chicago, Black Southerners, and the Great Migration*. Chicago: University of Chicago Press, 1991.

Gutman, Herbert G. *Power and Culture: Essays on the American Working Class*. New York: New Press, 1987.

Hahn, Stephen. *A Nation under Our Feet: Black Political Struggles in the Rural South from Slavery to the Great Migration*. Cambridge, MA: Harvard University Press, 2003.

Haley, Sarah. *No Mercy Here: Gender, Punishment, and the Making of Jim Crow Modernity*. Chapel Hill: University of North Carolina Press, 2016.

Hall, Jacquelyn Dowd. "Disorderly Women: Gender and Labor Militancy in the Appalachian South." In Ruiz and Du Bois, *Unequal Sisters*, 348–71.

———. "The Long Civil Rights Movement and the Political Uses of the Past." *Journal of American History* 91, no. 4 (2005): 1233–63.

Halpern, Rick. *Down on the Killing Floor: Black and White Workers in Chicago's Packinghouses*. Urbana: University of Illinois Press, 1997.

Harding, Vincent. *There Is a River: The Black Struggle for Freedom in America*. San Diego: Harcourt, Brace, 1981.

Harley, Sharon. "For the Good of Family and Race: Gender, Work, and Domestic Roles in the Black Community, 1880–1930." *Signs* 15 (1990): 336–49.

———. "When Your Work Is Not Who You Are: The Development of a Working-Class Consciousness among Afro-American Women." In *"We Specialize in the Wholly Impossible": A Reader in Black Women's History*, edited by Darlene Clark Hine, Wilma King, and Linda Reed, 25–37. Brooklyn, NY: Carson, 1995.

Harley, Sharon, and the Black Women and Work Collective, eds. *Sister Circle: Black Women and Work*. New Brunswick, NJ: Rutgers University Press, 2002.

Harley, Sharon, and Rosalyn Terborg-Penn, eds. *The Afro-American Woman: Struggles and Images*. Port Washington, NY: Kennikat Press, 1978.

Harris, LaShawn. "Dream Books, Crystal Balls, and "Lucky Numbers": African American Female Spiritual Mediums in Harlem, 1900–1945." *Journal of Afro-Americans in New York Life and History* 35, no. 1 (January 2011): 1–30.

———. "Madame Queen of Policy: Madame Stephanie St. Clair and African American Women's Participation in Harlem's Informal Economy." *Black Women, Gender & Families* 2, no. 2 (Fall 2008): 53–76.

———. "Marvel Cooke: Investigative Journalist, Communist and Black Radical Subject." *Journal for the Study of Radicalism* 6, no. 2 (Fall 2012): 91–126.

———. "Running with the Reds: African American Women and the Communist Party during the Great Depression." *Journal of African American History* 94, no. 1 (Winter 2009): 21–40.

———. *Sex Workers, Psychics, and Numbers Runners: Black Women in New York City's Underground Economy.* Urbana: University of Illinois Press, 2016.

Harris, William H. "A. Philip Randolph, Black Workers, and the Labor Movement." In *Labor Leaders in America,* edited by Melvyn Dubofsky and Warren Van Tine, 258–79. Urbana: University of Illinois Press, 1987.

———. "A. Philip Randolph as a Charismatic Leader, 1925–1941." *Journal of Negro History* 64, no. 4 (1979): 301–15.

———. "Federal Intervention in Union Discrimination: FEPC and West Coast Ship Yards during World War II." *Labor History* 22, no. 3 (1981): 325–47.

———. *The Harder We Run: Black Workers since the Civil War.* New York: Oxford University Press, 1982.

———. *Keeping the Faith: A. Philip Randolph, Milton P. Webster, and the Brotherhood of Sleeping Car Porters, 1925–1937.* Urbana: University of Illinois Press, 1977.

Hartman, Saidya. "The Belly of the World: A Note on Black Women's Labors." *Souls* 18, no. 1 (2016): 166–73.

Hartmann, Susan M. *The Other Feminists: Activists in the Liberal Establishment.* New Haven, CT: Yale University Press, 1998.

Heathcott, Joseph. "Black Archipelago: Politics and Civic Life in the Jim Crow City." *Journal of Social History* (2005): 705–36.

———. "The City Quietly Remade: National Programs and Local Agendas in the Movement to Clear the Slums, 1942–1952." *Journal of Urban History* 34, no. 2 (January 2008): 221–42.

———. "In the Nature of a Clinic in St. Louis: The Design of Early Public Housing." *Journal of the Society of Architectural Historians* 70, no. 1 (March 2011): 82–103.

Hewitt, Nancy A., ed. *No Permanent Waves: Recasting Histories of U.S. Feminism.* New Brunswick, NJ: Rutgers University Press, 2010.

———. *Southern Discomfort: Women's Activism in Tampa, Florida, 1880s–1920s.* Urbana: University of Illinois Press, 2001.

———. *Women's Activism and Social Change: Rochester, New York, 1822–1872.* Ithaca, NY: Cornell University Press, 1984.

Hickey, Georgina. *Hope and Danger in the New South City: Working-Class Women and Urban Development in Atlanta, 1890–1940.* Athens: University of Georgia Press, 2003.

Hicks, Cheryl D. *Talk With You Like a Woman: African American Women, Justice, and Reform in New York, 1890–1935.* Chapel Hill: University of North Carolina Press, 2010.

Higginbotham, Evelyn Brooks. "African-American Women's History and the Metalanguage of Race." In *"We Specialize in the Wholly Impossible": A Reader in Black Women's History,"* edited by Darlene Clark Hine, Wilma King, and Linda Reed, 3–24. Brooklyn, NY: Carlson, 1995.

———. *Righteous Discontent: The Women's Movement in the Black Baptist Church, 1880–1920.* Cambridge, MA: Harvard University Press, 1993.

Hill, Herbert. "The AFL-CIO and the Black Worker: Twenty-Five Years after the Merger." Industrial Relations Research Institute, University of Wisconsin–Madison, Reprint No. 241, 44–54. Reprinted from *Journal of Intergroup Relations* 10, no. 1 (Spring 1982).

———. *Black Labor and the American Legal System: Race, Work, and the Law.* Madison: University of Wisconsin Press, 1985.

———. "The Problem of Race in American Labor History." *Reviews in American History* 24, no. 2 (June 1996): 189–208.

———. "Racial Discrimination in the Nation's Apprenticeship Training Programs." *Phylon* 23, no. 3 (Fall 1962): 215–24.

Hill, Lance. *The Deacons for Defense: Armed Resistance and the Civil Rights Movement.* Chapel Hill: University of North Carolina Press, 2004.

Hill, Lauren Warren, and Rabig, Julia. *The Business of Black Power: Community Development, Capitalism, and Corporate Responsibility in Postwar America.* Rochester, NY: University of Rochester Press, 2012.

Hill, Robert A., ed. *The FBI's RACON: Racial Conditions in the United States during World War II.* Boston: Northeastern University Press, 1995.

Hine, Darlene Clark. "Black Migration to the Urban Midwest: The Gender Dimension, 1915–1945." In Trotter, *Great Migration in Historical Perspective,* 126–46.

———. "Black Professionals and Race Consciousness: Origins of the Civil Rights Movement, 1890–1950." *Journal of American History* 89, no. 4 (2003): 1279–94.

———, ed. *Black Women in America.* New York: Oxford University Press, 2005.

———. *Black Women in White: Racial Conflict and Cooperation in the Nursing Profession, 1890–1950.* Bloomington: Indiana University Press, 1989.

———. *Hine Sight: Black Women and the Reconstruction of American History.* Bloomington: Indiana University Press, 1997.

———. "The Housewives' League of Detroit: Black Women and Economic Nationalism." In *Visible Women: New Essays on American Activism,* edited by Nancy A. Hewitt and Suzanne Lebsock, 223–41. Urbana: University of Illinois Press, 1993.

———. "Rape and the Inner Lives of Black Women in the Middle West." *Signs* 14, no. 4 (1989): 912–20.

Hinton, Elizabeth. *From the War on Poverty to the War on Crime: The Making of Mass Incarceration in America.* Cambridge, MA: Harvard University Press, 2016.

Hirsch, Arnold R. *Making the Second Ghetto: Race and Housing in Chicago, 1940–1960.* 1978. Reprint, Chicago: University of Chicago Press, 1998.

Honey, Maureen, ed. *Bitter Fruit: African American Women in World War II.* Columbia: University of Missouri Press, 1999.

Honey, Michael, ed. *Black Workers Remember: An Oral History of Segregation, Unionism, and the Freedom Struggle.* Berkeley: University of California Press, 2002.

——— *Going down Jericho Road: The Memphis Strike, Martin Luther King's Last Campaign.* New York: W. W. Norton, 2007.

———. "The Power of Remembering: Black Factory Workers and Union Organizing in the Jim Crow Era." In Payne and Green, *Time Longer Than Rope,* 302–35.

———. *Southern Labor and Black Civil Rights: Organizing Memphis Workers.* Urbana: University of Illinois Press, 1993.

Horne, Gerald. *Black and Red: W.E.B. DuBois and the Afro-American Response to the Cold War, 1944–1963.* Albany: State University of New York Press, 1986.

———. *Communist Front? Civil Rights Congress, 1946–1956.* Rutherford, NJ: Fairleigh Dickinson University Press, 1988.

Horowitz, Roger. *"Negro and White Unite and Fight!": A Social History of Industrial Unionism in Meatpacking, 1930–1990.* Urbana: University of Illinois Press, 1997.

Horton, Myles, and Paulo Friere. *We Make the Road by Walking: Conversations on Education and Social Change.* Philadelphia: Temple University Press, 1990.

Hull, Gloria T., Patricia Bell Scott, and Barbara Smith, eds. *All the Women Are White, All the Blacks Are Men, but Some of Us Are Brave: Black Women's Studies.* Old Westbury, NY: Feminist Press, 1982.

Hunter, Tera W. "The 'Brotherly Love' for Which This City Is Proverbial Should Extend to All": The Everyday Lives of Working-Class Women in Philadelphia and Atlanta in the 1890s." In *The African American Urban Experience: Perspectives from the Colonial Period to the Present,* edited by Joe W. Trotter, Earl Lewis, and Tera W. Hunter, 76–98. New York: Palgrave Macmillan, 2004.

———. *To 'Joy My Freedom: Southern Black Women's Lives and Labors after the Civil War.* Cambridge, MA: Harvard University Press, 1997.

———. "Writing of Labor and Love: Gender and African American History's Challenge to Present Day Assumptions and Misinterpretations." *Souls* 18, no. 1 (2016): 150–54.

Isaac, Larry, and Lars Christiansen. "How the Civil Rights Movement Revitalized Labor Militancy." *American Sociological Review* 67, no. 5 (2002): 722–46.

Isaac, Larry, Steve McDonald, and Greg Lulmsik. "Takin' It from the Streets: How the Sixties Mass Movement Revitalized Unionization." *American Journal of Sociology* 112, no. 1 (2006): 46–96.

Isserman, Maurice. *Which Side Were You On? The American Communist Party during the Second World War.* Middletown, CT: Wesleyan University Press, 1988.

Jackson, Kenneth T. *Crabgrass Frontier: The Suburbanization of the United States.* New York: Oxford University Press, 1987.

———. "Race, Ethnicity, and Real Estate Appraisal." *Journal of Urban History* 6 (Summer 1980): 419–52.

Jackson, Lawrence P. *The Indignant Generation: A Narrative History of African American Writers and Critics, 1934–1960.* Princeton, NJ: Princeton University Press, 2011.

Jackson, Walter A. *Gunnar Myrdal and America's Conscience: Social Engineering and Racial Liberalism, 1938–1987.* Chapel Hill: University of North Carolina Press, 1990.

Jacobs, Meg. *Pocketbook Politics: Economic Citizenship in Twentieth-Century America.* Princeton, NJ: Princeton University Press, 2007.

James, Joy. *Transcending the Talented Tenth: Black Leaders and American Intellectuals.* New York: Routledge, 1996.

Janiewski, Dolores. "Seeking 'a New Day and a New Way': Black Women and Unions in the Southern Tobacco Industry." In Groneman and Norton, *"To Toil the Livelong Day,* 161–78.

———. *Sisterhood Denied: Race, Gender, and Class in a New South Community.* Philadelphia: Temple University Press, 1985.

Jolly, Kenneth S. *Black Liberation in the Midwest: The Struggle in St. Louis, Missouri, 1964–1970.* New York: Routledge, 2006.

Jones, Jacqueline. *American Work: Four Centuries of Black and White Labor.* New York: W. W. Norton, 1998.

———. *The Dispossessed: America's Underclasses from the Civil War to the Present.* New York: Basic Books, 1992.

———. "Encounters, Likely and Unlikely, between Blacks and Poor White Women in the Rural South, 1865–1940." *Georgia Historical Quarterly* 76 (1992): 333–53.

———. *Labor of Love, Labor of Sorrow: Black Women, Work, and the Family from Slavery to the Present.* Rev. ed. New York: Basic Books, 2010.

Jones, William P. "The Damnable Dilemma: African-American Accommodation and Protest during World War." *Journal of American History* 81, no. 4 (1995): 1562–83.

———. *The March on Washington: Jobs, Freedom, and the Forgotten History of Civil Rights.* New York: W. W. Norton, 2013.

———. *The Tribe of Black Ulysses: African American Lumber Workers in the Jim Crow South.* Urbana: University of Illinois Press, 2005.

———. "The Unknown Origins of the March on Washington: Civil Rights Politics and the Black Working Class." *Labor* 7, no. 3 (2010): 33–52.

Joseph, Peniel E. "The Black Power Movement: A State of the Field," *Journal of American History* (December 2009): 751–76.

———, ed. *The Black Power Movement: Rethinking the Civil Rights–Black Power Era*. New York: Routledge, 2006.

———, ed. *Neighborhood Rebels: Black Power at the Local Level*. New York: Palgrave Macmillan, 2010.

———. *Waiting 'Til the Midnight Hour: A Narrative History of Black Power in America*. New York: Henry Holt, 2006.

Karp, Michael. "The St. Louis Rent Strike of 1969: Transforming Black Activism and American Low-Income Housing." *Journal of Urban History* 40, no. 4 (2014): 648–70.

Katzman, David M. *Seven Days a Week: Women and Domestic Service in Industrializing America*. New York: Oxford University Press, 1978.

Katznelson, Ira. *Fear Itself: The New Deal and the Origins of Our Time*. New York: Liveright, 2013.

———. *When Affirmative Action Was White: An Untold History of Racial Inequality in Twentieth-Century America*. New York: W. W. Norton, 2005.

Kelleher, Daniel T. "The Case of Lloyd Lionel Gaines: The Demise of Separate but Equal Doctrine." *Journal of Negro History* 56, no. 4 (1971): 262–71.

Kelley, Blair L. M. *Right to Ride: Streetcar Boycotts and African American Citizenship in the Era of Plessy v. Ferguson*. Chapel Hill: University of North Carolina Press, 2010.

Kelley, Robin D. G. *Freedom Dreams: The Black Radical Imagination*. Boston: Beacon Press, 2002.

———. *Hammer and Hoe: Alabama Communists during the Great Depression*. Chapel Hill: University of North Carolina Press, 1990.

———. *Race Rebels: Culture, Politics, and the Black Working Class*. New York: Free Press, 1994.

———. "'We Are Not What We Seem': Rethinking Black Working-Class Opposition in the Jim Crow South." *Journal of American History* 80, no. 1 (1993): 75–112.

———. *Yo' Mama's Disfunktional!: Fighting the Culture Wars in Urban America*. Boston: Beacon Press, 1997.

Kelly, Brian. "Beyond the 'Talented Tenth': Black Elites, Black Workers, and the Limits of Accommodation in Industrial Birmingham, 1900–1921." In Payne and Green, *Time Longer Than Rope*, 276–301.

Kersten, Andrew E. *A. Philip Randolph: A Life in the Vanguard*. Lanham, MD: Rowman and Littlefield, 2007.

———. "Jobs and Justice: Detroit, Fair Employment, and Federal Activism during the Second World War." *Michigan Historical Review* 25, no. 1 (1999): 76–101.

———. *Labor's Home Front: The American Federation of Labor during World War II*. New York: New York University Press, 2009.

———. *Race, Jobs, and the War: The FEPC in the Midwest, 1941–1946*. Urbana: University of Illinois Press, 2000.

Kersten, Andrew E., and Clarence Lang, eds. *Reframing Randolph: Labor, Black Freedom, and the Legacies of A. Philip Randolph*. New York: New York University Press, 2015.

Kessler-Harris, Alice. *Gendering Labor History*. Urbana: University of Illinois Press, 2007.

———. *In Pursuit of Equity: Women, Men, and the Quest for Economic Citizenship in 20th-Century America*. New York: Oxford University Press, 2001.

———. "A New Agenda for American Labor History: A Gendered Analysis and the Question of Class." In *Perspectives on Labor History: The Problem of Synthesis*, edited by Caroll Moody and Alice Kessler-Harris, 217–34. DeKalb: Northern Illinois University, 1989.

———. *Out-to-Work: A History of Wage-Earning Women in the United States*. New York: Oxford University Press, 1982.

———. *A Woman's Wage: Historical Meanings and Social Consequences*. Lexington: University Press of Kentucky, 1990.

———. *Women Have Always Worked: A Historical Overview*. Old Westbury, NY: Feminist Press; New York: McGraw-Hill, 1981.

Kimbrough, Mark, and Margaret W. Dagen. *Victory without Violence: The First Ten Years of the St. Louis Committee of Racial Equality, 1947–1957*. Columbia: University of Missouri Press, 2000.

King, Deborah K. "Multiple Jeopardy, Multiple Consciousness: The Context of a Black Feminist Ideology." In *Words of Fire: An Anthology of African-American Feminist Thought*, edited by Beverly Guy-Sheftall, 294–317. New York: New Press, 1995.

K'Meyer, Tracy. *Civil Rights in the Gateway to the South: Louisville, Kentucky, 1945–1980*. Lexington: University Press of Kentucky, 2010.

Kohler-Hausmann, Julilly. "'The Crime of Survival': Fraud Prosecutions, Community Surveillance, and the Original 'Welfare Queen.'" *Journal of Social History* (Winter 2007): 329–54.

Kornbluh, Felicia. *The Battle for Welfare Rights: Politics and Poverty in Modern America*. Philadelphia: University of Pennsylvania Press, 2007.

Kornbluth, Joyce L. "'We Did Change Some Attitudes': Maida Springer-Kemp and the International Ladies Garment Workers Union." *Women's Studies Quarterly* 23, nos. 1–2 (1995): 41–70.

Korstad, Robert Rodgers. *Civil Rights Unionism: Tobacco Workers and the Struggle for Democracy in the Mid-Twentieth-Century South*. Chapel Hill: University of North Carolina Press, 2003.

Korstad, Robert Rodgers, and Nelson Lichtenstein. "Opportunities Found and Lost: Labor, Radicals, and the Early Civil Rights Movement." *Journal of American History* 75, no. 3 (1988): 786–811.

Kremer, Gary. *Race and Meaning: The African-American Experience in Missouri.* Columbia: University of Missouri Press, 2014.

Kremer, Gary R., and Antonio F. Holland. *Missouri's Black Heritage.* Rev. ed. Columbia: University of Missouri Press, 1993.

Kruse, Kevin M., and Thomas J. Sugrue. *The New Suburban History.* Chicago: University of Chicago Press, 2006.

Kruse, Kevin M., and Stephen Tuck, eds. *Fog of War: The Second World War and the Civil Rights Movement.* New York: Oxford University Press, 2012.

———. *Divided Arsenal: Race and the American State during World War II.* New York: Cambridge University Press, 2000.

Kusmer, Kenneth L., and Joe W. Trotter. *African American Urban History since World War II.* Chicago: University of Chicago Press, 2009.

Lang, Clarence. "Between Civil Rights, Black Power, and the Mason-Dixon Line: A Case Study of Black Freedom Movement Militancy in the Gateway City." In *Race Struggles,* edited by Theodore Koditschek, Sundiata Keita Cha-Jua, and Helen A. Neville, 231–54. Urbana: University of Illinois Press, 2009.

———. "Freedom Train Derailed: The National Negro Labor Council and the Nadir of Black Radicalism." In *Anticommunism and the African American Freedom Movement,* edited by Robbie Lieberman and Clarence Lang, 161–88. New York: Palgrave Macmillan, 2009.

———. *Grassroots at the Gateway: Class Politics and Black Freedom Struggle in St. Louis, 1936–1975.* Ann Arbor: University of Michigan Press, 2009.

———. "Locating the Civil Rights Movement: An Essay on the Deep South, Midwest, and Border South in Black Freedom Studies." *Journal of Social History* 47, no. 2 (2013): 371–400.

Lawson, Steven F. *Black Ballots: Voting Rights in the South, 1944–1969.* New York: Columbia University Press, 1976.

———. *Civil Rights Crossroads: Nation, Community, and the Black Freedom Struggle.* Lexington: University Press of Kentucky, 2014.

———. "Freedom Then, Freedom Now: The Historiography of the Civil Rights Movement." *American Historical Review* 96, no. 2 (1991): 456–71.

———. "Long Origins of the Short Civil Rights Movement, 1954–1968." In McGuire and Dittmer, *Freedom Rights,* 9–37.

———, ed. *To Secure These Rights: The Report of President Harry S. Truman's Committee on Civil Rights.* Boston: Bedford, 2004.

Leflouria, Talitha. *Chained in Silence: Black Women and Convict Labor in the New South.* Chapel Hill: University of North Carolina Press, 2015.

Letwin, Daniel. *The Challenge of Interracial Unionism: Alabama Coal Miners, 1878–1921.* Chapel Hill: University of North Carolina Press, 1998.

Levenstein, Lisa. "From Innocent Children to Unwanted Migrants and Unwed Moms: Two Chapters in the Public Discourse on Welfare in the United States, 1960–1961." *Journal of Women's History* 11 (Winter 2000): 10–33.

———. *A Movement without Marches: African American Women and the Politics of Poverty in Postwar Philadelphia*. Chapel Hill: University of North Carolina Press, 2009.

Lewis, David Levering, ed. *W.E.B. Du Bois: A Reader*. New York: Henry Holt, 1995.

———. *W.E.B. Du Bois: Biography of a Race, 1868–1919*. New York: Henry Holt, 1993.

Lewis, Earl. *In Their Own Interests: Race, Class, and Power in Twentieth-Century Norfolk, Virginia*. Berkeley: University of California Press, 1991.

———. "More Than Race Relations: A. Philip Randolph and the African American Search for Empowerment." *Reviews in American History* 19, no. 2 (1991): 277–82.

Lichtenstein, Alex. "Consensus? What Consensus?" *American Communist History* 11, no. 1 (2012): 49–53.

———. "The Other Civil Rights Movement and the Problem of Southern Exceptionalism." *Journal of the Historical Society* 11, no. 3 (September 2011): 351–76.

Lichtenstein, Nelson. *American Capitalism: Social Thought and Political Economy in the Twentieth Century*. Philadelphia: University of Pennsylvania Press, 2006.

———. *Labor's War at Home: The CIO in World War II*. Cambridge: Cambridge University Press, 1982.

———. *State of the Union: A Century of American Labor*. Princeton, NJ: Princeton University Press, 2002.

———. *Walter Reuther: The Most Dangerous Man in Detroit*. Urbana: University of Illinois Press, 1995.

Lipsitz, George. *American Studies in a Moment of Danger*. Minneapolis: University of Minnesota Press, 2001.

———. *How Racism Takes Place*. Philadelphia: Temple University Press, 2011.

———. *A Life in the Struggle: Ivory Perry and the Culture of Opposition*. Philadelphia: Temple University Press, 1988.

———. *The Possessive Investment in Whiteness: How White People Profit from Identity Politics*. Philadelphia: Temple University Press, 1998.

———. *A Rainbow at Midnight: Class and Culture in the 1940s*. Urbana: University of Illinois Press, 1994.

———. *The Sidewalks of St. Louis: Places, People, and Politics in an American City*. Columbia: University of Missouri Press, 1991.

Litwack, Leon F. *How Free Is Free? The Long Death of Jim Crow*. Cambridge, MA: Harvard University Press, 2009.

———. *Trouble in Mind: Black Southerners in the Age of Jim Crow*. New York: Vintage, 1999.

Lucander, David. *Winning the War for Democracy: The March on Washington Movement, 1941–1945*. Urbana: University of Illinois Press, 2014.

Lumpkins, Charles. *American Pogrom: The East St. Louis Riot and Black Politics.* Athens: Ohio University Press, 2008.

MacLean, Nancy. *Freedom Is Not Enough: The Opening of the American Workplace.* Cambridge, MA: Harvard University Press, 2006.

Makalani, Minkah. *In the Cause of Freedom: Radical Black Internationalism from Harlem to London, 1917–1939.* Chapel Hill: University of North Carolina Press, 2011.

Marable, Manning. "A. Philip Randolph and the Foundations of Black American Socialism." *Radical America* 14, no. 2 (1980): 7–29.

Marks, Carole. *Farewell—We're Good and Gone: The Great Black Migration.* Bloomington: Indiana University Press, 1989.

Martin, Waldo E. *No Coward Soldiers: Black Cultural Politics in Postwar America.* Cambridge, MA: Harvard University Press, 2005.

Materson, Lisa G. *For the Freedom of Her Race: Black Women and Electoral Politics in Illinois, 1877–1932.* Chapel Hill: University of North Carolina Press, 2013.

May, Elaine Tyler. *Homeward Bound: American Families in the Cold War.* Rev. ed. New York: Basic Books, 2008.

McCallum, Brenda. "The Gospel of Black Unionism." In *Songs about Work: Essays in Occupational Culture,* edited by Archie Green. Bloomington: Indiana University Press, 1993.

McDuffie, Erik S. "Black and Red: Black Liberation, the Cold War, and the Horne Thesis." *Journal of African American History* 96, no. 2 (2011): 236–47.

———. "Chicago, Garveyism, and the History of the Diaspora Midwest." *African and Black Diaspora* 8, no. 2 (2015): 129–45.

———. "Garveyism in Cleveland, Ohio, and the History of the Diasporic Midwest, 1920–1975." *African Identities* 9, no. 2 (May 2011): 163–82.

———. "'No Small Amount of Change Could Do': Esther Cooper Jackson and the Making of a Black Left Feminist." In Gore, Theoharis, and Woodard, *Want to Start a Revolution?,* 25–46.

———. *Sojourning for Freedom: Black Women, American Communism, and the Making of Black Left Feminism.* Durham, NC: Duke University Press, 2011.

McDuffie, Erik S., and Komozi Woodard. "'If You're in a Country That's Progressive, the Woman Is Progressive': Black Women Radicals and the Making of the Politics and Legacy of Malcolm X." *Biography* 36, no. 3 (Summer 2013): 507–39.

McElya, Micki. *Clinging to Mammy: The Faithful Slave in Twentieth-Century America.* Cambridge, MA: Harvard University Press, 2007.

McGuire, Danielle L. *At the Dark End of the Street: Black Women, Rape, and Resistance: A New History of the Civil Rights Movement from Rosa Parks to the Rise of Black Power.* New York: Vintage Books, 2011.

McGuire, Danielle L., and John Dittmer, eds. *Freedom Rights: New Perspectives on the Civil Rights Movement.* Lexington: University Press of Kentucky, 2011.

———. "Fighting for What We Didn't Have: How Mississippi's Black Veterans Remember World War II." In McMillen, *Remaking Dixie*, 93–110.

———, ed. *Remaking Dixie: The Impact of World War II on the American South.* Jackson: University Press of Mississippi, 1997.

Meier, August. "Toward a Synthesis of Civil Rights History." In *New Directions in Civil Rights Studies,* edited by Armstead L. Robinson and Patricia Sullivan, 211–24. Charlottesville: University Press of Virginia, 1991.

Meier, August, and Elliot Rudwick. *Along the Color Line: Explorations in the Black Experience.* Urbana: University of Illinois Press, 1976.

———. *CORE: A Study in the Civil Rights Movement, 1942–1968.* New York: Oxford University Press, 1973.

———. *From Plantation to Ghetto.* 3rd ed. New York: Hill and Wang, 1976.

Menifield, Charles E. "Black Political Life in the Missouri General Assembly." *Journal of Black Studies* 31, no. 1 (2000): 20–38.

Milkman, Ruth. *Gender at Work: The Dynamics of Job Segregation by Sex during World War II.* Urbana: University of Illinois Press, 1987.

———. "Women's Work and Economic Crisis: Some Lessons of the Great Depression." *Review of Radical Political Economies* 8 (1976): 73–97.

Millard, Jessica. "Black Women's History and the Labor of Mourning." *Souls* 18, no. 1 (2016): 161–65.

Mitchell, Michele. *Righteous Propagation: African Americans and the Politics of Racial Destiny after Reconstruction.* Chapel Hill: University of North Carolina Press, 2004.

Montgomery, David. *The Fall of the House of Labor: The Workplace, the State, and American Labor Activism 1865–1925.* Cambridge: Cambridge University Press, 1989.

———. "Labor and the Political Leadership of New Deal America." *International Review of Social History* 39, no. 3 (December 1994): 335–60.

———. *Workers' Control in America.* Cambridge: Cambridge University Press, 1979.

Moore, Jesse T. *A Search for Equality: The National Urban League, 1910–1961.* University Park: Pennsylvania State University Press, 1981.

Moore, Robert J., Jr. "Showdown under the Arch: The Construction Trades and the First 'Pattern or Practice' Equal Employment Suit, 1966." *Gateway Heritage* 15, no. 3 (1994–1995): 20–43.

Moreno, Paul D. *Black Americans and Organized Labor: A New History.* Baton Rouge: Louisiana State University Press, 2006.

———. *From Direct Action to Affirmative Action: Fair Employment Law and Policy in America, 1933–1972.* Baton Rouge: Louisiana State University Press, 1997.

Morris, Aldon D. *The Origins of the Civil Rights Movement: Black Communities Organizing for Change.* London: Free Press, 1984.

Moye, J. Todd. *Let the People Decide: Black Freedom and White Resistance Movements in Sunflower County, Mississippi, 1945–1986.* Chapel Hill: University of North Carolina Press, 2004.

Muhammad, Khalil Gibran. *The Condemnation of Blackness: Race, Crime, and the Making of Modern Urban America.* Cambridge, MA: Harvard University Press, 2010.

Mullen, Bill V. *Popular Fronts: Chicago and African American Cultural Politics, 1935–46.* Urbana: University of Illinois Press, 1999.

Mumford, Kevin. "Double V in New Jersey: African American Civic Culture and Rising Consciousness against Jim Crow, 1938–1966." *New Jersey History* 119, nos. 3–4 (2001): 22–56.

———. *Interzones: Black/White Sex Districts in Chicago and New York in the Early Twentieth Century.* New York: Columbia University Press, 1997.

Murch, Donna Jean. *Living for the City: Migration, Education, and the Rise of the Black Panther Party in Oakland, California.* Chapel Hill: University of North Carolina Press, 2010.

Myrdal, Gunnar. *An American Dilemma: The Negro Problem and Modern Democracy.* New York: Harper and Row, 1944.

Nadasen, Premilla. "Citizenship Rights, Domestic Work, and the Fair Labor Standards Act." *Journal of Policy History* 24, no. 1 (January 2012): 74–94.

———. "Domestic Worker Organizing: Storytelling, History, and Contemporary Resonances." *Souls* 18, no. 1 (2016): 155–60.

———. "Expanding the Boundaries of the Women's Movement: Black Feminism and the Struggle for Welfare Rights." *Feminist Studies* 28, no. 2 (Summer 2002): 270–301.

———. "From Widow to 'Welfare Queen': Welfare and the Politics of Race." *Black Women, Gender, and Families* 1, no. 2 (Fall 2007): 52–77.

———. *Household Workers Unite: The Untold Story of African American Women Who Built a Movement.* Boston: Beacon Press, 2015.

———. "'Sista' Friends and Other Allies: Domestic Workers United and Coalition Politics." In *New Social Movements in the African Diaspora: Challenging Global Apartheid*, edited by Leith Mullings, 285–98. New York: Palgrave Macmillan, 2009.

———. "'Tell Dem Slavery Done': Domestic Workers United and Transnational Feminisms." *Scholar and Feminist Online* 4, no. 8 (2009). http://sfonline .barnard.edu/work/nadasen_01.htm.

———. *Welfare Warriors: The Welfare Rights Movement in the United States.* New York: Routledge, 2005.

Naison, Mark. *Communists in Harlem during the Great Depression.* Urbana: University of Illinois Press, 2005.

Nelson, Bruce. "Class, Race, and Democracy in the CIO: The New Labor History Meets the 'Wages of Whiteness.'" *International Review of Social History* 41, no. 3 (1996): 351–74.

———. *Divided We Stand: American Workers and the Struggle for Black Equality.* Princeton, NJ: Princeton University Press, 2001.

———. "Organized Labor and the Struggle for Black Equality in Mobile during World War II." *Journal of American History* 80, no. 3 (1993): 952–88.

Nesbitt, Francis Njubi. *Race for Sanctions: African Americans against Apartheid, 1946–1994.* Bloomington: Indiana University Press, 2004.

Nieves, Angel David, and Leslie M. Alexander. *"We Shall Independent Be": African American Place Making and the Struggle to Claim Space in the United States.* Boulder: University Press of Colorado, 2008.

Norrell, Robert J. "Case in Steel: Jim Crow Careers in Birmingham, Alabama." *Journal of American History* 73, no. 3 (1986): 669–94.

———. *The House I Live In: Race in the American Century.* New York: Oxford University Press, 2005.

Northrup, Herbert R. *Organized Labor and the Negro.* New York: Harper, 1944.

Orleck, Annelise. *Common Sense and a Little Fire: Women and Working-Class Politics in the United States, 1900–1965.* Chapel Hill: University of North Carolina Press, 1995.

———. *Storming Caesar's Palace: How Black Mothers Fought Their Own War on Poverty.* Boston: Beacon Press, 2005.

Osofsky, Gilbert. *Harlem: The Making of a Ghetto: Negro New York, 1890–1930.* Reprint. Chicago: Ivan R. Dee, 1996.

Painter, Nell Irvin. *Exodusters: Black Migration to Kansas after Reconstruction.* New York: Alfred A. Knopf, 1976.

———. *Narrative of Hosea Hudson: The Life and Times of a Black Radical.* New York: W. W. Norton, 1994.

Palmer, Phyllis. *Domesticity and Dirt: Housewives and Domestic Servants in the United States, 1920–1945.* Philadelphia: Temple University Press, 1989.

Parris, Guichard, and Lester Brooks. *Blacks in the City: A History of the National Urban League.* Boston: Little, Brown, 1971.

Patterson, James T. *America's Struggle against Poverty, 1900–1994.* Rev. ed. Cambridge, MA: Harvard University Press, 1995.

Payne, Charles. *I've Got the Light of Freedom: The Organizing Tradition and the Mississippi Freedom Struggle.* Berkeley: University of California Press, 1995.

———. "Men Led, but Women Organized: Movement Participation in the Mississippi Delta." In *Women and the Civil Rights Movement: Trailblazers and Torchbearers,* edited by Vicki L. Crawford, Jacqueline Anne Rouse, and Barbara Woods, 1–12. Bloomington: Indiana University Press, 1993.

Payne, Charles M., and Adam Green, eds. *Time Longer Than Rope: A Century of African American Activism, 1850–1950.* New York: New York University Press, 2003.

Peiss, Kathy. *Hope in a Jar: The Making of America's Beauty Culture.* Philadelphia: University of Pennsylvania Press, 2011.

Phillips, Kimberley L. *Alabama North: African-American Migrants, Community, and Working-Class Activism in Cleveland, 1915–1945.* Urbana: University of Illinois Press, 1999.

———. *War! What Is It Good For? Black Freedom Struggles and the U.S. Military from World War II to Iraq.* Chapel Hill: University of North Carolina Press, 2012.

Poole, Mary. *The Segregated Origins of Social Security: African Americans and the Welfare State.* Chapel Hill: University of North Carolina Press, 2006.

Primm, James Neal. *Lion of the Valley: St. Louis, Missouri, 1764–1980.* 3rd ed. St. Louis: Missouri Historical Society Press, 1998.

Purnell, Brian. *Fighting Jim Crow in the County of Kings: The Congress of Racial Equality in Brooklyn.* Lexington: University Press of Kentucky, 2013.

Rainwater, Lee. *Behind Ghetto Walls: Black Families in a Federal Slum.* Chicago: Aldine, 1970.

Rainwater, Lee, and William L. Yancey. *The Moynihan Report and the Politics of Controversy.* Cambridge, MA: MIT Press, 1967.

Randolph, Sherie M. *Florynce "Flo" Kennedy: The Life of a Black Feminist Radical.* Chapel Hill: University of North Carolina Press, 2015.

Ransby, Barbara. *Ella Baker and the Black Freedom Movement: A Radical Democratic Vision.* Chapel Hill: University of North Carolina Press, 2003.

Redmond, Shana L. *Anthem: Social Movements and the Sound of Solidarity in the African Diaspora.* New York: New York University Press, 2014.

Reed, Christopher Robert. *The Rise of Chicago's Black Metropolis, 1920–1929.* Urbana: University of Illinois Press, 2011.

Reed, Merl. *Seedtime for the Modern Civil Rights Movement: The President's Committee on Fair Employment Practice, 1941–1946.* Baton Rouge: Louisiana State University Press, 1991.

Reed, Toure. *Not Alms but Opportunity: The Urban League and the Politics of Racial Uplift, 1910–1950.* Chapel Hill: University of North Carolina Press, 2008.

Reese, De Anna J. "Domestic Drudges to Dazzling Divas: The Origins of African American Beauty Culture in St. Louis, 1900–1930." In *Women in Missouri History: In Search of Power and Influence,* edited by LeeAnn Whites, Mary C. Neth, and Gary R. Kremer, 168–79. Columbia: University of Missouri Press, 2004.

Richards, Yevette. *Maida Springer: Pan-Africanist and International Labor Leader.* Pittsburgh: University of Pittsburgh Press, 2000.

———. "Race, Gender, and Anticommunism in the International Labor Movement: The Pan-African Connections of Maida Springer." *Journal of Women's History* 11, no. 2 (1999): 35–59.

Robnett, Belinda. *How Long? How Long? African American Women in the Struggle for Civil Rights.* New York: Oxford University Press, 2000.

Roediger, David. "Making Solidarity Uneasy: Cautions on a Keyword from Black Lives Matter to the Past." *American Quarterly* 68, no. 2 (June 2016): 223–48.

———. *The Wages of Whiteness: Race and the Making of the American Working Class.* Rev. ed. New York: Verso, 1999.

———. "What If Labor Were Not White and Male? Recentering Working-Class History and Reconstructing Debate on the Unions and Race." *International Labor and Working-Class History* 51 (Spring 1997): 72–95.

Roediger, David R., and Elizabeth D. Esch. *The Production of Difference: Race and the Management of Labor in U.S. History.* New York: Oxford University Press, 2012.

Roediger, David R., and Philip S. Foner. *Our Own Time: A History of American Labor and the Working Day.* New York: Greenwood Press, 1989.

Roll, Jarod. *Spirit of Rebellion: Labor and Religion in the New Cotton South.* Urbana: University of Illinois Press, 2010.

Rubio, Philip F. *There's Always Work at the Post Office: African American Postal Workers and the Fight for Jobs, Justice, and Equality.* Chapel Hill: University of North Carolina Press, 2010.

Rudwick, Elliot. *Race Riot at East St. Louis: July 2, 1917.* Carbondale: Southern Illinois University Press, 1964.

Ruiz, Vicki L. *Cannery Women, Cannery Lives: Mexican Women, Unionization, and the California Food Processing Industry, 1930–1950.* Albuquerque: University of New Mexico Press, 1987.

Ruiz, Vicki L., and Ellen Carol Du Bois. *Unequal Sisters: A Multicultural Reader in U.S. Women's History.* 3rd ed. New York: Routledge, 2000.

Sacks, Karen. *Caring by the Hour: Women, Work, and Organizing at Duke Medical Center.* Urbana: University of Illinois Press, 1988.

Sandage, Scott A. "A Marble House Divided: The Lincoln Memorial, the Civil Rights Movement, and the Politics of Memory, 1939–1963." *Journal of American History* 80, no. 1 (1993): 135–67.

Sandweiss, Eric. *St. Louis: The Evolution of an American Urban Landscape.* Philadelphia: Temple University Press, 2001.

Santamarina, Xiomara. *Belabored Professions: Narratives of African American Working Womanhood.* Chapel Hill: University of North Carolina Press, 2005.

Schrecker, Ellen. *Many Are the Crimes: McCarthyism in America.* Princeton, NJ: Princeton University Press, 1998.

Schultz, Kevin M. "The FEPC and the Legacy of the Labor-Based Civil Rights Movement of the 1940s." *Labor History* 49, no. 1 (2008): 71–92.

Scott, Daryl Michael. *Contempt and Pity: Social Policy and the Image of the Damaged Psyche, 1880–1996.* Chapel Hill: University of North Carolina Press, 1997.

Scott, Michelle R. *Blues Empress in Black Chattanooga: Bessie Smith and the Emerging Urban South.* Urbana: University of Illinois Press, 2008.

Self, Robert O. *American Babylon: Race and the Struggle for Postwar Oakland.* Princeton, NJ: Princeton University Press, 2005.

Sharpless, Rebecca. *Cooking in Other Women's Kitchens: Domestic Workers in the South, 1865–1960.* Chapel Hill: University of North Carolina Press, 2010.

Shaw, Stephanie J. "Black Club Women and the Creation of the National Association of Colored Women." *Journal of Women's History* 3 (1991): 10–25.

———. *What a Woman Ought to Be and to Do: Black Professional Women Workers during the Jim Crow Era.* Chicago: University of Chicago Press, 1996.

Shockley, Megan Taylor. *"We, Too, Are Americans": African American Women in Detroit and Richmond, 1940–1954.* Urbana: University of Illinois Press, 2004.

Simmons, LaKisha M. *Crescent City Girls: The Lives of Young Black Women in Segregated New Orleans.* Chapel Hill: University of North Carolina Press, 2015.

Singh, Nikhil Pal. *Black Is a Country: Race and the Unfinished Struggle for Democracy.* Cambridge, MA: Harvard University Press, 2004.

Sitkoff, Harvard. *A New Deal for Blacks: The Emergence of Civil Rights as a National Issue.* 1978. Reprint, New York: Oxford University Press, 2008.

———. *Toward Freedom Land: The Long Struggle for Racial Equality in America.* Lexington: University Press of Kentucky, 2010.

Sklaroff, Lauren Rebecca. *Black Culture and the New Deal: The Quest for Civil Rights in the Roosevelt Era.* Chapel Hill: University of North Carolina Press, 2009.

———. "'Buy Where You Can Work': Boycotting for Jobs in African-American Baltimore, 1933–1934." *Journal of Social History* 27 (Summer 1994): 735–61.

Skotnes, Andor. *A New Deal for All? Race and Class Struggles in Depression-Era Baltimore.* Durham, NC: Duke University Press, 2013.

Smith, Peggie R. "Regulating Paid Household Work: Class, Gender, Race, and Agendas of Reform." *American University Law Review* 48, no. 4 (April 1999): 851–923.

Sparrow, James T. "Freedom to Want: The Federal Government and Politicized Consumption in World War II." In Kruse and Tuck, *Fog of War,* 15–31.

Spear, Allen. *Black Chicago: The Making of a Negro Ghetto, 1890–1920.* Chicago: University of Chicago Press, 1967.

Spector, Bert. "Early Interracial Protests: St. Louis Congress of Racial Equality, 1948–1955." *Social Science Quarterly* 2 (1974): 14–17.

Spero, Sterling D., and Abram L. Harris. *Black Worker: The Negro and the Labor Movement.* New York: Columbia University Press, 1931.

Springer, Kimberley. *Living for the Revolution: Black Feminist Organizations, 1968–1980.* Durham, NC: Duke University Press, 2005.

Stein, Judith. *Running Steel, Running America: Race, Economic Policy, and the Decline of Liberalism.* Chapel Hill: University of North Carolina Press, 1998.

Storrs, Landon R. Y. *Civilizing Capitalism: The National Consumers' League, Women's Activism, and Labor Standards in the New Deal Era.* Chapel Hill: University of North Carolina Press, 2000.

Strickland, Arvarh. *History of the Chicago Urban League.* Columbia: University of Missouri Press, 2001.

Sugrue, Thomas J. *The Origins of the Urban Crisis: Race and Inequality in Postwar Detroit.* Princeton, NJ: Princeton University Press, 1996.

———. *Sweet Land of Liberty: The Forgotten Struggle for Civil Rights in the North.* New York: Random House, 2008.

Sullivan, Patricia. *Days of Hope: Race and Democracy in the New Deal Era.* Chapel Hill: University of North Carolina Press, 1996.

———. *Lift Every Voice: The NAACP and the Making of the Civil Rights Movement.* New York: New Press, 2010.

Summers, Martin. *Manliness and Its Discontents: The Black Middle Class and the Transformation of Masculinity, 1900–1930.* Chapel Hill: University of North Carolina Press, 2004.

Taylor, Quintard. *In Search of the Racial Frontier: African Americans in the American West, 1528–1990.* New York: W. W. Norton, 1998.

Taylor, Quintard, and Shirley Ann Wilson Moore. *African American Women Confront the West, 1600–2000.* Norman: University of Oklahoma Press, 2003.

Theoharis, Jeanne, and Komozi Woodard, eds. *Freedom North: Black Freedom Struggles outside the South, 1940–1980.* New York: Palgrave, 2003.

———. *Groundwork: Local Black Freedom Movements in America.* New York: New York University Press, 2005.

Thompson, Heather Ann. *Whose Detroit? Politics, Labor, and Race in a Modern American City.* Ithaca, NY: Cornell University Press, 2004.

Tranel, Mark, ed. *St. Louis Plans: The Ideal and the Real St. Louis.* St. Louis: Missouri Historical Society Press, 2007.

Trotter, Joe William, Jr. *Black Milwaukee: The Making of an Industrial Proletariat, 1915–45.* Urbana: University of Illinois Press, 1985.

———. *Coal, Class, and Color: Blacks in Southern West Virginia, 1915–32.* Urbana. University of Illinois Press, 1995.

———. "From a Raw Deal to a New Deal?" In *To Make Our World Anew: The History of African Americans,* edited by Robin D. G. Kelley and Earl Lewis, 409–44. New York: Oxford University Press, 2000.

———, ed. *The Great Migration in Historical Perspective: New Dimensions of Race, Class, and Gender.* Bloomington: Indiana University Press, 1991.

Trotter, Joe W., and Patricia Cooper. "Introduction, Urban and Labor History: Old and New Connections." *Journal of Urban History* 30 (2004): 327–38.

Tuck, Stephen. *We Ain't What We Ought to Be: The Black Freedom Struggle from Emancipation to Obama.* Cambridge, MA: Harvard University Press, 2010.

Tyson, Timothy B. *Radio Free Dixie: Robert F. Williams and the Roots of Black Power.* Chapel Hill: University of North Carolina Press, 1999.

Van Deburg, William L. *New Day in Babylon: The Black Power Movement and American Culture, 1965–1975.* Chicago: University of Chicago Press, 1992.

Vapnek, Lara. *Breadwinners: Working Women and Economic Independence, 1865–1920.* Urbana: University of Illinois Press, 2009.

Vargas, Zaragosa. *Labor Rights are Civil Rights: Mexican American Workers in Twentieth-Century America.* Princeton, NC: Princeton University Press, 2005.

———. "Tejana Radical: Emma Tenayuca and the San Antonio Labor Movement during the Great Depression." *Pacific Historical Review* 66, no. 4 (1997): 553–80.

Venable, H. Phillip. "The History of Homer G. Phillips Hospital." In *Early, Ain't but a Place,* 324–27.

Von Eschen, Penny. *Race against Empire: Black Americans and Anticolonialism, 1937–1957.* Ithaca, NY: Cornell University Press, 1997.

Walker-McWilliams, Marcia. *Reverend Addie Wyatt: Faith and the Fight for Labor, Gender, and Racial Equality.* Urbana: University of Illinois Press, 2016.

Wallace-Sanders, Kimberly. *Mammy: A Century of Race, Gender, and Southern Memory.* Ann Arbor: University of Michigan Press, 2008.

Washington, Mary Helen. "Alice Childress, Lorraine Hansberry, and Claudia Jones: Black Women Write the Popular Front." In *Left of the Color Line: Race, Radicalism, and Twentieth Century Literature of the United States,* edited by Bill V. Mullen and James Smethurst, 183–204. Chapel Hill: University of North Carolina Press, 2003.

———. *The Other Blacklist: The African American Literary and Cultural Left of the 1950s.* New York: Columbia University Press, 2014.

Weiss, Nancy J. *Farewell to the Party of Lincoln: Black Politics in the Age of FDR.* Princeton, NJ: Princeton University Press, 1983.

———. *The National Urban League, 1910–1940.* New York: Oxford University Press, 1974.

Welky, David. *Marching across the Color Line: A. Philip Randolph and Civil Rights in the World War II Era.* New York: Oxford University Press, 2013.

Wesley, Charles H. *Negro Labor in the United States, 1850–1925.* New York: Vanguard Press, 1927.

Wesley, Doris A., Wiley Price, and Ann Morris. *Lift Every Voice and Sing: St. Louis African Americans in the Twentieth Century.* Columbia: University of Missouri Press, 1999.

White, Deborah Gray. *Too Heavy a Load: Black Women in Defense of Themselves, 1894–1994.* New York: W. W. Norton, 1998.

Whites, Lee Ann, Mary C. Neth, and Gary R. Kremer, eds. *Women in Missouri History: In Search of Power and Influence.* Columbia: University of Missouri Press, 2004.

Wilkerson, Isabel. *The Warmth of Other Suns: The Epic Story of America's Great Migration*. New York: Vintage Books, 2010.

Williams, Rhonda Y. "Black Women, Urban Politics, and Engendering Black Power." In Joseph, *Black Power Movement*, 79–103.

———. *The Politics of Public Housing: Black Women's Struggles against Urban Inequality*. New York: Oxford University Press, 2004.

———. "'Something's Wrong Down Here': Low-Income Black Women and Urban Struggles for Democracy." In Kusmer and Trotter, *African American Urban History*, 316–36.

———. "We're Tired of Being Treated like Dogs: Poor Women and Power Politics." In "Black Power Studies: A New Scholarship," special issue, *Black Scholar* (Fall–Winter 2001): 31–41.

Wilson, Francille Rusan. *The Segregated Scholars: Black Social Scientists and the Creation of Black Labor Studies, 1890–1950*. Charlottesville: University of Virginia Press, 2006.

Wolcott, Victoria W. *Remaking Respectability: African American Women in Interwar Detroit*. Chapel Hill: University of North Carolina Press, 2001.

Wright, John A. *Discovering African American St. Louis: A Guide to Historical Sites*. 2nd ed. St. Louis: Missouri Historical Society Press, 2002.

———. *St. Louis: Disappearing Black Communities*. New York: Acadia, 2004.

———. *The Ville: St. Louis*. Chicago: Arcadia, 2001.

Zieger, Robert. *The CIO: 1935–1955*. Chapel Hill: University of North Carolina Press, 1995.

———. *For Jobs and Freedom: Race and Labor in America since 1865*. Lexington: University Press of Kentucky, 2007.

Theses and Dissertations

Beatty-Brown, Florence R. "The Negro as Portrayed by the St. Louis Post-Dispatch from 1920 to 1950." PhD diss., University of Illinois, 1951.

Boxerman, Lawrence Harvey. "The St. Louis Urban League: History and Activities." PhD diss., St. Louis University, 1968.

Brunn, Paul Dennis. "Black Workers and Social Movements of the 1930s in St. Louis." PhD diss., Washington University, 1975.

Christensen, Lawrence O. "Black St. Louis: A Study in Race Relations, 1865–1916." PhD diss., University of Missouri, 1972.

Cummings, Charles Kimball. "Rent Strike in St. Louis: The Making of Conflict in Modern Society." PhD diss., Washington University, 1975.

Dowden, Priscilla. "Over This Point We Are Determined to Fight." PhD diss., Indiana University, 1997.

Feurer, Rosemary Ann. "Left Unionism in the Heartland: A History of United Electrical Workers Union District Eight, 1937–1949." PhD diss., Washington University, 1997.

Grant, Louise Elizabeth. "The St. Louis Unit of the March on Washington Movement: A Study in the Sociology of Conflict." Master's thesis, Fisk University, 1944.

Greene, Debra Foster. "Published in the Interest of Colored People: The St. Louis Argus Newspaper in the Twentieth Century." PhD diss., University of Missouri, 2003.

Harrison, William Jefferson. "The New Deal in Black St. Louis: 1932–40." PhD diss., St. Louis University, 1976.

Henry, Deborah Jane. "Structures of Exclusion: Black Labor and the Building Trades in St. Louis, 1917–1966." PhD diss., University of Minnesota, 2002.

Jolly, Kenneth Stuart. "It Happened Here, Too: The Black Liberation Movement in St. Louis, Missouri, 1900–1960." PhD diss., University of Missouri–Columbia, 2002.

Lang, Clarence E. "Community and Resistance in the Gateway City: Black National Consciousness, Working Class Formation, and Social Movements in St. Louis, Missouri, 1941–1964." PhD diss., University of Illinois, 2004.

Index

Civil Rights and the Struggle for Black Equality
in the Twentieth Century

Series Editors
Steven F. Lawson, Rutgers University
Cynthia Griggs Fleming, University of Tennessee

Civil Rights Crossroads: Nation, Community, and the Black Freedom Struggle
Steven F. Lawson

Selma to Saigon: The Civil Rights Movement and the Vietnam War
Daniel S. Lucks

In Remembrance of Emmett Till: Regional Stories and Media Responses to the Black Freedom Struggle
Darryl Mace

Freedom Rights: New Perspectives on the Civil Rights Movement
edited by Danielle L. McGuire and John Dittmer

This Little Light of Mine: The Life of Fannie Lou Hamer
Kay Mills

After the Dream: Black and White Southerners since 1965
Timothy J. Minchin and John A. Salmond

Faith in Black Power: Religion, Race, and Resistance in Cairo, Illinois
Kerry Pimblott

Fighting Jim Crow in the County of Kings: The Congress of Racial Equality in Brooklyn
Brian Purnell

Roy Wilkins: The Quiet Revolutionary and the NAACP
Yvonne Ryan

Thunder of Freedom: Black Leadership and the Transformation of 1960s Mississippi
Sue [Lorenzi] Sojourner with Cheryl Reitan

For a Voice and the Vote: My Journey with the Mississippi Freedom Democratic Party
Lisa Anderson Todd

Art for Equality: The NAACP's Cultural Campaign for Civil Rights
Jenny Woodley

For Jobs and Freedom: Race and Labor in America since 1865
Robert H. Zieger

CPSIA information can be obtained
at www.ICGtesting.com
Printed in the USA
LVHW110206040619
620058LV00003B/59/P